BATTLE
A HISTORY OF CONFLICT ON LAND, SEA AND AIR

Alistair Revie · Thomas Foster · Burton Graham

Marshall Cavendish

LAND BATTLES

PICTURES SUPPLIED BY:

Associated Press 90
Bapty & Co. Cover
British Museum Newspaper Library 48,
50, 54
Bundesarchiv, Koblenz 84
Photo Giraudon 32
Robert Hunt Picture Library 4-5
Imperial War Museum 36, 48, 62, 63, 64,
65, 68, 70, 76, 81, 82, 83, 101, 102, 105,
106, 118
Mansell Collection 6, 7, 11, 20, 21(rt), 22,
30, 31, 52, 53
J. G. Moore Collection 14, 15, 36, 41, 46
Musée de Versailles 28-29
National Army Museum 27, 33, 34
Novosti Press Agency 87, 90, 97
National Portrait Gallery 50, 55
Public Archives of Canada 120, 123
RAC Tank Museum 126
Radio Times-Hulton Picture Library 52
Scala, Milan 8-9
M. A. Snelgrove 16-17
Staatsbibliothek 78, 85, 98
Süddeutscher Verlag 60, 66, 72, 76
USAF 105
US Army 100, 103, 108, 112, 117, 124,
125, 128
US National Archives 26, 52, 54, 56, 62,
74, 86, 92, 94
Washington-Lee University 21
Yale University Art Gallery 24
Zeitgeschichtliches Bildarchiv 112-113

Maps by Allard Design Group

Diagrams by James Bamber 60, 61, 69, 81,
88, 90, 91, 103, 104, 116
Tony Bryan 114
Peter Sarson/Tony Bryan 80

AIR BATTLES

PICTURES SUPPLIED BY:

Camera Press Ltd 36-37, 37
Camera Press Ltd/P. Endsleigh Castle/
Observer 23 (left)
Victor Flintham 119, 120-121, 122-123,
124-125, 125, 126-127, 128
Fox Photos 84, 87
Fujifotos, Japan 58, 92-93, 93, 96, 97,
100-101
Robert Hunt Picture Library 14
Imperial War Museum Front Cover, 18,
20-21, 22, 23 (right), 26-27, 26, 34, 35,
38-39, 40, 41, 42 (bottom right), 44-45,
46, 47, 48, 49, 50-51, 52-53, 62-63, 64,
65, 66-67, 70-71, 73, 76-77, 80, 81, 88
89, 98-99 102-103
Imperial War Museum/Chris Barker 13,
16-17, 90-91
Keystone Press Agency 59
J. G. Moore Collection 6-7, 11, 15
Popperfoto 107, 112
Punch/Mary Evans 11 (bottom)
Royal Aeronautical Society 8-9 (top)
Search Ltd/Chris Barker 28, 32, 36
Suddeutscher Verlag 8-9 (top), 10, 42
Ullstein GmbH 30
USAF 74, 78-79, 82-83, 105, 106-107,
110-111, 112-113, 114-115, 116-117
US Navy 54-55, 56-57, 60-61

SEA BATTLES

PICTURES SUPPLIED BY:

Camera Press Ltd. 71, 79, 100, 102
The County Studio 8, 16, 36, 48, 76, 84,
102, 108, 120
Fujifotos 58, 59, 60, 63, 64
Sonia Halliday 17
Imperial War Museum 4, 70, 74, 78, 82,
86, 87, 90, 94, 95, 98, 101, 105, 106, 110,
112, 113, 114
Imperial War/Museum Chris Barker
72-73
Mansell Collection 6, 7, 10, 11, 12, 14, 18,
24, 31, 44, 46
J. G. Moore Collection 38, 71
National Maritime Museum, London 20,
26, 28, 30, 40, 44, 52, 92
National Maritime Museum, London/
Chris Barker 34
Dudley Pope 50
P & O Steamship Company 86, 88-89
Ullstein GmbH Front Cover
US Navy ,Washington 116, 118, 123, 124,
126, 128
Victoria & Albert Museum 68
Ray Woodward/Blandford Press Ltd. 22,
32, 42, 81, 96

Maps by Roger Kelly

Published by
Marshall Cavendish Books Limited
58 Old Compton Street
London W1V 5PA

© Marshall Cavendish Limited 1974 – 84

ISBN 0 86307 171 6

Printed and bound by Dai Nippon Printing Company, Hong Kong

This is the big one, a giant book that covers that giant subject—war.

From a forced march by Roman legions to Hitler's fast-moving Panzer troops, from galleys to battleships, from Zeppelins to supersonic fighters, *Battle* is the history of conflict on land, sea and air.

For the knowledgeable enthusiast or the interested tyro, *Battle* is your full guide to the most important battles of all time: why they were fought, the leaders—and the men— involved, the tactics and the weapons they used.

The authoritative and highly-readable text has all the information you require, specially-drawn maps give you a clear guide to the action, detailed diagrams flesh out the technical specifications of guns, tanks, ships and planes and dozens of illustrations, many in full colour, bring you the excitement, the danger— and the sadness—of war.

Battle will take you right into the world of the great commanders, the great heroes and the great fighting machines. Put it on your bookshelf and you will consult it again and again.

CONTENTS

LAND BATTLES

SEA BATTLES

AIR BATTLES

METAURUS

Rome in 207 B.C. lay open before the Carthaginian armies of Hannibal and Hasdrubal. Yet the Consul Nero out-bluffed Hannibal and then, after the toughest forced march in history, defeated and slew Hasdrubal beside the river Metaurus.

The Romans of classical times were brutal as they were brave. In winning for Rome the most important battle of the two Punic Wars fought against the Carthaginians, their elected consul Gaius Nero not only mercilessly slaughtered the second Carthaginian army on a river bank by the Adriatic in northern Italy; he also hacked off the enemy general's head and carried it on a short-sword to Canusium in the extreme south of the land; and at Canusium, he contemptuously tossed the gory skull into the camp of the first Carthaginian army.

It was one of the most fitting dramatic gestures in military history.

The tousled, glassy-eyed head was that of Hasdrubal.

The camp into which it bounced like a football was the headquarters of Hasdrubal's equally famous brother Hannibal . . . they of the surname Barca, meaning Thunderbolt.

These two sons of Hamilcar the Great, ruthlessly raised, like lions' whelps, had taken a vow at their father's knee to hate Rome and to make war on her, not for prizes but for prestige and revenge. They had succeeded to the point that Hannibal roamed Italy almost at will and brave senators trembled at sight of a double H. Now the tables of power were turned with a vengeance.

Hannibal and Hasdrubal had been about to link armies to crush Rome once and for all, and to make the Punic power supreme over all na-

tions. But Nero's inspired interception had unexpectedly changed history. The Roman Empire was shaking itself free, and it had the will to be great.

As he brushed the matted locks away from the brother's face he had last seen 11 years before, Hannibal wept; and when he raised his head it was to groan aloud in bitterness, saying: 'All is lost. Rome will now be mistress of the world.'

Hannibal comes to Italy

Hannibal had earlier pointed up his greatness in making his incredible elephant march across the Alps in 218 B.C. This had been enterprise and showmanship of the highest order. On its completion, his name rang round the Mediterranean like that of a god.

But the march had also been a grim ploy in which he lost about half his seasoned troops. And the truth was it had been necessary because Carthage no longer commanded the seas.

In the event, it worked wonders. His descent into the heart of Italy, then controlled by the City State of Rome, together with the brilliance of his cavalry-led tactics, enabled him to slaughter two Roman armies, totalling over 100,000 men, and their consuls with them. Thus depleted, the Romans did not dare say boo to him; apart from other factors, about two-thirds of their million troops were 'allies', not always reliable in adversity.

But Hannibal was also fallible; and he made the big mistake (probably because he lacked siege equipment) of not attacking the city of Rome. Instead he chose to impoverish much of Italy and so bankrupt the Romans.

The 'game' between Hannibal and Rome was in many respects the precursor of that between Napoleon and England, with an individual of genius taking on a great power. In both cases, the individual lost the last battle; after 17 years in Hannibal's case; after 16 in Napoleon's.

Yet, as with Napoleon, Hannibal's thirst for satisfaction was never even temporarily quenched, for the Roman Republic's Senate magnificently refused to accept the true situation.

Left The ancient 'tank' against Roman legionaries. To disable it either the underbelly had to be stabbed or the legs hamstrung. It might, however, panic anyway.

The stern spirit of Roman resolution was ever highest in adversity or danger.

Hasdrubal follows Hannibal

While Hannibal rampaged Italy, his brother Hasdrubal had been engaging the Romans in Spain, and had then followed his brother's ploy by marching his elephants, horses and men across the Pyrenees and the Alps. His route was surer and his losses were smaller; indeed, he was able to gather strength, every league of his journey, in recruits from among the mountain tribes, attracted by the high rates of pay he offered.

Hasdrubal's 50,000 were also speeded by the excellence of the engineering works Hannibal's experts had laid; in due course, they emerged

Below Nero made the savage gesture of throwing Hasdrubal's head into the camp of Hannibal, his elder brother, on a night six days after the battle.
Overleaf Africanus confronts Hannibal across a river five years after Metaurus where the consul Nero defeated Hasdrubal, Hannibal's brother, and destroyed Hannibal's last hope of victory in Italy. The Carthaginian was forced to return home in 202 B.C.

SCIPIO ET ANNI
SVPER ADV
AD INVICEM
CONVENIVNT

from the Alpine valleys much sooner than had been anticipated. They crossed the Po in good weather and advanced beyond Ariminum on the Adriatic, over the Metaurus, and as far as the little town of Sena to the south-east of that river (not far from the modern resort of Rimini).

The alarm in Rome was extreme. There were to be two Hs now in Italy, one to the north, one to the south, gnawing at the republic's vitals and ruining her economy. The best mobile troops in the southern plains were rushed north to engage Hasdrubal's invaders. Joint consuls (or generals) were chosen, to command in north and south respectively. One was Marcus Livius – a grim, moody, taciturn old soldier, with a chip on his shoulder about past injustices. Chosen as 'plebeian consul', representing the people as the law required, he was rushed to Sena.

The other chosen consul was Caius Claudius Nero, a patrician or aristocrat from one of the families of the great Claudian house. He had previously served against both Hannibal and Hasdrubal, but appeared rather young and inexperienced for so great a task as commanding the army. The leading senators fortunately noted in Nero the energy, shrewdness and spirit the situation required, and the people of Rome – who had the final say – wisely concurred. Nero went at once to Canusium, to play a cat-and-mouse game with Hannibal.

Three of Rome's six armies were in the north, but one was pinned down, restraining the disaffected Etruscans. Livius promptly welded the two disengaged armies into one, and placed them near enough to be 'in touch' with Hasdrubal's forward troops.

At this stage Hasdrubal suffered an unaccustomed stroke of ill luck. Knowing that his brother would be anxious to have detailed information of his movements and plans, and particularly as to whether he would move into Etruria or down the Adriatic coast, he prepared some letters and sent trusted messengers south with them.

But the Carthaginian messengers were intercepted by Nero's cavalry scouts and the letters were laid in Nero's hands instead of Hannibal's. They gave full particulars of Hasdrubal's camp, the strength of his forces and his intended line of march. And they revealed that the meeting place was to be South Umbria, whence together they could wheel round against Rome.

Nero saw at once how grave the crisis had become, with the two sons of Hamilcar only 200 miles apart and ready to take the city at last.

Nero makes his move

There was a law forbidding a consul to make war or march beyond his province without written permission. Nero knew he had no time to comply. Pausing only to send a messenger to Rome to lay Hasdrubal's letters before the senate, he ordered 7,000 of his finest men, a thousand of them horsed, to hold themselves in readiness for a secret attack on one of Hannibal's garrisons, while the rest of his army maintained its watch on the Carthaginian's principal forces.

It was bluff. He had set out on a southern tack, but at nightfall he wheeled the 7,000 around, and pressed with all speed north towards Picenum, to link with Livius. He also sent horsemen ahead along his proposed line of march to tell local communities to leave stores, provisions and refreshments by the nearest roadsides. All the while he hoped he had out-bluffed the archbluffer; that Hannibal was and should remain ignorant of his feint and its true purpose.

Also, like Montgomery in World War II, Nero was a great believer in trusting his troops. When they were a league or two on the way, he halted in a natural ampitheatre and explained to the 7,000 what was in his heart, as well as what was in his mind.

Toughest march in history

'It may prove the toughest forced march in history,' Nero explained, 'but if we can do it swiftly and secretly, Rome will be saved, and you will be able to tell your grandchildren you took part in our greatest-ever victory.' And he asked them to fear nought. 'There has never been a design more seemingly audacious and more really "safe",' he concluded. Surprise would be theirs. The Carthaginians would know nothing until the Romans appeared on the battlefield.

The men responded as never before. It was to be a march unparalleled in military annals. The men caught the full spirit of their leader. Night and day they pressed on, taking meals on the march, and resting by relays in following waggons supplied by country people.

Several times, couriers passed secretly and

safely between Nero and Livius (Livius was now encamped within half-a-mile of Hasdrubal), and among the messages was one advising Nero to time his arrival so as to reach the camp by night. When the marchers reached their goal, the 7,000 were smuggled silently into the tents of their Livius-commanded comrades, each according to his rank, so that no enlargement of the camp could give the game away to the enemy.

A council of war was held at once, with Livius's officers urging rest for the weary marchers. But Nero understood the importance of striking while the bluff held. 'We must fight without undue delay,' he said, 'while both the foe here and the southern foe are ignorant of our subterfuge. Having destroyed Hasdrubal, I must be back in Apulia before Hannibal awakes from his torpor.' And the most he would agree to was one day's rest.

He need not have worried. No spy or deserter had informed Hasdrubal of Nero's arrival. Nor had his departure become known to Hannibal.

In the morning, however, there was a moment when the deceit at Metaurus was all but rumbled. As Hasdrubal rode out with the dawn patrol, he noticed there things: the armour of some of the soldiers seemed unusually dull and stained, which was strange, as Livius was known to be a spit and polish merchant; some of the horses,

Carthaginian elephants engage Roman javelin men while infantry wait to exploit the ponderous assault. But Hasdrubal lost six of his ten elephants.

too, were dirtier and more rough of coat than was normal; and the trumpets giving orders to the Roman legions sounded once oftener than usual, suggesting the arrival of a consul of greater importance than Livius.

It was the third observation that confused Hasdrubal into error. There was no actual sign of an increase in the numbers before him. The trumpet calls had to mean that there was to be a change of command ... and that was of no great consequence; he could out-think the best of them. Anyway, it was time to put his master plan into operation. This was to retreat by night to friendly country and then fight.

Hasdrubal's plan crumbles

So it was that that night, at the time of the first watch, Hasdrubal led his army silently out of their entrenchments, and northwards to the Metaurus, to place the river between himself and the Romans before his move was discovered.

But his locally-recruited guides betrayed him. They led him away from the only ford, made their escape in the dark and reported to Nero. They had been 'planted' on Nero's instructions by his advance men.

Hasdrubal's army was floundering in confusion along the steep banks, and falling in numbers into deep water. By dawn they had altogether halted in confusion, indiscipline, fatigue and frustration.

The Roman cavalry arrived on the scene at first light, to be followed shortly by the legions, marching swiftly towards instant engagement.

Hasdrubal could do little but rapidly survey the ground and get his troops into something resembling Carthaginian battle order, assembled according to the nationalities or capabilities of the men.

The armies line up

Before the whole army, he quickly lined up his ten colossal elephants, with their Ethiopian 'boy's' as a chain of mobile advanced fortresses, placed to the centre and right fore. The elephant boys were armed with a sharp spike and a mallet. If any beast threatened to run amok, it was to be killed by a blow at the junction of head and spine.

In the centre of the army proper were Hasdrubal's best warriors – Carthaginians and Phoenici-Africans. These were surrounded by half-naked Gauls, with targets, long javelins or broadswords; white-clothed Iberians; savage Ligurians; plus farther-travelled Nasamones and Lotophagi. On the wings, troops of Numidian horsemen, from all the tribes of the desert, swarmed and swanned about on unsaddled Arab horses. The van was soon occupied by Balearic slingers.

Around him, personally, Hasdrubal had a picked troop of veteran Spanish infantry, protected by helmets and shields, and armed with short cut-and-thrust swords.

Because of the rugged nature of the terrain, Hasdrubal hoped the Roman right wing would be delayed while he made some impression, with his veterans, on the Roman left.

On Nero's side, the two main divisions of legionary were drawn up ten-deep, with three feet between files (which were alternate, like men on a draught or checkers board) and three feet between the ranks. This allowed javelins to be showered on the enemy, with one line succeeding the other twice over before swords were drawn. They wore breastplates, or coats of mail, according to rank or wealth; each had brazen greaves or leg-protectors, and a brazen helmet, with a lofty, upright crest of black or scarlet feathers; each bore an oblong shield and was armed with two javelins and a short sword. The third division was held in reserve and consisted entirely of veterans. Each of these carried a spear, instead of javelins, and a cut-and-thrust sword. For the rest, the Roman army consisted of lightly-armed skirmishers, and some hundreds of highly-trained cavalrymen.

Nero commanded the right wing, as senior consul, and Livius the left, with the praetor in the centre.

As the battle opened, Livius charged the Spaniards and Africans. There was great butchery on both sides, but neither prevailed. The elephants greatly troubled the Romans, breaking their front ranks and causing their ensigns to fall back.

Meanwhile, as Hasdrubal had anticipated, Nero's right flank had to labour up a steep hill and had difficulty maintaining contact with the Gauls. Hasdrubal therefore threw even more of his forces against Livius on the left of the Roman army.

Nero's master stroke

Hasdrubal's tactics were sensible, but did not allow for Nero's genius, who, when he could not get at the Gauls, wheeled a brigade of his best men round the rear of the other two-thirds of the Carthaginian army. He then fiercely charged the flank of the Spaniards and Africans.

This charge was as successful as it was unexpected. It rolled the enemy back in sudden disorder, and, although the Spaniards and their Ligurian colleagues bravely chose to die rather than retreat, they could not stem the Roman charge with their bodies.

Instead, the way was opened to make the Gauls accessible to Nero; and he now butchered them mercilessly. Thereupon, the remaining elements of the Carthaginian second army, including its surviving elephants, fled in panic, or fell into the now-bloody waters of the river Metaurus, which was to give the great battle its name.

Hasdrubal then showed the stuff he was made of as a man. He had always schooled his men to die fighting, rather than to gratify, as captives, Roman cruelty and pride. So, having done all that a general could be expected to do in the circumstances, and knowing that there could be no hope of further resistance or of subsequent regrouping, he saw no other choice than to go down with his army.

So it was that Hasdrubal spurred his horse into the midst of a Roman cohort, where, sword in hand, he met the gory death he considered worthy of the son of Hamilcar and the brother of Hannibal.

Although Nero gained a glorious victory, his name has been almost forgotten, overshadowed by the misdeeds of the Emperor Nero who reigned 250 years later. Lord Byron, the English poet, wrote of 'the consul Nero, who made the unequalled march which deceived Hannibal and defeated Hasdrubal, thereby accomplishing an achievement almost unrivalled in military annals.

'To this victory of Nero's it might be owing that his imperial namesake reigned at all. But the infamy of the one has eclipsed the glory of the other. When the name of Nero is heard, who thinks of the consul? But such are human things.'

With the longest forced march in history, Nero deceived Hannibal for long enough to defeat Hasdrubal. The final master-stroke was taking his crack troops behind Livius.

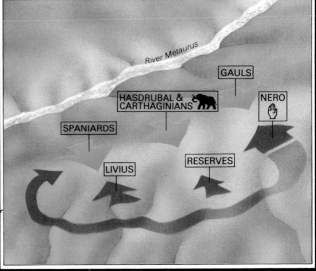

AGINCOURT

At Agincourt in France in 1415, Henry V and 5,500 troops defeated 20,000 French. The modern concept of missiles backed by infantry — the English massed archers and foot-slogging men-at-arms — was already showing its superiority over the romantic cavalry charges.

Shakespeare immortalized the classic Jack-the-Giantkiller victory of the English over the French at Agincourt with: 'We few, we happy few, we band of brothers,' in the alleged words of Henry V before the battle.

And Shakespeare could have anticipated Churchill's words about the Battle of Britain by adding: 'Never in the history of English arms were so many slaughtered by so few,' for Agincourt was also one of the world's bloodiest battles.

But there is a basic ringing difference between the two events.

Whereas Churchill was capturing an everlasting truth in a phrase, Shakespeare was sugaring an unpalatable pill, to give it the semblance of eternal virtue. That he succeeded is his magic rather than that of the event itself.

Henry taunts the French

The stubborn, strong-willed Henry V, like Edward III in his prime, had a natural gift of

leadership, but tended to use it as a means towards perverse ends. He was as foolish as he was brave, and was fortunate to have luck going for him a lot of the time. By all the odds, he never

Opposite Henry V was a warrior king, happy to join the fighting, but he was fortunate to win at Agincourt.

Below The English might well pray on the morning before battle for they faced a French army four times their size.

Right The long-bow and 3,000 archers gave Henry the advantage. The five-foot bow loosed a three-foot, steel-tipped arrow that could stop cavalry at 300 yards.

Overleaf In fighting at Agincourt the French forgot their own principle of victory through avoiding battle. Bogged down and with their horses floundering in the mud they died in thousands.

should have won at Agincourt. After the idiocy of his lengthy, pointless and flesh-wasting siege of Harfleur, in which he not only lost half his army as casualties, but weakened the rest with malnutrition and dysentery, he should have sailed back to England, thankful to have made one half-baked point. But this could not be, because he had dismissed his sea transports, determined to go home the hard way, to 'show' the French his contempt for their fighting qualities.

Not that the Dauphin's noble generals were any more rational. Henry's slow march, or 'Edwardian' parade, towards and across the Somme was clearly signposted. All the French had to do to destroy the tired, ragged and hungry English army was to employ against it the strategy taught them by the Constable du Guesclin. If they had kept their emotions in check, victory was theirs. The drill – by which du Guesclin had, in five years, reduced the vast English possessions in France to a slender strip between Bordeaux and Bayonne – was to *avoid* battle with the main English army, while exploiting mobility and surprise, nibbling away at the marchers to their utter dismay, always taking the line of least expectation and mostly doing so by night.

Just as other generals, in common with moneylenders, had maintained the principle of 'no advance without security', so du Guesclin's shrewd teaching had been 'no attack without surprise'.

The French mistake

Instead of following du Guesclin's ideas, the Dauphin, the French prince, was goaded by Henry's arrogance even into forgetting the lesson of Crecy, the battle 80 years earlier where Edward III's outnumbered army had beaten the French. He insisted that, with a four-to-one superiority of force, it would be shameful to use his army for anything other than a direct confrontation.

So it was that, after Henry had passed the small river of Ternoise, at Blangy in Picardy, about 40 miles from Calais, he was astonished to see the entire French army drawn up across his path, amply provisioned and heavily armed.

The scene was set for a major showdown, and the 'stars' were worthy of the scenario. Henry

had his noblest barons with him; the Dauphin – in the absence, due to madness, of his father, the king – was supported by all the princes of the blood. The underlying rivalry, jealousy, and gamesmanship had earlier been established when the Dauphin, hearing that Henry was coming to fight against him, had sent a box of tennis balls, urging the English monarch to amuse himself with them at home instead of making the 'foolish' invasion. Henry's response had been to say he would lob back gun stones instead of balls.

At Agincourt, Henry prudently drew up his army on a half-mile funnel of ground between two woods which guarded his flanks. He was wisely mindful of the fact that his situation was similar to those of Edward at Crecy, and of the Black Prince at Poitiers, and by God he was ready to show himself as fine a soldier king.

The French were foolishly posturing, their tongues rudely thrust out and their fingers to their noses, so to speak. There were over 20,000 of them against barely 5,500 on the English side.

Henry, having heard mass, rode along the lines, inspiring and jollying his weary warriors. A magnificent, instantly-recognizable extrovert figure, he had a gold crown upon his helmet, and wore a coat over his armour embroidered not only with the leopards of England, but with the lilies of France. He then dismounted and took his place among his soldiers, with the royal standard waving over him. It was October 25, Saint Crispin's Day, and the clear dawn showed the two armies already in battle positions, but contrasted ones. The French clung old-fashionedly to the idea that cavalry should dominate the field; the English put their faith in the more modern concept of massed archers and foot-slogging men-at-arms. Both sides had guns, but these were to play little part in the battle.

Overnight rain had stopped and the armies could each see the other clearly. They had plenty of opportunity for rumination, for the initial stalemate lasted for four hours.

The rout begins

At 11 a.m., Henry grew weary of the eyeball-to-eyeball business and suddenly gave the order: 'Banners Advance!' whereupon, with trumpets shrilling, the English army advanced to cries of 'St. George! St. George!'

The soggy clay on the French side had been

churned into a quagmire overnight by their thousands of horses; it was much firmer at the English end. When Henry's army was within bow-shot range of the enemy, he gave the order to halt, and the 3,000 archers thrust their palisades into the ground, forming an anti-cavalry fence behind which they could fire. In a moment there was a whooshing sound, as of water rushing, and the sky was filled with a forest of English arrows.

The French horses, already floundering in the mud, took fright the more easily as arrows fell like rain; some rushed onwards to impale themselves on the stakes, throwing their riders at the feet of the bowmen, where they were clubbed to instant death; most of the others either rolled on the ground to get the arrows out of their flesh or bolted in all directions, scattering dismounted men-at-arms and throwing their armoured riders, who remained where they fell in the mud.

The mass of the French men-at-arms ploughed on but were so crowded together as the field narrowed towards the English end that they could scarcely raise their weapons.

As dismay gave place to confusion, Henry chose exactly the right moment to advance again. His men were comparatively light and unencumbered; and being fewer in number, they had room to manoeuvre. As the English foot-soldiers began knocking down and cutting up the 'Frogs' in their hundreds, the English archers threw down their bows, took up their battleaxes and joined in with gusto. Tasting blood, they excitedly butchered their way through the first French line and straight into the second.

No prisoners to be taken

Within an hour, the piles of corpses and dying men were head high in places and Henry's unstoppable army had to climb over them to round up the remnants behind. At first these were taken as prisoners for ransom money, but at about mid-day, the king – who had fought on foot as bravely as any three men – gave the bloody order: 'No prisoners are to be taken.' He did this, it is said, because the French third line, mainly cavalry, was standing back, undecided; apparently Henry wanted to 'show' them further resistance would be madness. The fact is that the wholesale cruel slaughter went on, and even the houses to which some of the

Agincourt

The French faced a British army weakened by lengthy forced marches. But their cavalry could not charge on the soggy ground while the British advanced within bow-shot.

wounded had been carried by their comrades were razed to the ground by fire. The third line was then rounded up, more or less intact.

When the count was taken, some said only 40 Englishmen were killed, and some said 100. Certainly, the French dead numbered over 7,000, including the highest nobles in the land, and Henry was master of at least twice as many prisoners.

Henry's army was by now too worn out to pursue its advantage. Henry returned with them to tremendous acclaim in England, and his ascendancy, as a result of the one great battle, was sufficiently assured to prevent trouble at home for the rest of his short life.

There was even a 'pop' ballad written, *The Agincourt Song*, which caught the public's imagination and helped to establish the battle in history as a great and glorious event.

BUNKER HILL

On the bloody slopes of Bunker Hill, in 1775, a thousand American farmers stood against the professional soldiers of the British Army. Their highly-successful 'guerilla' action helped kindle the American War of Independence.

The grisly battle of Bunker Hill, which fanned the sparks of American independence into a forest fire, came 18 months after the Boston Tea Party and nine months after the first Continental Congress.

Delegates from every province in the colonies but one had assembled in Philadelphia on 4 September, 1774, in the persons of almost all the ablest men in America; they had drawn a series of state papers, defining and defending the position of the colonies, with such caring that these were declared superior to the masterpieces

Left Well dug-in, with the hill slope and cannon helping, American militia held off 3,000 regulars.

Above George Washington as a young man crowned the victory won on Bunker Hill by forcing a British evacuation of Boston.

of Greek or Roman statecraft; and they had drafted the splendid Declaration of Rights.

These men, although firmly against Imperial taxation, the quartering of troops, and the three recent coercion acts, made a declaration that was nonetheless far from aggressive towards the mother country.

September, 1774, was therefore the moment when inspired statesmanship could have prevented what was to become 'the most painful of all subjects for an Englishman to dwell on' – the War of Independence.

Instead, the obstinacy of the despotic King George III, the folly of his advisers and the natural pride of the freeborn sons of freeborn pioneers spoiled the moment.

The King believed the colonists could and should be beaten into obedience; they valued their freedom more than their lives; Eastern Massachusetts had risen in arms against Boston; and events moved swiftly toward the confrontation on the Charlestown peninsula through which the quarrel would pass from words to blood.

Paul Revere rides all night

The overture to the drama of Bunker Hill was in April, 1775, when patriot Paul Revere had ridden all night, as for his life, through the lanes of Massachusetts awakening villagers. His message was that they had to bar the road to Concord, near Boston, where other patriots were collecting arms and stores.

The British redcoats got no satisfaction in Concord and, on their forced withdrawal to Boston, after the unfortunate shooting of eight American minutemen at Lexington, suffered 293 casualties, killed or wounded by the shotgun blasts of hedgerow-hidden farmers.

In 1775, Britain had only 7,000 troops in all of North America, where the population numbered about $2\frac{1}{2}$ million. In England and Scotland there were fewer than 10,000 able-bodied soldiers to defend Britain and to reinforce the American garrisons; and it usually took three or four months to cross the Atlantic.

The British, brainwashed by the King and his obsequious ministers, had been astounded at the turn of events, following the first Congress. Like 'German George', they did not understand the American mind, nor did they try to learn about it. They regarded the colonists as Britons across the sea, whereas the Americans had become a very different sort of people – a rebel people, ready to shake off the mass of traditions that meant so much to an Englishman.

Americans take Bunker Hill

On the morning of 17 June, 1775, General Thomas Gage, commander-in-chief of the British military force in America, an effete, supine and mild-mannered man with little grasp of the realities of the situation, sat drinking tea with his American-born wife, as he doodled with the wording of a 'progress report to the King'. He could scarcely believe the words of his adjutant who interrupted to give him news that the embattled farmers of Massachusetts had overnight occupied and fortified two hills on the Charlestown peninsula, just over the narrow Charles River from Boston. So dominant were these features that it became immediately apparent, even to the sluggish-minded Gage, that unless the redcoats could recapture the hills, holding Charlestown and maybe Boston, too, would become impossible.

The two hills, interconnected by a ridge, were Breed's Hill and Bunker Hill. They had been taken over silently by a body of about 1,000 men, under the command of William Prescott, a hero of the French war. The occupation of the Boston suburb of Charlestown was eagerly desired by the colonists, and the two hills – which should have been fortified by Gage's troops, but were not – were the vital first step strategically.

Prescott's expedition acted with such speed and carried out its work so quietly that, although the peninsula was surrounded by the British ships of war, not one watching sailor was alerted to what was going on a few hundred yards away in the dark.

Prescott more than once walked down to the shore during the night and reassured himself that his ploy was unobserved; he wrote later that he could clearly hear the British sentries going their rounds and changing guard.

Spurred into unaccustomed action, the diffident Gage set about recovering the hills. Shortly after noon on June 17, he assembled 3,000 British troops in Boston, and they were quickly ferried across the river. At the same time, the guns of a man-of-war, *The Lively*, opened fire on the American positions, and so did a battery from Copp's Hill.

'Prescott's Thousand' continued their toil through all the pounding, apparently inspired and undismayed, encouraged by Israel Putnam, second-in-command of all Massachusetts volunteers, a courageous if illiterate farmer, and by Joseph Warren, the youthful president of the colony's Congress.

When it was found that the mass gunfire was having no effect on the colonists, Gage reluctantly decided that there was nothing for it but to have the hills stormed.

British redcoats attack

Just after three o'clock that afternoon, the 3,000 British redcoats, under the command of General William Howe, ascended Bunker Hill to make a frontal attack on the American trenches. Not a sound came from the entrenched volunteers until Howe's men were within 50 yards. Then Prescott

Right Colonel Israel Putnam, a French and Indian war veteran, ordered his men to fire at the white British gaiters and then 'at the white of their eyes'.

Bunker Hill

CANADA

Boston •

AMERICAN
New York•
Philadelphia •
Atlantic Ocean
COLONIES

BOSTON AND BUNKER HILL.

Left *The occupation of Bunker and Breed's hills 550 yards from Charleston threatened British Boston. The British had to counter-attack.*

Overleaf *Cold steel prevails at the third attempt. Howe and Clinton took the hill by a flank attack with artillery support, when the Americans ran out of ammunition.*

lustily gave the single crisp order: 'Fire!'

Under the terrible instant volley, the first British troops were cut to rags. Many others paused, reeled and wavered; some even ran back down Bunker Hill, all the way to the river bank.

'Do you still say the Yankees are cowards?' yelled the hill's defenders as the redcoats fell back. Americans were regarded in England as less than brave, for some odd reason, and it had been thought they would flee like sheep the moment they saw redcoats advancing under any circumstances.

Howe was a tough and single-minded general. He led his men on the attack, miraculously escaping personal injury. Twice more they were driven off before the murderous massed colonial fire. At one point, Howe found himself virtually alone on the field, and he had no choice but to withdraw, to rally and reassemble his frightened men. Every member of his personal staff had been felled, and his silk stockings were blood-spattered.

In their improvised bunkers on Bunker Hill, the men Gage had called 'the rabble of New England' were jubilant, as they awaited their third test by fire. They were as mixed a bunch – farmers, labourers and merchants – as could have been plucked from the countryside in a socio-economic sample. Maybe they were not going to be able to capture Charlestown and threaten Boston from the north, as had been the object of the exercise; maybe they were soon going to have to retreat firing, as minutemen should; but, by God, they had shown their marksmanship as well as their sheer guts. They had struck a noisy blow for freedom that day which many would hear and would follow.

This was something Gage and his fellow-sneerers had badly misjudged. The countrymen of the colonies were scant in military training, but they were probably unequalled in the world in their speed and accuracy as marksmen; the wild and wily game they tackled as individuals was much trickier to shoot than any gang of highly-disciplined redcoats.

Prescott's Thousand

As they waited for the next charge, clutching their sporting guns and old flintlocks, their powder horns by their sides, their 'uniforms' as disparate as their personalities, the insurgents' sole thoughts were how best to put a bullet in the heart of a red breast and to hell with the subtleties of battle.

There was a movement at the foot of the hill, and 'Old Put' in his command post sent a hoarse whisper echoing around the dugouts: 'Fire when you see the whites of their eyes and then retire.'

'Aye, that we will,' muttered Angus Gordon, a tough hook-nosed crofter. He raised his shotgun and spat on the ground, where his blood would soon mingle with that of a red-coated cousin from Inverness.

The embattled countrymen were all but out of bullets, and some were at the stage of improvising with nails, bolts and bits of scrap iron. But Howe did not know this, as he prepared for another assault.

Regrouped and lightened of their knapsacks, with bayonets fixed, his men again swept up Bunker Hill, with the general in the fore – six feet tall, in days when this was rare – and, although picked off by the insurgents in scores, the British succeeded in over-running the first trenches, whereupon the minutemen behind melted across the neck of the peninsula, like snow on the first day of spring.

When they had gone, the carnage on the hill was terrible to behold.

The Battle of Bunker Hill had ended as a British victory, but it was a dearly-bought one. British casualties numbered 1,054, out of 3,000 men engaged. Of Prescott's Thousand, 441 had fallen on the battlefield and others were carried away wounded.

Bunker Hill may have been a 'defeat' for the patriots, but it disproved the assumption that a farmers' army could not stand up to a regular army. And it lowered morale at Boston.

The news was carried to the second Congress in Philadelphia, where the importance of the event was at once appreciated. The Americans had shown they could and would fight for all they believed in. Three days before Bunker Hill, they had promoted Colonel George Washington to general and had made him commander-in-chief. He left at once for Boston. The War of Independence had begun.

Gage was recalled to England. Howe took charge in his stead but he was not to hold the trophy of Bunker Hill for long. He was compelled, by the superior generalship of Washington, to evacuate the hill, the peninsula, Charlestown and Boston itself in less than a year.

The second wave of British troops crosses the Charles river as Charleston burns. American reinforcements descend Bunker hill to join the men on Breed's hill.

AUSTERLITZ

The chance in 1805 to crush both Austrians and Russians forced Napoleon to fight an army bigger than his own — and stimulated his military genius to the full. Six months of brilliant strategy and confident tactics culminated in victory at Austerlitz.

French infantry advance in closely dressed ranks with muskets crooked at 'Support arm'. This tight tactical control brought as many as possible of these close-range, inaccurate weapons to bear on the enemy.

Overleaf *Napoleon's magnificent victory at Austerlitz firmly established his regime and prepared the way for further conquests.*

Austerlitz was the French Emperor's greatest battle and 1805 was Napoleon's year despite Lord Nelson's victory at Trafalgar.

After several years of uneasy peace, the curtain that had fallen on the French Revolutionary wars was now rising on a new act – the Napoleonic war, fought by Bonaparte in his new role of Emperor.

Mainly, he had built his reputation as the greatest general of his era in two ways: by compelling each foe to fight at a numerical disadvantage; and by building his own legend through self-advertisement. Always put up a bold arrogant front and you're half-way there, was his outlook.

Austerlitz was exceptional in that for once he was outnumbered in the field; for once, he risked all to win at odds of 8:7 against. But on this one occasion, the demands of the political situation overrode military calculations.

The battle was in December, 1805. Napoleon had been Emperor for 18 months. Earlier in the year he had mesmerized his enemies into a state of fumbling apprehension. In May, he had been made king of Italy in the cathedral of Milan, with the iron crown of the Lombard Kings; at the same time he had 'acquired' the republic of Genoa. He tore up treaties and contemptuously tramped on small states. Having neutralized Prussia, he felt ready by July to invade Britain. Only the Royal Navy stood in his way, and he had plans to dispose of that. Spain and the five German states were subservient allies. His appetite for aggrandizement seemed insatiable.

Like Hitler, his ambitions would drown through his ultimate inability to cross the English Channel. Like Hitler, he underrated the British and did not read the signs correctly. When the news of Trafalgar would reach dictator Napoleon, on the eve of Austerlitz, he was to regard it as an accute irritant rather than the writing on the wall; for his preoccupations had become European.

Napoleon went out among his soldiers on the morning before battle and their enthusiastic welcome heralded a day of triumph.

He had failed in only one other way in 1805, and that was in his efforts to separate the Austrians from the Russians on the principle he lived by, which stated: 'Divide, in order to subsist; concentrate, in order to fight.' Now his chance was coming to crush both in one blow, so the superior odds against him had to be faced. It was far too good a chance to miss.

Napoleon takes his chance

On August 28, the French army of about 200,000 which had been lined up, with flat-bottomed landing craft, to invade England from Boulogne, was given the order 'About turn!' and was force-marched towards the Rhine. It was characteristic Napoleonic opportunism.

He calculated that the Austrians would send an army into Bavaria to block the Black Forest exits, and he planned a wide manoeuvred march around their northern flank, across the Danube (which he reached in six weeks) and on to the Lech. He explained to his troops in advance this intended strategic barrage across the Austrians' rear.

It worked brilliantly, and this closing down of the rear led to the almost bloodless surrender of the outnumbered Austrians, under their 'paper tiger', General Mack, at Ulm, and the taking of 30,000 prisoners.

But Ulm had not finally crushed the Austrians, the more so as they knew the Russians were on the march to save them, and other Austrian armies were due to return from Italy and the Tyrol.

One of Napoleon's worries was that in crossing Austria he had gathered thousands of pressed soldiers and the size of his army was threatening to become inconvenient. The space between the Danube and the mountains to the south-west was

French cannon bombard the helpless 5,000 Austro-Russian troops trapped on the marshes below Platzen. Two hundred men and 25 guns drowned in icy water.

too cramped for any local indirect approach and there was not time for an Ulm-like wide-ranging manoeuvre.

And already the Russians were drawn up upon the Inn to shield the Austrians until their 'foreign' armies could have time to join them, from the south, through Carinthia.

The indirect approach

Napoleon's answer was to use a series of variations on the ancient theme of the indirect approach—the grand strategy which, as used in the overthrow of Persia by Alexander, and Carthage

Left Napoleon's energy was his great asset. His strategic speed and surprise at Austerlitz was unsurpassed.

Below One of the 7,000 French cavalry at the battle. They successfully fought off 15,000 enemy horsemen.

by Scipio, had given birth to the Macedonian and Roman empires. This was the moment for him firmly to establish his European empire by doing likewise.

First, by subtly forcing the Russians to move eastwards he was able to separate them from the Austrian army returning from its successes in Italy. He advanced directly east towards Vienna, while sending a corps under Mortier along the north bank of the Danube. This forced the Russian general, Kutosov, his communications threatened, to fall back northeastwards to Krems.

French general Joachim Murat was then sent dashing across Kutosov's new flank towards Vienna, which he took without a struggle on November 13. Thence, Murat moved northwards on Hollabrunn, to menace the Russian army's left rear, and they were driven into another scrambled retreat north-east, almost to their own frontier, at Olmutz, where they were able to draw reinforcements; but they had been forced by Napoleon to abandon their original role of protecting Austria until the Italian-based army arrived.

Time was now of the essence for Napoleon, because Prussia had turned-coat and seemed likely to bring an army of 180,000 to the help of the allies before long. Also, his general position remained less than secure; his corps were scattered in a gigantic semi-circle, from Pressburg almost to Brunn, with winter under way.

Napoleon therefore pursued the indirect approach he had been following by feigning weakness and retreat. This tempted the two Russian armies, as he had hoped, into taking the offensive.

He concentrated a mere 50,000 of his troops at Brunn, against the enemy's 80,000, and pushed out isolated detachments towards Olmutz. He also sent emissaries to plead for peace talks, and, when the enemy swallowed this poisoned bait, he recoiled before them to a position he had carefully pre-studied near Austerlitz, which could form a natural snare for his too-unwary foes.

Czar and Emperor

The allies were led, titularly, by two autocratic emperors—the young Czar Alexander of Russia (a German by descent and by marriage) and the Emperor Francis II of Austria. Their plan—put to them by the Austrian general Weirother, a favourite of the Czar—was to turn the right wing of the French army and so cut off their connections with Vienna. Napoleon, again reading their ponderous minds, had encouraged their design by abandoning the Platzenberg, a move which persuaded them he still intended to retreat, with his meagre force of 50,000. The allies rejoiced, believing that, for once, they had had the Corsican pig on the run, because of their superior numbers, and they foolishly ignored the lesson—demonstrated for a decade—that French troops under Napoleon could be made to march two miles to anybody else's one.

Ensnared, although they did not know it, the two emperors and their staff officers took over Austerlitz castle at the end of November and on December 1 established their armies on the nearby defensible plateau of Platzen—where their centre could be weakened with impunity—exactly as the cunning Corsican had wanted.

Meanwhile, in the 60 hours before the battle, Napoleon brought up a division at the trot, from Pressburg, 70 miles to the south, and a corps from Iglau, 50 miles to the east—all unknown to the allies—to the point that he had nearly 70,000 men to the allies' 80,000. This he deemed just

about enough for his purposes, his tactics could offset his rare deficiency in numbers.

Napoleon celebrates

So confident was Napoleon on the morning of December 2 that he went out to visit the soldiers at the bivouacs, and they were no less enthusiastic. Someone had recalled that December 2 was the anniversary of the emperor's coronation and spontaneously the troops gathered up the straw upon which they had been sleeping, made it into bundles, and lit these at the end of poles, in celebration of the event.

This sudden pre-dawn blaze was taken on the allied side to be a further indication of the impending flight of the French forces. Before the

A chasseur à cheval from one of 24 regiments. These light horse were used in pursuit and scouting, especially to screen Murat's movements before Austerlitz.

Austerlitz

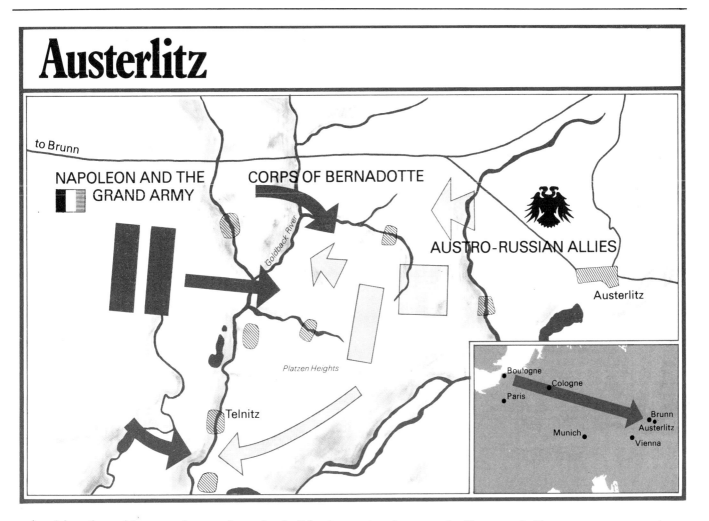

to Brunn

NAPOLEON AND THE
GRAND ARMY

CORPS OF BERNADOTTE

Goldback River

AUSTRO-RUSSIAN ALLIES

Austerlitz

Platzen Heights

Telnitz

Boulogne
Cologne
Paris
Brunn
Austerlitz
Munich
Vienna

early bitterly-cold morning mists had lifted, 30,000 of the Austro-Russian troops sought to hasten this retreat by hurling themselves against the French right, driving it from the village of Telnitz and across the Goldbach. This was as Napoleon had predicted to his soldiers. He encouraged the allies thus to extend their left against his retreating right, until they found themselves stretched over a long arc, with their possession of the outside lines a handicap.

This was the moment Napoleon was waiting for; he swung round his centre against the weakened 'joint'; storming the heights of the Platzenberg, a French corps held off all attempts by the Russian horse and foot to retake this key position.

The allied armies were falling apart at the centre, where Napoleon was personally leading the infantry of the guard, and the corps of Bernadotte; and the extended right wing was not only unable to help, but failed to extricate itself from a trap set for it, and was swept into frozen marshes, where hundreds fell through the ice and drowned as French cannon balls landed at their sides.

By the close of the winter day, the two allied

Napoleon marched his army half-way across Europe then tempted 85,000 Austro-Russians into trying to crush him against the river Goldback. Reinforced, he split them on the Platzen Heights.

emperors had abandoned the bloody battlefield in despair. Behind them, they could hear French cries of victory as the cavalry pursued the vanquished; around them were the groans of the wounded and the imprecations of the fugitives.

Austerlitz had been taken over by the conquerors. The emperors sought safety in the imperial castle of Halitsch, and sent Prince John of Lichtenstein to ask from Napoleon an armistice and an interview.

Austerlitz shattered the Czar's confidence, and forced Francis to abandon the coalition.

Napoleon again summoned his troops the next day and said: 'Soldiers, I am satisfied with you ... In France, my people will see you again with joy, and it will suffice for you to say: "I was at the battle of Austerlitz," to receive the reply: "There indeed is a hero!"'

BALACLAVA

'Someone had blundered' says the poem about the Charge of the Light Brigade at Balaclava in the Crimea in 1854. It was only the last of a series of idiocies in a battle redeemed solely by the courage of the common soldier.

Idiotic diplomacy begat the Crimean war. Massive inefficiency characterized its conduct. It was a lustful, useless war, which Britain, France and Russia drifted into, and which scarcely anyone wanted. Even when the drift had become irreversible, the generals had difficulty in deciding where or how it should be fought. And when the Crimea had been chosen, because Napoleon III feared he might be as unlucky as his uncle if he went anywhere near continental Russia, what should have been a short sharp victory became instead a tragic series of bungled nonsenses in a year of misery for all concerned.

Victory to the soldiers

Yet the common British soldier – frozen, undernourished, badly clothed and frequently flogged – fought with such bravery at Balaclava, for no cause other than that of pride, that the pointless and inconclusive battle is still talked of as a great and glorious victory.

He did this led by old and useless generals; by pink young men who had bought their commissions.

The allied armies had landed in the Crimea, during September 14 to 16, 1854, to begin the war which had been six months declared.

The Czar's naval forces had declined battle with the British and French fleets in the Black Sea, and had retired to Sebastopol harbour, so that the Crimean operations were almost exclusively military.

The British were led by General Lord Raglan,

The 17th Lancers lead the 'Gallant Six Hundred' into the 'Valley of Death'. Lord Cardigan, on the left, in his 11th Hussars uniform heads the Light Brigade.

and the French by Marshal Leroy de St-Arnaud. Raglan was brave but mediocre and stupid as well as old; St-Arnaud was dying. They quarrelled constantly, not least because Raglan, in his dotage, kept referring to the French as 'the enemy'. This was the more odd because he had previously never even commanded a battalion in the field, having been behind a desk for 40 years and more.

Somehow, an equally-muddled Russian army was defeated at the Alma on September 20. St-Arnaud promptly died, to be replaced by the equally-uninspired General F. C. Canrobert. The allies could and should have followed through promptly. They could have entered Sebastopol from the north; instead, after characteristic arguments and indecisions, they eventually marched to the south, and camped around the harbour of Balaclava, the ancient Portus Symbolon.

This allowed the Russians, under General Todleben, to throw up defensive works at Sebastopol – an immensely strong fortress – and these would hold the allies at bay for another 12 months; it would also enable the Russians to build up from 40,000 to 100,000 men. Nor were the allies equipped for a siege of *any* length.

Disease and frost

In the bitterly cold and desolate wastes around the insanitary allied tents and trenches, disease and vermin caused almost incredible conditions. Lice, bugs and fleas were everywhere; scurvy, cholera and dysentery claimed hundreds of lives. Britain had been at peace for 40 years, and everyone had forgotten how to plan a war. While the troops shivered and starved at Balaclava, stores of unreachable clothing and food were piling up in the wrong ports; when a shipload of boots arrived at the proper port, they were found to be all for the left foot. Terrible storms wrecked other supply vessels. The same storms blew away the Balaclava tents, so that the troops had to sleep on wet straw in the snow and frost, and this in cold so dreadful that rifle barrels froze to men's hands and tore away the skin when removed. In the crowded hospitals (before the arrival of Florence Nightingale and her 38 nurses after the battle) the dirt, horror and indifference were dreadful.

Such was the scene in Balaclava on the eve of the battle.

Because it was 39 peacetime years since

Waterloo, the army was also rusty and un-professional in its officer class. The youngest of all possible generals, from whom Raglan was chosen, were in their sixties.

The way to the top

Lord Cardigan had achieved command of the Light Brigade of Cavalry, without ever seeing a shot fired in anger, by a fairly typical route. He had bought his way to the top of the 15th Hussars for £30,000, and had lost his command after a scandal; he had then paid £40,000 for the top rank in the 11th Light Dragoons, and had, this time survived until promotion had to be given him. General Scarlett, his opposite number with the Heavy Brigade, was equally ignorant, languid and 'green'.

The commander of the Cavalry Division, Lord Lucan, Cardigan's brother-in-law, was probably even more vapid than the other two. Like 'Major Major Major Major' in *Catch 22*, Lord Lucan (known to the troops as Look-on) was the ultimate in mediocrity.

Nor were cavalry activities in the campaign helped by a bitter feud Lucan and Cardigan had been engaged in since childhood, which both considered more pressing, even on the battlefield, than any face-to-face with the Russians. Indeed, Lord Wolseley (when commander-in-chief) would say of these two: 'If they had been private soldiers, no colonel would be stupid enough to promote them to the rank of corporal!' And a French general said of all three cavalry officers: 'They were brave because they were too dim to discern an alternative.'

Cavalry has its day

Balaclava is remembered for its horses as much as for its men. In 1874, cavalry were still a large part of the cult of the conqueror, horse-worship having long been a part of the British way of life. The theory was that the man on the horse was not only more powerful and bigger than the infantryman, but he was faster and more robust. He was also a superior being, to be horse-borne

In close-order British infantry are drilled with iron discipline. First and 4th Divisions marched in such a manner and failed to fire a shot in the battle.

at all, and it is worthy of note that, to this day, cavalry regiments take precedence over infantrymen of the British Army

The unpalatable truth, generally ignored, is that, in point of military history, cavalry has had a very up and down record as against infantry. Nothing can kill the cult and the 'glamorized' legend of British 'warhorses' and their association with the aristocracy, as at Balaclava. It is no chance that the Queen takes the salute, at the Trooping the Colour parade, on horseback (rather than standing by the Mausoleum, like a Russian military leader), and the British still refuse to eat horsemeat, for no coherent reasons.

The Russians had about 50,000 troops available for the attack on Balaclava, and the allies had 66,000, but only a few thousand British and Russian mounted troops, and some guns were involved in the curiously unreal battle, during the last great war to be fought in scarlet and gold, according to the military equivalent of the Queensberry Rules of the Ring. Nor were the French and Turks involved to blur the pattern.

Lord Raglan's headquarters were on the Sapoune Ridge, some five miles out from Balaclava, and about 25,000 of his besieging troops were around him. Balaclava itself was but lightly guarded and the British could have been cut off from their supplies at almost any time by any force less dim than the Russians.

File to your lines

In the pre-dawn half-light, on October 24, the anniversary of Agincourt, half the Russian army (consisting of 20,000 infantry, 3,000 cavalry, and 78 guns) was seen to be advancing through the eastern approaches towards the North Valley which faced the British. The Cavalry Division, which had been 'standing to horses', was ordered to 'file to your lines' and was drawn up at the other end of the valley, just outside Russian gun range, the Light Brigade to the left, the Heavy to the right, directly under Raglan's 'eyrie', whence he proposed to watch the battle through his spy-glass.

A British horse battery of two howitzers and four six-pounders unlimbered near the Causeway to the right of the valley, between the second and third redoubt. Another battery of guns was established to the north of the Causeway.

Cardigan, who was still asleep in his private

Above Lord Raglan, the British commander at Balaclava who lost his right arm at Waterloo, still sometimes thought he was fighting the French.

Right Two squadrons of the Royal Scots Greys (2nd Dragoons) lead the charge of the Heavy Brigade.

yacht in the bay, was roused; various wives were sent for so that they could 'enjoy' the sight of the battle from Raglan's hill-top hq, just as a Russian cannonade of some power opened the proceedings. A small party of Turks in the most forward redoubt on Canrobert's Hill, hopelessly outgunned and seeing no hope of relief from the British, fell back, as did their compatriots on the Causeway Heights, from the second of the six redoubts. These latter were pursued by Cossack cavalry and many were cut to pieces without mercy.

Too many Russians

Seeing the port of Balaclava threatened, the British sent troops from the northern flank to reinforce the small garrison; this exposed the third (strategically most important) redoubt in the heart of the North Valley. Its Turkish occupants fled screaming 'Too many Russians', as did those of the fourth redoubt at the other end of the valley, in front of the cavalry division. The British NCOs who had led them remained long enough to spike the guns of the second, third and fourth redoubts. All this negative

activity had taken up the first hour of the battle, and some time had been gained to get most of the British officers to the scene. By the laws of war (British version) nothing positive could happen in the game until the captains of the teams were present.

Raglan's first order, sent at some leisure by foot from his almost inaccessible post, was to the cavalry, and it was for them to retreat behind the 'safe' sixth redoubt, still nearer to him.

At this point, the Russians, with great superiority of numbers, could have overwhelmed the

The 1st Division took a roundabout route to the plain, to avoid any confrontation with the Russians, and was astonished, when on the Sapoune heights, to see an immense body of Cossacks, in close formation, accompanied by artillery and followed by infantry, moving up the North Valley. In due course, Raglan, with the

The 17th Lancers have reached the 12 Russian guns, but Cossacks are counter-charging. Blunt sabres and lances reduced losses in such melees.

British, but they were ditherers, too, and they did nothing. A lull of some hours descended on the battlefield, while Raglan gave the order for a frugal breakfast for the troops, to be washed down with a welcome tot of rum, and called in two reserve divisions, the 1st and 4th, in support; but the 4th was delayed because its commander, Sir George Cathcart, refused to hurry his breakfast and sat in his tent drinking coffee for 40 minutes after the order had reached him. It would have been funny had it not been so tragic.

over-cautious Canrobert beside him, saw this, too, with panic in his heart.

Heavy Brigade in action

Thinking the Russians were headed direct for Balaclava, by-passing him, Raglan ordered eight squadrons of the Heavy Brigade to attack the Russians, who were now in sight, over the causeway ridge. The 'Heavies' were at a tactical disadvantage, on lower ground; they were strung out in two lines; and they were led by a courageous but short-sighted inexperienced dolt, Scarlett. They were also about 300 strong against the Russian's 2,000 or more horses, now not more than half a mile away.

Stupidly ignoring the Russians' rapid approach, Scarlett and his officers placed themselves in front of their troopers, their backs to the enemy, put out markers, and unhurriedly dressed them by the right, as they had learned to do on the parade grounds of Hounslow and Phoenix Park in Britain. Nor was the ritual hurried when the trumpeter, on Lucan's order, sounded the charge.

Again the Russians had the chance of a lifetime. Again they allowed themselves to be astounded to see Scarlett, his aide-de-camp, his trumpeter and his orderly charging towards them at full tilt, while the squadrons behind them got slowly into movement, through the walk, the trot and the gallop, as was the correct drill.

A Russian retreat

The fearless four arrived at the Russian fore a full 60 yards ahead of the rest and somehow slashed their way through the massed ranks. The arrival of the British squadrons was also allowed to happen without real resistance, other than a few wild carbine shots, and for minutes the disorganized, bewildered Russians waited for an

The Thin Red Line of the 93rd Argyll and Sutherland Highlanders stopped the Russians from reaching the port of Balaclava.

bamboozled by the British pantomime. They halted in tight formation, about 400 yards away from Scarlett's backside, staring blankly, unbelievingly to their front. And they watched for long minutes while Scarlett completed the drill, gave 'Eyes front!' and turned to face them.

They were still stationary when the commander of the Heavy Brigade suddenly ordered the 'Charge'. He did this in such a way that only those nearest to him heard it at first, with the result that the Russians were still further

order that was never given. Their general was speechless, apparently affronted. The Scots Greys and the Inniskillings cut and hacked their way into the enemy, fighting like heroes, soon to be followed by several squadrons of Dragoons. Too late the Russian general realized the mistake he had made in receiving the charge standing still, instead of at the counter-charge, and he led the retreat to safety behind the lines of the sheltering guns along the Causeway.

The English had muddled through once again.

All this while, the Light Brigade had stood to one side, 500 yards away, motionless. It would not have been 'cricket' for them to interfere, and, in any event, Lord Cardigan had not yet arrived from his yacht. Even when the Russians fled and

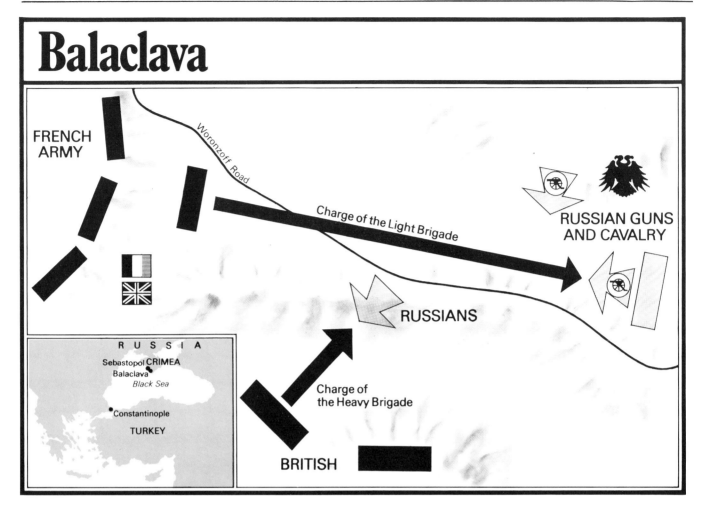

Balaclava

FRENCH ARMY

Woronzoff Road

Charge of the Light Brigade

RUSSIAN GUNS AND CAVALRY

RUSSIANS

R U S S I A

Sebastopol CRIMEA
Balaclava
Black Sea

Charge of
the Heavy Brigade

•Constantinople
TURKEY

BRITISH

positive action, in the form of pursuit, was obviously called for, neither Lucan nor Cardigan *did* anything, and Scarlett chose to re-muster his squadrons.

In due course, however, the Light Brigade was to have its moment of bloody pantomime, and, through it, Balaclava was to be immortalized in Alfred Lord Tennyson's epic poem of the Charge.

Charge of the Light Brigade

Lord Raglan and his party had been seated on rocks, like playgoers in the circle, watching the battle. He now decided it was time to bring the infantry into play, as well as the Light Brigade into the action. He sent a characteristically unclear order down the hill. It got thoroughly garbled. Lord Lucan interpreted it as an order for his remaining cavalry brigade to charge down the valley (actually Raglan had wanted him to recapture the redoubts on the heights). Cardigan protested that it was suicidal so to proceed. But

The Light Brigade were supposed to exploit the success of the 'Heavies' by recapturing the Causeway Heights but instead advanced straight down North Valley – the 'Valley of Death'.

he nevertheless went through all the drills and led the charge across the mile and a half of frozen soil towards the Russian batteries straight ahead, and through the flanking cross-fire of other guns and riflemen, only to have to double back again through the mayhem of the plain.

In half an hour, nearly 500 of the 673 officers and troopers had been killed, wounded, or dishorsed, in the inferno of fire. Cardigan was spared to walk his horse round the rear, across the valley to safety, partly because the Russian Prince Radzivil had recognized him as a society acquaintance, as he rode between the guns, and had ordered that he should be captured rather than killed. He had done enough, he felt. A hot bath was called for. He was apparently indifferent to the shambles he had left behind. But first he wrapped himself in a blanket and slept exhausted on the ground near the Brigade camp – overcome by his exertions.

Bravery was all; intelligence, knowledge and organization were of no account.

The operations were then suspended. The wretched Russians, with apparently no more heart for the fight, were allowed to hold on to the three redoubts. And the siege, interrupted only by the Battle of Inkerman, continued for the best part of a year.

Balaclava was a victory *manqué*. Nor was the Crimean War a success. Certainly, as far as political objectives were concerned, it accomplished virtually nothing.

The casualties were terrible to contemplate, and 88 per cent of the 20,000 British victims of the war fell to disease and deprivation.

The 'rag trade' probably benefited most from the lah-de-dah fashions of the officers concerned. The battle and the campaign begat the Raglan coat sleeve, the Cardigan and the Balaclava helmet.

*Overleaf The Light Brigade had 195 mounted survivors, leaving 113 dead and 134 wounded with 231 unhorsed men. But the rigours of camp **below**, the climate and lack of medical care killed far more.*

SECOND BULL RUN

The bonfire of captured stores lit by 'Stonewall' Jackson's Confederate troops after defeating the Northerners at Bull Run in 1862 could be seen in Washington, capital of the North. It was the high spot for the South during the American Civil War.

Second Bull Run

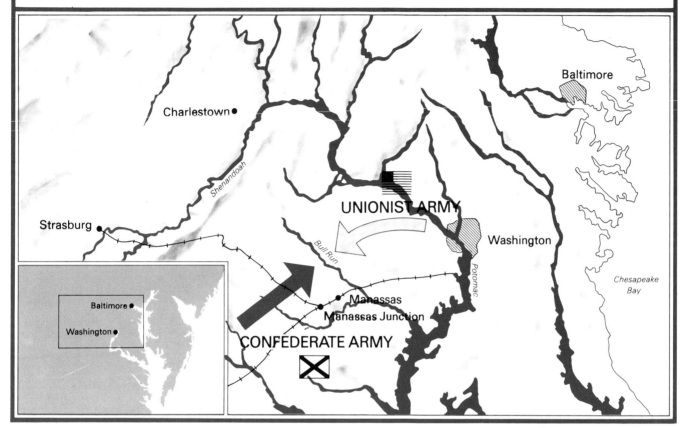

There are many shades between black and white in any argument, but the clash between the northern and the southern states in America, in the 1860s, clearly sprang from the question of slavery, whatever nuances there may have been. Largely condemned in the relatively progressive and democratic North, slavery was the basis of a distinctive aristocratic society in the South.

The actual Civil War which stemmed from this was fought, when Abraham Lincoln was made President, to decide whether the South had the right to secede from the Union and pursue its own ways in a separate republic, the Confederate States, under its own man, Jefferson Davis.

The high-water mark

The Second Battle of Bull Run, sometimes called Second Manassas, in August 1862, was a high-water mark for the Confederates. It was also the beginning of a dreary record of defeat for the Union cause in Virginia, in which the North's commanders were outwitted and outfought by

Left 'Stonewall' Jackson whose daring raid on Manassass Junction 'set up' a second Southern victory at Bull Run.

Above A new Union army formed to threaten the Southern capital found itself defeated 23 miles from its own.

brave bands of Confederates, under General Robert E. Lee's restlessly-ambitious crop of lieutenants: Longstreet, the Hills, Ewell, Stuart, and the astonishing Thomas 'Stonewall' Jackson.

The First Battle of Bull Run had been in July 1861, when 20,000 Union men, under General McDowell, had been humiliated into a panic-stricken rout, to the point that the fall of the capital became a sudden frightening possibility. After the battle, the frightened northerners had built up a well-equipped army of 150,000 men, and had decided on an 'Anaconda' strategy for 1862 which would hinge on Northern pincer offensives in both the west and east, following the blockade of the entire Southern coast.

Politics, however, smothered the good intentions of the North's strategists, and fumbling

SECOND BULL RUN

Left Supplies for the campaign of 1862 at Yorktown which had been captured by Federal troops.

Below Manassass junction after Jackson's visit on August 27th. The rail bridge was broken and anything that could not be carried off was burnt that night.

Overleaf Sigel's German Union corps furiously assaults Jackson on the first day of Second Bull Run.

defence rather than driving attack was becoming the order of the day by mid-1862. Their dictatorial commander-in-chief, young George B. 'Little Napoleon' McClellan had his wings clipped, when Congress reduced him in rank to commander of the Army of the Potomac. He was ordered to remain on the Virginia Peninsula and defend Washington.

Lincoln called John Pope from the west to command a new army to march from Washington to Richmond. McClellan was then ordered to leave the Peninsula and pull back to Washington. The intention was that he should unite with Pope and resume the drive on the Confederate capital. General Lee guessed what was afoot. His response was to deal first with Pope. On August 9, Stonewall Jackson intercepted a detachment of Pope's army at Cedar Mountain and routed it. There followed a series of manoeuvres which forced Pope's main forces to retreat to the apparent security of the north side of the Rappahannock River, where he proposed to wait until McClellan's troops reinforced him.

Lee's counter-plan was brilliant, if risky. Against all text-book rules, he divided his army. One half, under 'Stonewall' Jackson, was sent hot-foot to the north-west, around Pope's flank, while the other half, under General James Longstreet, was kept facing Pope to hold his attention. and camouflage the diversion.

Stonewall Jackson

Jackson's fast-moving infantry, making record time, swung off behind Bull Run mountains –

which he knew well. He had got his heroic name in the first battle of Bull Run, when General Bee had said: 'Look at Jackson! There he stands, like a stone wall.'

Thence he speeded east through Thoroughfare Gap, whence he was able to surprise and overwhelm the Unionists' supply base at Manassas junction, in Pope's rear. This caused the Union army to turn away defensively from Longstreet, which, in turn, gave Lee and Longstreet the chance to slip away to join Jackson east of the mountains. It was bluff, counter-bluff, and it succeeded brilliantly.

John Pope now became thoroughly confused. He had a stubborn energetic courage, but he was somewhat slow-thinking, and Lee had always been able to read his intentions. Pope chased his mobile army 'around the houses', looking for Jackson, who had, in truth, moved his 25,000 men out from Manassas as swiftly as he had pounced. And he had, unknown to Pope's scouts, taken up concealed positions in the hills and in the natural cover of the wooded thickets of the winding stream of the familiar battlefield at Bull Run. So well hidden were the Confederates that Pope's infantrymen thoroughly exhausted themselves

Left *Federal General John Pope who boasted that his HQ was 'in the saddle'. Lee retorted 'headquarters on his hindquarters!'*

Below *A Union battery of artillery is about to fire. The men are ramming home the powder and shot.*

and his cavalry got in a lather, whipping from hill to hill without catching sight of even one southerner.

When the Northern army finally made contact with the Southern on the slopes of Bull Run on August 29, it was more by good luck than judgement. Pope was by now like an enraged bull. He forced his tired, partly-trained militia – Irishmen from New York and Boston; Germans from St. Louis; Pennsylvanian farm boys clutching flintlocks; and some well-schooled career soldiers – to battle up the hill in headlong assault.

In the skirmishing that followed, the North did so well that the Southerners held their entrenched ground with great difficulty and some considerable loss, before apparently retreating.

In fact, as darkness fell, Jackson had chosen deliberately to withdraw to a second line of defence. And the foolish Pope misread the situation to the point that he sent a messenger galloping off to Washington, 23 miles away, with a dispatch which read: 'Enemy in full retreat; am preparing to pursue and harry.'

The Confederates attack

In the morning, he woke up with egg on his face. Jackson's losses had been bearable. He had regrouped and was holding the same hill just as strongly, a bit higher up. Lee and Longstreet had arrived on the scene. They nibbled at Pope's flank,

and at the same moment Stonewall Jackson switched from defence to attack.

His men were devoted to him; he was probably better loved than any general of the period. A West Point man, he was a general at the age of only 38. He had, above all things, the sort of honest, open style of command that ensured absolute loyalty.

Nor did any Confederate officer or soldier fail him at this important moment of the war. He had trained them well in small arms – having been a professor at Lexington Military Institution just before the war – and he led his cumbersome army personally, without fear or hesitation. Stonewall was steady as a rock in the heart of the battle.

Each opposing force tried to turn his opponent's left flank, and for a time North and South were locked in hand-to-hand skirmishing, men on both sides waving flags when not in contact, and each side trying to out-shout the other in its version of a popular song of the day, 'Flag of the Free'. Irish immigrants on opposing sides shouted Gaelic expletives at each other as they hacked away with a will. 'It was very unreal,' said an eye-witness, 'this fighting between brothers, cousins and ex business friends. The Northerners seemed to have less heart in the proceedings than the men of the South, but that was probably because of the superiority of the South's leadership.'

Jackson breaks through

Although in the last hours of the battle, some of McClellan's divisions succeeded in joining up with Pope's army, Jackson's frontal attack finally broke through and reduced the Union army to disorder. Crushed and dispirited, it fled to the north of Bull Run and all the way back to Washington.

It was a remarkable Confederate victory. General Pope had lost the day, his reputation as the scourge of the west, his nerve and his prospects. He had also lost some 16,000 of his army – dead, wounded and prisoners – plus many horses and all his artillery.

Confederate losses were serious but less heavy. Jackson's men were in great good spirits. They went on to deal the final humiliation of Pope's defeat when they captured intact all the Union army's stores and the general's headquarters, in a brilliant post-battle move, schemed by Stonewall Jackson. The stores, filling a train of cars two miles long, were burned after the Confederates had taken all the plunder they could carry . . . and the light of the extravagant bonfire could be clearly seen at the White House in Washington.

A Union gun crew stand by their field-gun. It is probably a 3-inch Parrott rifled muzzle-loader which fired a ten pound smooth metal banded shell spun by the rifling. A light, accurate gun it had a range of 1,900 yards. The man on the right is about to fire the piece by a long lanyard that enables him to stand away from the gun's recoil. On the right of the breach is the Parrott's pendulum sight.

SOMME

Slaughter on a scale never seen before or since was the trade-mark of the offensive on the Somme in France of 1916 as the British, under General Haig, and French tried to drive the Germans back by sheer weight of numbers — and paid the price.

Below Two British machine-gunners, wearing gas helmets, fire at a German communication trench. The fire-power of the machine-gun took a fearsome toll of any infantry advance – this Vickers .303-inch Mark I fired about 500 rounds a minute.

Right Five miles was the gain from 140 days of fighting through the blood-soaked mud of the Somme – five miles and honours for the generals.

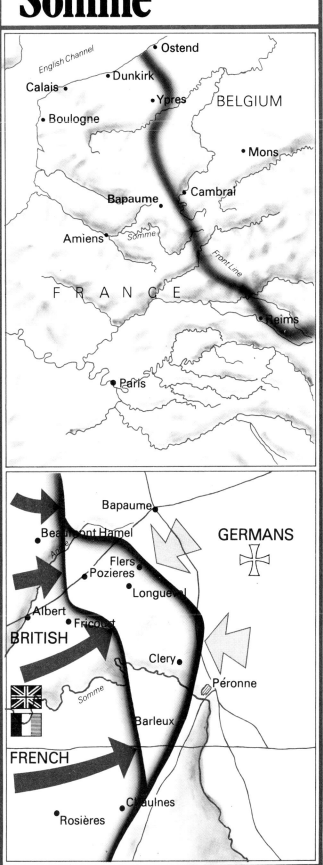

Somme

The battle of the Somme should have sickened mankind of warfare forever. The sheer bestiality of deadlocked trench fighting on this scale is almost unimaginable: slime, blood, rats, thirst, filth, gas, metal showers, fear of death, despair and madness . . . these things are so beyond the normal as to demand revolt. And yet, on the Somme during 1916, men on both sides went on enduring them for months. There were, indeed, mutinies in the French army, but not in the British.

The period between July 1, 1916, and April, 1917, which embraced the Somme offensive and the retreat which followed, was the bloodiest of the whole bloody war.

The Western Front, where the Somme river lay, was the critical front, and everyone on both sides of it knew, by the end of June, 1916, that it was about to be put to the test. At this moment, the German line stretched in sickle-shape from Switzerland to the shores of Belgium.

The sector of the line that seemed to offer the best outcome to successful attack was that covering Ypres and Compiegne. Here the lines of communications of the German army in France and Belgium could be cut.

The British held about 90 miles of the front, from above Ypres to the Somme. The French were in an adjacent sector, to the south. Amiens, the city on the Somme, the spider in the centre of a web of communications stretching all over Normandy, was to be the base from which the

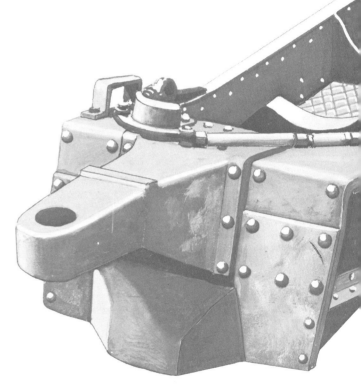

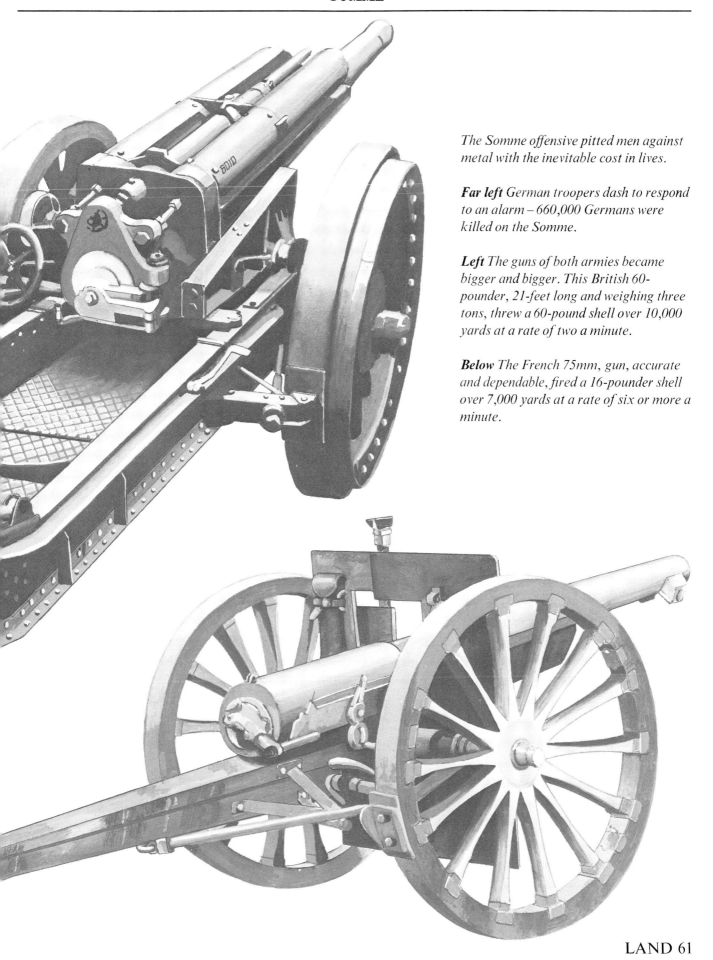

The Somme offensive pitted men against metal with the inevitable cost in lives.

Far left German troopers dash to respond to an alarm – 660,000 Germans were killed on the Somme.

Left The guns of both armies became bigger and bigger. This British 60-pounder, 21-feet long and weighing three tons, threw a 60-pound shell over 10,000 yards at a rate of two a minute.

Below The French 75mm, gun, accurate and dependable, fired a 16-pounder shell over 7,000 yards at a rate of six or more a minute.

Allies would strike.

The Germans were massed beyond the low hills which sheltered the plains. This meant the British had to attack up steep slopes in generally hostile country.

Bombs, gas and guns

The most ambitious campaign in which the British had ever been engaged opened with several days of bombardment, by artillery and from the air. Poison gas was dropped at least 40 times. Aerial photographs were taken of the German lines on the north bank of the river. The light field guns had a special task: to destroy the miles of woven barbed wire, devised as an initial obstacle to advancing troops.

The heavy guns concentrated on concrete redoubts with steel emplacements for machine guns. Trench mortars of all sizes accounted for observation posts and first line trenches, while howitzers attacked the second and third lines of defence. But no artillery was capable of dealing with the underground burrows and shelters, up to two-thirds of a mile deep, which ran into

Opposite Deadlocked trench warfare earned the name The Sausage Machine because it took in men, churned out corpses and stayed firmly screwed in place.

Above A German trench gun in action – gunners crawled from dug-outs to fire at advancing infantry.

Left The landscape suffered – and so did the soldiers. They bravely fought their way through blood, mud and slime.

mountains of slag and clinker. These featured impregnable underground caverns, from which 'fresh' German machine gunners could quickly emerge against an infantry attack.

Come on, British pigs

The plan was that battle should commence on June 28, but bad weather prevented this, and it was three more days before the word was given. Of course, by this time the Germans knew what was going on to the point that they raised banners and placards announcing: 'Come on, British pigs; we are ready for you.'

On Saturday, July 1, the British attacked at 7.30 on a sultry summer morning. Mainly involved was 5 Corps of General Rawlinson's Fourth Army, with 7 Corps of General Allenby's Third Army on its left. There were 19 divisions allotted to the attack, making 200,000 infantry. There were also nearly 100,000 British artillery-men involved, and these fired 13,000 tons of shells in support on July 1 alone.

On the German side, General Fritz von Below was in command of the Second Army.

At the appointed hour, platoon commanders blew their whistles almost in unison, summoning the largely untrained troops to leave their trenches and brave the smudged, cratered wastes of No Man's Land. A series of extended lines advanced – two paces between men and 100 yards between ranks.

The greatest catastrophe

On the other side, the moment the British barrage eased for the infantry assault, German machine gunners rushed from their dugouts and ran to the nearest shell craters, establishing a line of rapid-fire defence. Their moment soon came when the rapidly-advancing thousands reached the German barbed wire and tragically found it uncut by shells along two-thirds of the front. They were aunt-sallies. There was no way forward, and they could not go back because of the press of line after line behind.

The enemy machine guns opened up and mowed down the British at will. The slaughter was on a scale never seen before or since and it was the greatest single catastrophe of 'the great war'. On that first day of the battle of the Somme, British casualties totalled 57,470, Of these, more than 20,000 died where they lay.

Little ground had been gained. Nothing worthwhile had been achieved. There was no chance of a break-out. Yet the offensive continued on Sunday, July 2 . . . on Monday, July 3 . . . on July 4 . . . . On and on went the battering ram, without finesse and with inevitable useless slaughter at around 10,000 a day, through July, August, September, October and into November.

General Douglas Haig, British commander in chief, ordered his troops to press on 'without intermission'; the Germans observed that the British army were 'lions led by donkeys'; and Colonel Winston Churchill protested that 'the open country towards which we are struggling by inches is utterly devoid of military significance. There is no question of breaking the line, or letting loose the cavalry in the open country behind, or of inducing a general withdrawal of the German armies in the West.'

Left *From left to right General Joffre, Sir Douglas Haig and General Foch decided Allied strategy at the Somme: their recipe – more men, more guns.*

Below *Some of the guns in action. This is a British battery of eight-inch howitzers used for shelling artillery positions, trenches and so on.*

Blood and slime

In the midst of the offensive, but without any attempt at co-ordination, a large French contingent, under General Ferdinand Foch, fought on the right of the British, and were able to advance, where the British could not, before eventually becoming just as stuck in the blood-soaked mud – their casualties equally heavy.

Later, during the 140 days of the Somme, torrential rain played its part. The entire battlefield became a slough where the wounded could disappear into slime in an instant, where attacks were pressed with men wading up to their hips, where men drowned in trenches from sheer weariness. The landscape was murdered, as well as its human moles. And always there were guns, aircraft, balloons, bombs and poison gas.

The brave and the dead

Tales of daring were fed back to the public, and there was bravery in the midst of the filth and stagnancy. But mostly the deeds most worthy of medals were done unseen by the medal-givers. There was also muddle and inefficiency on a massive scale, from the miscalculations of the leaders to the British patrols who lost their way at night and found themselves in German trenches in mistake for their own.

The Somme offensive began as a British push, but before it ended nearly all the Empire had taken part. The South Africans joined in at Delville Wood; the Australians were involved at Pozieres and Warlencourt; the New Zealanders fought bravely to the west of Gueudecourt; the Canadians took over at Pozieres; there were even Indians on horseback south of High Wood.

The long battle petered out on November 19, when the Allies managed to reach the southern half of the Bapaume to Peronne road, having achieved little territorially. It was claimed that Haig's plan had ground down the enemy towards his eventual collapse. The cold figures showed that the Allied casualties totalled some 630,000 against 660,000 on the German side.

Both sides fought a battle of attrition. Here the crews of German 21 cm. howitzers survey the resulting devastation.

CAMBRAI

Mobile armoured warfare exploded at Cambrai, France in 1917. For the first time ever, squadrons of tanks roared towards the German lines, striking terror into the hearts of the defenders, and paving the way for the Panzer thrusts of World War II.

Looming out of the mist the British tanks so frightened the Germans that they christened them 'devil coaches'. At Cambrai, massed squadrons of Mark IVs stormed directly towards the German lines. A great improvement on earlier models that had operated in small numbers from September 1916, the Mark VI carried heavier armour plating and mounted two long-barrelled six-pounders and four machine-guns – the 'female' version had just machine-guns. Its maximum speed was around four miles an hour. The wooden bar above the body could be carried round by the tracks to give leverage in muddy conditions.

At the first battle of Cambrai, on November 20, 1917, no fewer than 324 tanks were used, in circumstances of maximum surprise, and the effect on the Germans was as sensational as if flying saucers had descended. The boost to British morale, on the other hand, was as welcome as it was necessary.

This was the first major engagement for the British invention which was to transform tactical planning on land. Named the 'tank' in development in 1915 as a security precaution, it had appeared briefly in small numbers on the Somme on 15 September, 1916, but few had seen it and little had since been said.

In the winter that followed the long battle of the Somme, the Germans had secretly withdrawn slowly from the river to base themselves on a prepared position some miles behind, known as the Hindenburg Line. Hindenburg and Ludendorff had become joint commanders of the German armies.

Thereafter, the Germans made no great effort on the Western Front in 1917. Secure in the knowledge that they had air superiority, they remained defensive, whereas the Allies embarked on two major and extremely costly offensives – both characteristic failures.

Two mistakes by the Allies

First, the French attacked on the Aisne, to the south of Cambrai between Soissons and Rheims. Security was so bad, the Germans knew the battle orders in advance. The French, under General Robert Nivelle, gained a small part of the heights above the Aisne, but at a terrible cost. There was also a serious mutiny in the French army. Nivelle was replaced by General Philippe Pétain.

Second, the Third Battle of Ypres, or Passchendaele, to the north of Cambrai, began

in July, and was to became the crowning horror of the trench warfare of the Western Front.

In the Ypres salient the most unthinkable conditions prevailed. The drainage system had broken down from continual shell fire, and the entire battlefield was a swamp, blasted and cratered like a moonscape.

Grimly and unfeelingly, Sir Douglas Haig had forced his infantry – British, Canadian and Australian – again and again across this waterlogged wasteland. Attack after attack – watched in disbelief by the German supremo, Ludendorff himself – petered out among the mud and blood of the Passchendaele Ridge. Haig had created a treadmill of horror and he kept it going with seeming masochism . . . but from a distance. He never once visited the battlefield.

As the months of slaughter, or 'grinding down' as Haig chose to call it, went on, the Germans were killing three soldiers for every man they lost themselves, but Haig somehow managed to go on finding replacements for his dead. By the time the Ypres fighting had at last died down from sheer mutual exhaustion, the British and their Empire had gained a couple of thousand yards at a cost of 300,000 casualties, 'the flower of our manhood'.

Men of vision

But there were some military men of vision. One was General Sir Julian Byng, who was among the first to grasp the importance of the tank as a weapon. Shortly after General Haig had reluctantly broken off his futile offensive, Byng's Third Army, at the instigation of General Ferdinand Foch, about to become generalissimo, launched the surprise tank attack at Cambrai –

the most important centre of German communications in the West at that time.

The Cambrai plan had been produced by Britain's chief tank expert, Colonel Fuller, and Byng had gone along with him on the idea that it could bring dramatic mobility to the static front, with its grim positional warfare. Both agreed the country chosen was ideal for tanks.

Inevitably, the original plan, prepared in August, 1917, changed considerably in discussion. Inevitably, also, when Haig was told, he would have none of it. He did not have much faith in the tank, which he called 'a useful, if mechanically unreliable supporting weapon, but one that could never be considered a decisive one in its own right'.

Eventually, the pro-tank men presented the Cambrai plan to Haig as 'tanks supporting infantry' in a way that got his grudging sanction on October 13.

300 tanks and 1,000 guns

A week later Byng was ready for the crossing of the Hindenburg Line and the capture of Cambrai. He had assembled six infantry divisions, five cavalry divisions, nine tank battalions and 1,000 guns for the drive. Secrecy had been well maintained, with all tank movements taking place at night.

The day dawned misty and at 0630 hours all the tanks, commanded by General Elles, led six divisions of infantry into No Man's Land, supported above by nearly 300 strafing aircraft. The plan worked with incredible smoothness. The tanks broke through the successive belts of

Tanks needed infantry to back them up. Here men of the 11th Inniskilling Fusiliers advance over the captured German second line near Havrincourt. The Germans thought the line impregnable.

German wire, which were of great strength and depth, so that the English, Scottish and Irish regiments which followed were able to sweep over the enemy's outposts and storm the first defensive system of the Hindenburg Line on the whole front. They then pressed on in the shelter of the tanks, and captured the Hindenburg Support Line more than a mile ahead.

The tanks acted like small animated forts, moving through villages and in effect occupying them. At Lateau Wood, a tank even charged a battery of 5.9 mm artillery, pushed between and amongst them, scattering the crews and capturing the guns.

Haig reports victory

The following day Haig sent a report of the battle to London speaking of an amazing victory. It read:

'Yesterday morning the Third Army, under the command of General the Hon. Sir Julian Byng, delivered a number of attacks between St Quentin and the river Scarpe. These attacks were carried out without previous artillery preparation, and in each case the enemy were completely surprised. Our troops have broken into the enemy's positions to a depth of between four and five miles on a wide front, and have captured several thousand prisoners with a number of guns. At the hour of assault on the principal front of the attack a large number of tanks moved forward in advance of the infantry, and broke through the successive belts of German wire, which were of great depth and strength.

'Following through the gaps made by the tanks, English, Scottish, and Irish regiments swept over the enemy's outposts, and stormed the first defensive system of the Hindenburg Line on the whole front. Our infantry and tanks then pressed on in accordance with programme, and captured the German second system of defence more than a mile beyond. This latter is known as the Hindenburg support line.

'In the course of this advance East-country troops took the hamlet of Bonavis and Lateau Wood after stiff fighting. English rifle regiments

Tanks 'cleared the way' by smashing through barbed wire, opening up the softer defences of the Hindenburg Line.

and light infantry captured La Vacquerie, and the formidable defences of the spur known as Welsh Ridge.

'Other English country troops stormed the village of Ribecourt, and fought their way through Coutlett Wood. Highland Territorial battalions crossed the Grand Ravine and entered Flesquieres, where fierce fighting took place.

'West Riding Territorials captured Havrincourt and the German trench systems north of the village, while Ulster battalions covering the latter's left flank moved northwards up the west bank of the Canal du Nord. Later in the morning our advance was continued, and rapid progress was made at all points.

'English, Scottish, Irish, and Welsh battalions secured the crossings of the canal at Masnieres and captured Marcoing and Neuf Wood. The West Riding troops who had taken Havrincourt made remarkable progress east of the Canal du Nord, storming the villages of Graincourt and Anneux, and with the Ulster troops operating west of the canal carried the whole of the German line northwards to the Bapaume-Cambrai road.

'West Lancashire Territorials broke into the enemy's position east of Epehy, and Irish troops

have captured important sections of the Hindenburg Line between Bullecourt and Fontaine-les-Croisilles. The number of prisoners, guns, and material captured cannot yet be estimated.

'The spell of fine dull weather which favoured our preparations for our attacks broke early yesterday. Heavy rain fell during the night and the weather is now stormy.'

In truth, in the first six hours Byng's army had captured more ground than 51 British divisions had done at Third Ypres in four months of desperate fighting.

The tanks had driven at will through the German lines to a distance of 10,000 yards.

As British tanks advance towards the attack on Bourlon Wood, they pass German guns already captured in earlier attacks. The Germans lost 142 guns and a total of 50,000 killed, missing or wounded.

The terrifying tank

On the German side it was a traumatic experience. The tank has become known as a blitzkreig weapon of great versatility – as flamethrower, mine-exploder, cavalry recce vehicle, armoured amphibian, mobile destroyer and so on – but it terrified the Germans at Cambrai. Many crossed themselves and surrendered on their knees.

It must have been utterly unnerving for them to be faced, without warning or explanation, by steel monsters which crushed vast wire entanglements, like so much straw, crashed through dugouts, smashed machine-guns to bits, and ploughed on across the mud with flames darting from their steaming exhaust pipes.

Nearly 9,000 German prisoners and 100 German guns were captured that day and British losses were comparatively negligible. And one of the strongest sectors of the German Western Front had been broken in a single blow.

Ludendorff was beside himself. The surprise of the event completely shattered him. He frantically ordered up several divisions for a counter-attack. But he was grimly aware that this would take a week or so to stage.

In fact, he need not have worried. Haig who, earlier in the year, had so confidently assembled his cavalry behind the Ypres swamps for the expected easy victory ride to the coast, had had no expectation of success with Byng's tanks, and had concentrated no reserves to exploit success in front of Cambrai. Indeed, most of the troops he should have used were rotting in the Passchendaele mud.

By November 29, Ludendorff was ready. His counter-attack was completely successful. By the next day the British had lost all and more of the ground they had won in the great massed tank victory of November 20.

Top left *Tanks line up ready to advance.*

Left *Defenders at Cambrai found rifles and grenades useless before the terrifying tanks – but the Germans were developing anti-tank flame-throwers and guns.*

Right *In six hours, 324 tanks captured more ground than 51 division had taken in four months of fighting at Ypres.*

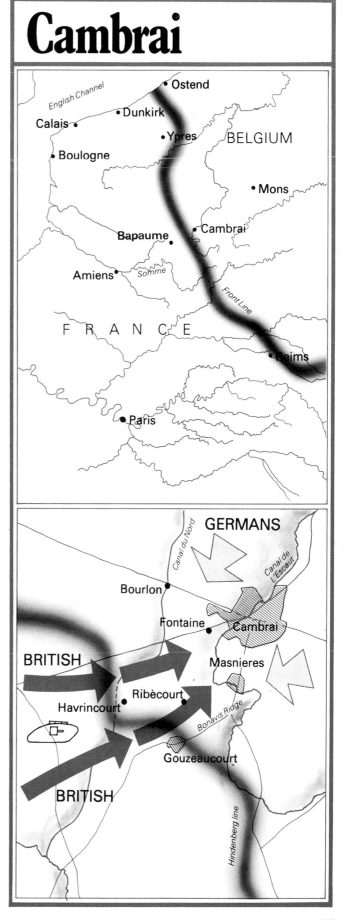

GAZALA

In the deserts of North Africa, during the drive on Tobruk in 1942, Rommel displayed the fast-moving tactical brilliance that has made his campaigns famous — if the British had read his book on tank warfare they might have made fewer mistakes.

At Gazala, Rommel took the initiative. Churchill had pressed for an Allied offensive – but while they prepared, Rommel struck. His daring paid off. As he poured forward the tanks, troop carriers, armoured half-tracks, Kubelwagens, lorries, and motorcycles of the Afrika Korps and the Italians, the Gazala line crumbled and Tobruk fell.

Many of the British troops who took part in the Battle of Gazala in the Western Desert were 'militiamen'. They had been called up three years before, in the summer of 1939, simply because they were 20 years of age. After training, they had been shipped out to the desert to fight the Italians. They were the 'brave amateurs' of World War II – muddling through to win in the end.

Below *The mighty 88 was the wonder-gun of the Desert War. With the base dug in, the gun presented a small target to tanks and could pierce 99 mm. armour at 2,200 yards. It was highly accurate and the Germans deployed it with skill, forming an anti-tank screen behind which armour could operate. The 25-foot long gun could throw an 88 mm. shell nearly 11,000 yards at a rate of six a minute.*

So ill-prepared had the cavalry arm of the British Army been at the start of the war that some regiments in the desert had only horses and swords with which to harry the Italians. Nor had things improved all that much by the summer of 1942.

Reconnaissance regiments – vital in desert warfare – were equipped with South African made armoured cars that had been used in World War I, or with Rolls-Royce, Daimler and Humber vehicles of similar vintage. Tank regiments had mainly slow, obsolete Valentines or stop-gap Honeys. Virtually all the armoured cars and tanks in use had 'pea-shooter' guns, known as two-pounders.

There were a few American Grant tanks at Gazala, with larger 75mm guns but these were in

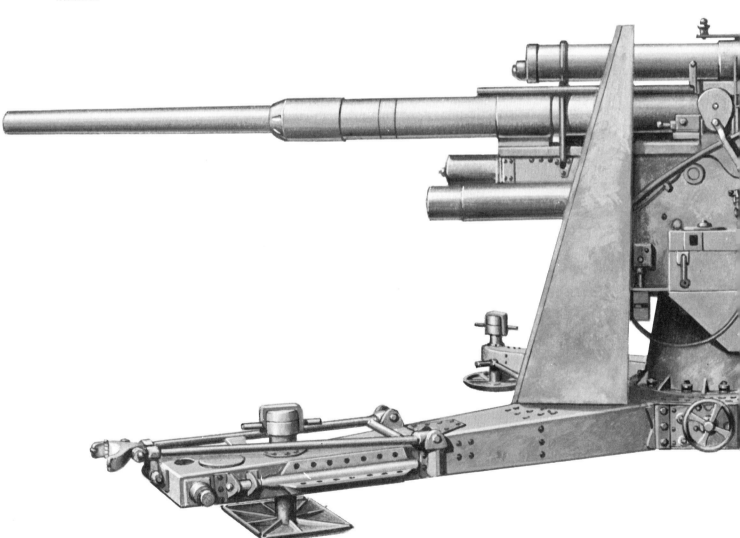

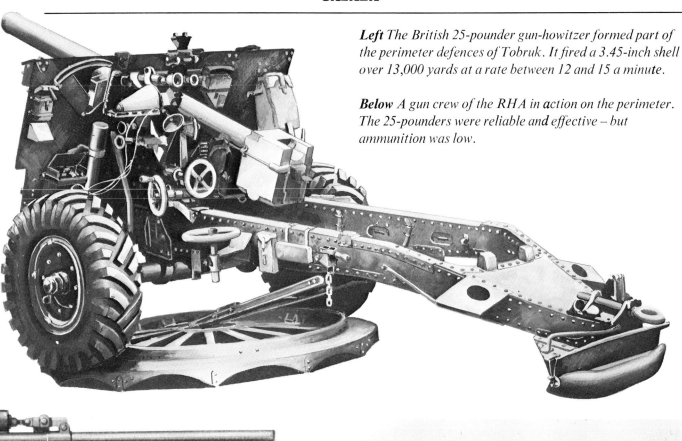

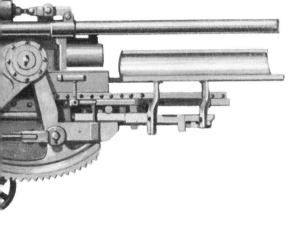

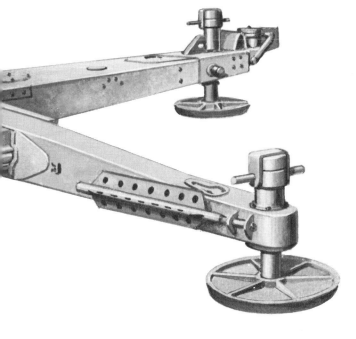

Left The British 25-pounder gun-howitzer formed part of the perimeter defences of Tobruk. It fired a 3.45-inch shell over 13,000 yards at a rate between 12 and 15 a minute.

Below A gun crew of the RHA in action on the perimeter. The 25-pounders were reliable and effective – but ammunition was low.

fixed turrets; and the Grant, which could not 'cruise', was vulnerable and liable to break down.

The mighty 88

All tanks in Rommel's Africa Korps could outgun almost anything the British possessed. His Panzer Mark IIIs and Mark IVs had 75mm guns (or 50mm at worst) and adaptations were appearing with 88mm – the finest gun of the war. These could knock out British armour at 1,500 yards; British two-pounder shells bounced off

German armour at anything over 1,000 yards. This was like David taking on Goliath, but with both hands tied behind his back until the last moment. Rings of German anti-tank guns – also 88mm – wrought similar havoc.

Not only was British armour outgunned and outpaced; it also tended to 'brew up'. Auxiliary 40-gallon drums of high-octane fuel, to give range, were often strapped to the flanks of the tank or armoured car. Incendiary bullets could cause an instant inferno from which no crewman could hope to escape. Charred bones in blackened iron 'coffins' were grim symbols of this phase of the desert war.

Such was life as the British Eighth Army, commanded by Lieutenant-General Neil Ritchie, faced the Africa Korps, and its Italian allies, under Field Marshal Erwin Rommel, the Desert Fox.

Gazala, point of no return

Germany dominated the central Mediterranean at this time and had good port facilities for the desert campaign. The two thorns in her flesh were Malta, whence her shipping was harried, and Tobruk, the Eighth Army's only nearby supply port. These were Hitler's two objectives in the area in the early part of 1942.

But Gazala, 40 miles to the west of Tobruk, was a sort of point of no return for both sides, half-way across the bleak deserts of Cyrenaica, in the centre of the long Mediterranean coast of Africa; their land supply and communication lines were stretched to the maximum.

Building up to battle

So, for the first few months of 1942, Rommel halted on the Tmimi-Mechili Line, facing Gazala until he could reinforce – notably with replacement Panzers through Tripoli.

During this same period Ritchie, a com-

The British defence was a series of 'boxes' which fought virtually independently, holding off attacks until supplies ran out.

paratively inexperienced staff officer thrust into the breach by Auchinleck, who preferred to command from Cairo, was building a strong Gazala Line. This consisted of a series of defended boxes – based on the British 'square' of Waterloo fame, but adapted to armoured fighting – linked to a vast minefield that stretched southwards from the sea to the Bir Hacheim Foreign Legion fortress. Each 'box' was garrisoned by an artillery-supported brigade group.

The desert war up to that point had been one of shuttling see-saw successes – three to each side. Rommel had been the latest to advance to reconquer the western half of Cyrenaica. Now he was building up to take Tobruk, without which, he knew, the British would have to retreat to the Egyptian frontier. Meanwhile, attempts were to be made by other German forces to capture the island of Malta.

The British plan was that the Eighth Army would attack, when ready, from the boxes of the Gazala line. In fact, Rommel struck first, on May 27.

On paper both sides were fairly matched: about 130,000 men and just over 700 tanks each.

The lesson of the Desert Fox

At first, it went fairly well for Britain, with Rommel frustrated in his break-through attempts for five days. One of the factors was a new anti-tank gun Britain was trying out, a useful six-pounder, nearer in bore to the German 88s. The RAF, too, was attacking every German supply convoy.

But losses of British tanks were heavy, partly because Ritchie failed to keep the two armoured divisions – the 1st and the 7th – together. He evidently had not read Rommel's tank lectures. 'If the enemy is foolish enough to allow any

The big guns of the defence pound the German positions. But with the British tank forces scattered and picked-off surrender was inevitable.

scattering of his tank forces,' the Fox had written, 'it will be easy to destroy them piecemeal.'

The 7th Armoured Division, the famous Desert Rats, suffered heavy casualties when its brigades were fighting separately, on orders from the top, instead of together.

As time went on, the British became concerned to defend their vast stores at a railhead that had been built at Belhamed. But Ritchie failed sufficiently to co-ordinate his forces for adequate counter-attack, or even to build up a clear picture of what was going on.

Rommel breaks through

Rommel meanwhile had carried out a right hook around the minefields, and had secured his rear by forcing a gap through the mines at Trigh Capuzzo, in case he had to withdraw west. He has also sent mobile columns to take Bir Hacheim from Koenig's brave Free French. Its defence was the first sign of a revival in French fighting vitality since the 1940 debacle.

Gazala and Tobruk

Tobruk Perimeter

British Minefields

Ain el Gazala

Tobruk

BRITISH

Acroma

Pilastrino

ROMMEL'S ADVANCE

'Knightsbridge'

El Adem

Mediterranean Sea

AFRICA

'The Cauldron'

Bir Hakeim

FREE FRENCH TROOPS

On the night of June 4, the British attacked through the minefields in an area nicknamed The Cauldron. One South African division was standing by, together with both armoured divisions. The Cauldron attack was abortive and unnecessarily expensive. By nightfall, 60 British tanks were destroyed, and the ground troops annihilated or routed. Four regiments of field artillery were also lost.

On June 10 news came through that Bir Hacheim had fallen at last, and the Gazala Line was cut in two. At this stage, Rommel had about 150 first-line tanks left, plus 60 inferior Italian ones, to Britain's 180, so the numbers were fairly even.

On June 11, Rommel drove out towards a direct attack on Tobruk. On that day, on a bloody, sand-stormed, fire-raked battlefield, by a 'box' known as Knightsbridge (because gentlemen guardsmen who spent their time in that area of London had been holding it) the rest of the British armour was outgunned and destroyed.

Tobruk's South African defenders could hold out only until June 20, when the port fell, 33,000 prisoners with it.

Ritchie gave the order: 'Abandon the Gazala Line' and the British withdrew to a depression known as Alamein while Malta held-out stubbornly towards her George Cross.

Left Rommel directed his forces with skill and energy forcing the Allies to fight on the retreat.

Below left The sweep to Tobruk, through successful, was held up by the Gazala minefield, the Free French at Bir Hakeim and dogged resistance at Knightsbridge.

Below A German gun crew in action. Rommel's tactics were to keep his tanks together, protected by artillery, and launch a series of concentrated attacks.

STALINGRAD

At Stalingrad, Russia in 1942, Hitler, threw his military machine against the resistance of an embattled people. In one of the greatest battles of all time, the million-strong Soviet Army lured the Wehrmacht into a trap then swooped down and annihilated it unit by unit.

Hitler had no-one to blame but himself for the situation the Wehrmacht, the German army, got itself into at Stalingrad, when it sustained its greatest-ever defeat. Up to Moscow, and the nightmare winter of 1941–42, all had gone as planned. The Moscow crisis had been an interruption, not an end, to Hitler's run of strategic successes. A new year meant a new life-force. So ran his tantrums.

His political and military strategy for 1942 was final. It called for the defeat of Soviet forces in the south, the conquest of the Caucasus, an advance to the Volga River, and the seizure of Stalingrad. These were the strangling fingers that would throttle the USSR as a state. The swift seizure of the Caucasian oilfields alone would bring the Soviet war machine to a standstill; and on all fronts, he *knew*, the Russian reserves had been exhausted.

So ran Hitler's visionary dream.

Hitler's impossible dream

In truth, on the German side of the Russian fronts, what with the bitter winters, the failure to anticipate them, the long supply lines, the exhaustion of the troops, the decline in reserves, and other factors, it was the impossible dream. But no-one could tell this to the German dictator. He treated his advisors with contempt. His god-like trances became more numerous.

Hitler had always believed that victory was a matter of will-power, and had proved it by carrying to success plans all others had condemned. And certainly, by June 1942, it must have seemed, to all around him, that Hitler was right once more.

The Wehrmacht was cruising fast and freely to the Caucasus and had destroyed 300,000 Soviet troops at Kharkov and Kiev in three armies; the Japanese were over-running the Far East, and looked like linking soon in the drive against the USSR; the Eighth Army were in headlong retreat towards the Egyptian border; King Farouk was preparing to welcome Mussolini at Alexandria; there had been no Allied invasion of Europe.

*German soldiers **left** fought Russian infantry and guerillas **right** inch by inch through Stalingrad's wilderness of broken buildings.*

The road to Stalingrad

Elated and confident, Hitler set his forces on the road to Stalingrad, in an 'inspired' move to gain the ultimate conquest in the east before the Allies were ready to open the promised 'second front' in the west. He had gambled on a short sharp war in eastern Europe, and that was what it had to be.

Hitler's hatred of Soviet Russia transcended all his other hatreds. But he had to settle them soon. All his writings had warned against fighting on two fronts at once. Not even he could split his will-power for such a situation.

So the USSR had to be brought quickly to heel. There were ideological compulsions, as well as strategic ones. In *Mein Kampf*, Hitler had summed up his greatest dream, thus: 'When we speak of new territory to take, we must first think of Russia. Destiny itself points the way there.'

In the mid-summer of 1942, Stalin, Soviet supreme commander as well as dictator, expected a new Nazi thrust on Moscow, from the Bryansk area. Instead, the Wehrmacht struck south again and took the naval base of Sebastopol on the tip of the Crimea. Having completed the conquest of the famous peninsula, they freed a whole army for use elsewhere, some divisions of which began to drive, with blitzkrieg speed, towards the Don River bend and Stalingrad, adding to the threat of Russia being cut in two, if the Volga was taken.

Stalin at once reorganized his forces and sent some of his most trusted political leaders to the front at Stalingrad. They included such famous names as Malenkov, Kruschev and Malychev.

Stalin chooses Zhukov

But still the Nazis drove forward, and, on August 27, 1942, the ruthless but simplistic Marshal Georgi Konstantinovich Zhukov, victor of Moscow – and perhaps the greatest soldier of the century – was summoned from the Western Front and named Deputy Supreme Commander-in-Chief, to Stalin. It was a measure of Zhukov's standing that there never had been a deputy supreme commander before, and there never would be again.

Stalingrad's fate, inseperable from Russia's, was placed in Zhukov's hands – and rough, strong hands they were.

Zhukov's style of leadership was simple. He had to be obeyed absolutely. There was nothing refined or likeable about him. He was a bull-like man, who would issue near-impossible orders, accompanied by the simple command: 'Do it now, or face the firing squad.' Nor were they empty words. Officers and men were indeed shot at his whim.

There was a constancy, as well as a simplicity, about Zhukov's tactics of necessity throughout the war. In non-urban areas, he subscribed wholeheartedly to the traditional Russian ploy: trade space for time. Otherwise, even in cramped

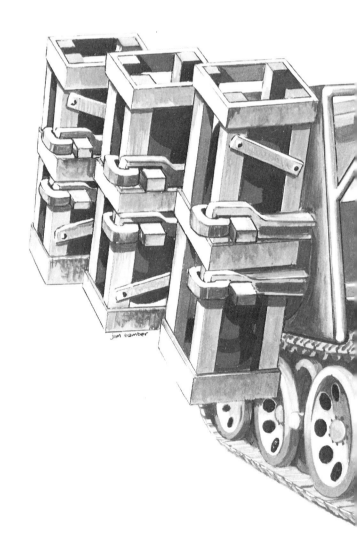

Shifting embattled 'freedom fighters' from buildings they knew well took special weapons. The German Sdkfz 251/1 was a half-track troop carrier carrying six adjustable racks designed to hold and fire 28 or 32 cm. rockets direct from their packing crates. In use, the rocket carrier could be driven close to an occupied building and was aimed by pointing the entire vehicle.

Close-quarter fighting required close-quarter weapons.

Above left *The German ERMA MP40 submachine gun was exactly suited to fast-moving, near hand-to-hand fighting. Its folding stock and plastic fore-grip combined lightness with strength and gave it high combat effectiveness. The submachine gun took a 32-shot magazine and fired 9 mm. bullets at the rate of 500 a minute.*

Left *As a German infantry man smashes his way into a sniper's hide-out a submachine gunner stands ready.*

Above *The PPSL-41 was the Russian equivalent to the MP40. The drum magazine took 71 rounds of 7.62 mm. ammunition and the cyclic rate of fire was 900 a minute.*

Below *In fighting at the approaches to Stalingrad, the Russian defenders made full use of the submachine gun.*

circumstances, he believed in letting the enemy extend themselves; he would wait until the last moment of offensive momentum and would then grind them down in rough, bloody, interlocking encounters as they neared their objective, while holding back substantial reserves for a speedy, powerful counter-attack, the moment he judged the enemy strength to be all-but spent. In the process, he did not care how many lives he sacrificed, as long as he won in the end.

The opposing forces that summer, along the entire eastern front, from the Barents Sea to the Black Sea, were slightly in Germany's favour numerically – and so weighty as scarcely to be comprehensible to any but the top-brass.

With defenders as fanatical as those at Stalingrad every inch of cover counted when moving into position.

Snipers by day, grenades and Molotov cocktails by night – the Germans had to guard against vicious attacks 24 hours a day.

Six million men in battle

The Axis powers had 217 divisions and 20 brigades, of which 178 divisions, eight brigades and four air forces were German. This represented 80 per cent of the total Nazi forces.

The Wehrmacht totalled six million men (including 800,000 allied troops), 3,250 tanks and self-propelled guns, 55,000 guns and mortars; and the eastern Luftwaffe had 3,500 planes.

But the new factor in mid-1942 was that the front was now so wide as to produce a reduction in operational density everywhere, despite the incredible numerical totals.

In an effort to prevent the Germans from reaching the Volga River, Stalin had, on July 12, set up a new Stalingrad Front, instead of the overall South-western Command. This was obvious but sensible anticipation. Directive No. 45, of the German High Command, dated July 23 ordered Army Group B and the Fourth Air Force to seize Stalingrad and gain a stronghold on the Volga River. This would give victory by cutting off the oil-rich Caucasus from the rest of the Soviet Union.

Within a few weeks, the Stalingrad Front consisted of 38 divisions, of low strength (perhaps equivalent to 18 normal divisions). The total front strength was 190,000 men, 350 tanks, 340 planes and 8,000 guns or mortars.

Against this, Germany was attacking Stalingrad with 250,000 men, 750 tanks, 1,200 planes, and 7,500 guns or mortars.

The Germans break through

On July 26, German armour broke through the Soviet defenses in the Don River bend and reached the river, and on August 23, the German Sixth Army and the Fourth Panzer Army, both under the command of General Friedrich Paulus, broke through again at the same point and cut the Stalingrad sector in two, before reaching the vitally important supply waterway, the Volga itself, just north of Stalingrad. This resulted in the Russian Stalingrad Front being divided. The part cut off, including Stalingrad proper, became known as the South-east Front. The German advance had succeeded in the centre partly because most of the Soviet strength was still on the flanks. But Paulus had not paused to wipe out Russian pockets as he stormed forward, so that Russia was able to retain bridgeheads on the right bank of the Don, as well as an important foothold west of Serafimovitch. This meant Paulus's flanks were weaker than he realized.

Meanwhile hundreds of German bombers were keeping up non-stop raids on the city of Stalingrad, in which its factories and much of its housing were reduced to grim demolition sites or to rubble. Thousands of civilians died in the raids.

The city's famous tractor plant, in the northern outskirts, was attacked by the Wehrmacht, but factory workers defended it without fear for their lives, and the attack was temporarily repulsed. Meanwhile strong diversionary Soviet efforts on other fronts drew off some of the reserves intended for Stalingrad.

As Zhukov conferred with Stalin, before taking complete control on August 27, it was learned that the Wehrmacht had crossed the Don in force, and were at the city named after Stalin. Advancing on a broad front, Paulus had succeeded, by the evening of August 23, in driving his Sixth Army left through the northern outskirts, to the right bank of the Volga. And within two weeks, the Fourth Panzer Army would cut an opening to the river through the southern suburbs, whereupon Hitler would impress on Paulus that the rest of the city had to be taken, and the armies joined, without delay.

Meanwhile, Stalin and Zhukov had moved everything they could, except for the newly-formed strategic reserves, intended for a subsequent counter-offensive, into the Stalingrad area for the coming crunch on which so much depended.

'Comrade, kill your German'

In Stalingrad, the population set about joining its defending troops in making the invader's positions as untenable as cunning and bravery would allow. 'Comrade, kill your German' became the universal catchphrase. In the wilderness of broken buildings, Russian infantry or guerillas sniped at any member of the German Sixth Army foolish enough to leave his trench or billet. Grenades were tossed into any Nazi dugouts or premises that could be reached in darkness and Molotov cocktails (bottles of petrol with simple wick fuses, as used by rebels to this day) crashed on vehicles by the hour. Also, night after night, until the river froze over in November, supplies and reinforcements were smuggled across in small boats.

The garrison and the civilians defended the ruins of central Stalingrad, street by street, house by house, and won the astonished admiration of the free world. As the German Sixth Army tried again and again to quell this resistance, once and for all, they little knew that Zhukov was assembling, in two groups of six armies, a million men, 800 tanks and 10,000 guns for the Stalingrad counter offensive. By the middle of November the Soviets had eight armies on the Don-Volga front.

The Russians counter-attack

In Stalingrad and the adjoining areas of the Don and the Volga, in the wearing-down period of the summer and autumn of 1942, the Nazis had already lost three-quarters of a million men, 900 tanks, 1,800 guns and 1,500 planes. They were being reinforced by unreliable Italians, Rumanians and Hungarians. But Hitler was confident they could quell any counter-attack in November, hold Stalingrad and then release troops for taking the Caucasian oilfields as planned. After all, did not Germany by November, 1942 occupy no less than 750,000 square miles of Russia – an area with a pre-war population of 80 million? And was not Goebbels telling the world every day the truth that the German race was infinitely superior to all other races?

On November 19 and 20, the Russian counter-attack, in the rear of the German forces at Stalingrad, was launched on a scale never seen before anywhere. Again, in numbers, there was not much to choose between Slav and Teuton on the general Stalingrad Front. But where Russian weapons had been getting better, the Wehrmacht had little new to offer in offence or defence. It was the same old weapons in the same old well-rehearsed highly-professional routines.

The Rumanian Third Army was devoured in record time, and the Soviet soldiers then fell upon the left of the Sixth Army, the Rumanian Fourth Army and the Fourth Panzer Army, which had failed to relieve the Stalingrad Germans. Once both Rumanian armies had succumbed, Soviet armour was able to race through and attack the Sixth Army's rear, capturing the bridge it used for its supplies en route.

In just over four days, the Russians captured 250,000 Axis troops in and to the west of Stalingrad, having smashed two broad holes in either flank of the huge salient before the city.

Paulus was then about to attempt to fight his way out of the city to the south-west with what was left of his army, but Hitler had other ideas. Goering had promised to fly in 500 tons of supplies a day to Stalingrad's two airports, and the Fuehrer gave the order to Paulus to remain and continue fighting for the city.

Air deliveries to Stalingrad fell hopelessly below Goering's promises, and were as little as 20 to 30 tons a day instead of 500. Meanwhile Stalingrad guerillas were blowing up stores as they arrived, while those without dynamite derailed trains or set fire to lorries.

Before Zhukov's massive forces had closed the noose completely around the Sixth Army, Paulus could have linked up with another German army, Manstein's 6th Armoured division, which had forced itself to within 25 miles of the city. But Paulus dithered and finally decided a break-out was not feasible.

Meanwhile, part of the Luftwaffe had been withdrawn to defend Tunisia against the British and Americans, so Paulus got less and less support or help from the air.

By January 8, Zhukov had completed the stranglehold and called on Paulus to surrender. Somehow, with his starving and fearful army, he held on until January 30. But then the Russian armies broke into the centre of Stalingrad, from north-west and west, amidst incredible scenes of rejoicing among the city's remaining population. The next day, the newly-promoted tall, gaunt Field Marshal Paulus capitulated, with 25 other generals and the remnants of his army. Their march to Zhukov's head-quarters led them through mounds of German bodies which new snow was mercifully covering.

Since November 19, 32 divisions and three brigades had been destroyed completely, while the remaining 16 divisions of the Wehrmacht had lost up to 75 per cent of their strength. Total German losses in the Don, Volga and Stalingrad sectors had totalled one and a half million men, together with nearly six months' arms production in the Reich.

Russia had broken Hitler's spell. Even non-blind Nazis could see for the first time their 'invicible' party and leader were frail and human. For the first time since the 1930s a dark cloud had appeared foreshadowing things to come.

Stalingrad

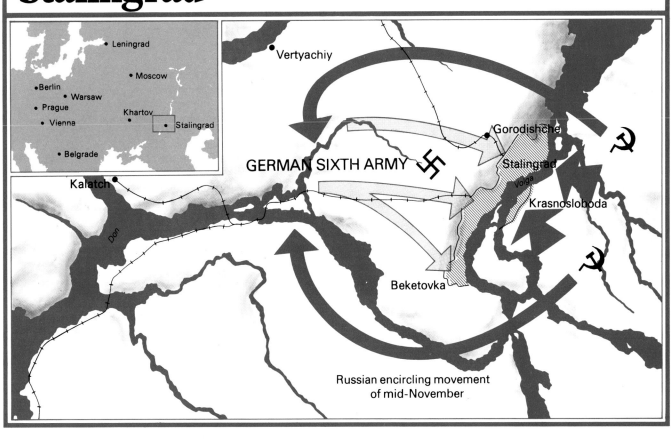

Vertyachiy

Leningrad
Moscow
Berlin
Warsaw
Prague
Khartov
Vienna
Stalingrad
Belgrade

Kalatch

Don

GERMAN SIXTH ARMY

Gorodishche
Stalingrad
Volga
Krasnosloboda

Beketovka

Russian encircling movement
of mid-November

Below After six months hard fighting the
Red Flag flies over Stalingrad again. The
German losses totalled one and a half
million men: Stalingrad had become a
decisive turning point of World War II.

Above Marshall Zhukov sucked the Germans into
Stalingrad, making them fight all the way, and then fell
upon Paulus's Sixth Army, forcing it to surrender and
taking the strategic initiative for the Soviets.

Hitler believed the capture of Stalingrad
would compensate for the defeat before
Moscow in the disastrous winter of
1941–42. But the German war machine
was over-stretched and although the
advance to Stalingrad went well at first,
under the severe conditions of a Russian
winter the Wehrmacht faced a better-
equipped opponent.

CASSINO AND ANZIO

In the theatrical setting of the Italian mountains in 1944, the Allies fought doggedly to shift the Germans from their eyrie atop Monte Cassino. At Anzio and in assaults on the peak itself Allied forces combined to achieve the breakthrough.

Observation is the key to a modern land battle, and Italy's Monte Cassino was an eyrie from which young eagle-eyed Germans were able for months to direct artillery or air arm fire on anything that moved in the two wide valleys which met at right angles below. This was a classic case where the battleground shaped the battle.

Cassino itself was a market town of 25,000 inhabitants, sited between the Rapido river valley and the steep massif behind. It stood, and stands, about halfway between Naples and Rome. It had begun its life as Casinum about the third or fourth century B.C., and it had been fought over many times since then, for the very good reason that it is one of the most perfect defensive positions in Europe, a natural barrier between northern and southern Italy.

Through its 1,700 foot high mountain, Cassino

*Below Allied artillery, here an American 57 mm. anti-tank unit had to winkle out **right** the German defence, here a light anti-aircraft gun, from well dug-in positions on Monte Cassino.*

Infantry took the brunt of the fighting at Monte Cassino and the .303-inch Bren was their standard light machine gun. Effective up to 800 yards, it could fire the 30 rounds in the magazines at a rate of 500 a minute.

had another outstanding claim to fame. It was atop Monte Cassino that the monk Benedict had founded the Benedictine Order in the sixth century, and a massive abbey had been established there ever since, poised and erect against the awe-inspiring backdrop of the Appenines which rose tier upon tier into the magic of the cloud-capped snowline.

Hitler forecasts wrong

After Rommel and his armies had been swept from Africa, it was obvious that the Allies would maintain the momentum of their success. But, not for the first time, Hitler mis-read Churchill and moved defensive forces to the Balkans. Even when, early in September 1943, the British Eighth Army and the Fifth American Army (half of it British) landed in the east, at Taranto in the foot curve of Italy, and at Salerno, in the west, near Naples, respectively, Hitler thought this to be a bluff to cover the real objective – the Balkans.

Notwithstanding the Fuehrer's theory, Field-marshal Albert Kesselring, who had read his history books, kept his strength up in Italy, and immediately prepared a plan by which he would lead the Allies by stages to Monte Cassino, to hold them there.

Kesselring picks his ground

Italy, with its backbone of mountains, had always been a country in which the defender chose the battlefield, and Kesselring made no mistake in his choice. At Cassino, the Allies would have no room to manoeuvre, and, unless the mountain fell, Rome was safe. To overcome this natural barrier by a frontal attack would be costly in the extreme.

But for extra insurance, Kesselring entrusted the defence line to the mainly young and fearless troops of the 14th Panzer Corps of the Tenth Army, under General von Senger und Etterlin.

The Cassino decision having been taken in good time – when the Fifth Army was 60 miles to the south – General von Senger was able to blast emplacements in the mountain's granite, set machine gun nests behind rocky outcrops and construct mortar emplacements in the safety of gullies. The mountainsides were then sown with mines and protected with barbed wire. Trip wires attached to flares and mines were placed at all

Above Commanders at Cassino from left to right, General Dwight D. Eisenhower, Lt.-Gen. Richard L. McCreery and Lt.-Gen. Mark W. Clark.

Below The German Nebelwerfer launched 150 mm. rockets – one at a time to prevent the weapon overturning – and took a minute and a half to reload. The rockets weighed about 70 pounds and had a range of 7,000 yards.

possible approaches. All key positions were reinforced with steel and concrete. A network of tunnels was created, and the town of Cassino heavily fortified. Finally, the Rapido was dammed so that, when the rains came, the entire valley would become a sea of mud, marsh and water. Only the Monastery was left untouched.

Mud and mountains

To allow plenty of time, the rearguards had delayed and nibbled at the Fifth Army, under General Mark Clark, making them fight for every river and hill in the approaches. Three vital months were gained this way, while Clark's men forded the Volturno and Biferno rivers and tackled Monte Camino, a smaller mountain before Cassino.

The Eighth Army meanwhile, having advanced some 600 miles up the Adriatic side of the Italian peninsula and having bravely crossed four rivers, culminating in the formidable Sangro, was stuck in the mud and the mountains, where it would have to remain for the rest of the winter. It lost its inspiration, too, when General Montgomery left to take charge of the invasion of France and was succeeded by General Sir Oliver Leese.

The Eighth and Fifth Armies were both responsible to General Sir Harold Alexander, as commander in chief of the land forces.

The Italians had, by this time, deserted their Axis partners and some were already fighting alongside the Allies, as part of the surrender agreement.

The main purpose of the landings had not been to subdue all Italy but to capture her airfields and use them against Germany. Those in the south fell quickly and came into use. But Eisenhower was determined there should be no delay in taking those in the north (as well as the psychologically important city of Rome) to help in softening up German positions in France for the Normandy landings. But dates had to be revised again and again, as the Fifth Army regularly threw itself against the mountain only to be promptly thrown back.

No amount of shelling and bombing had had any apparent effect on the defenders. Tanks, too, proved themselves useless. Large numbers had been landed, but mostly they lay by the roadsides or among the olive groves.

The troops of the Fifth Army involved in seeking to climb Benedict's mountain were Americans (of all colours and persuasions) British, Canadians, Poles, Indians, French, Moroccans, and New Zealanders. They tried everything they knew, and mules suffered with them, carrying ammunition, but to little effect. The one splendid thing, from a wider Allied point of view, was that the attacking armies had attracted to Germany's southern front many valuable divi-

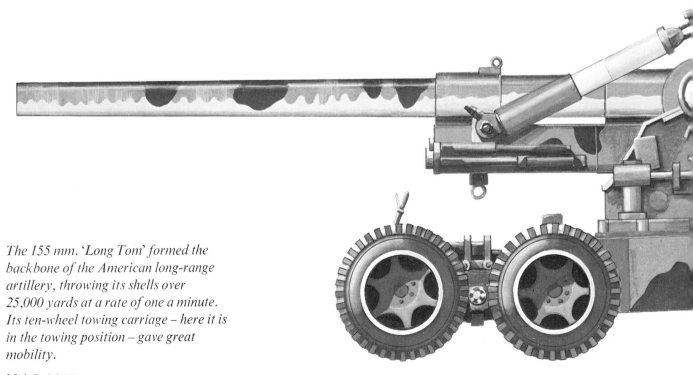

The 155 mm. 'Long Tom' formed the backbone of the American long-range artillery, throwing its shells over 25,000 yards at a rate of one a minute. Its ten-wheel towing carriage – here it is in the towing position – gave great mobility.

sions that Hitler could have used elsewhere.

Flower of the Hitler Youth

But as week followed weary week, into January, more and more lives were lost with absolutely nothing in the way of progress to show for it. One of the reasons was that members of the 1st German Parachute Division were the main suicidal defenders of Cassino. These were Hitler's brainwashed, insensitive bulls – the fanatical products of his master-race youth programme. They had been brought up, from childhood, to believe their lives to be dedicated to the Fuehrer. Normally the toughest of hill positions would have fallen to the tough New Zealanders. But even they died in vain on the mountainside. Blind fanatical faith in the shape of blonde young Aryans beat them back each time. The Hitler-youths were as eager to die for Fascism on Cassino as the Japanese suicide pilots. Their bunkers enabled them to wait underground during the barrages, and then they would emerge to die in bunches attacking from and defending the machine gun positions.

Day after endless day; night after endless night, the Fifth Army gave all it had in the most appalling conditions of snow, frost and slimy mud. But the natural fortress sanctuary and its fervid fighting moles did them down every time.

*Top Bombing raids left the monastery atop Monte Cassino in ruins but **below** the infantry still had to winkle out defenders from their fortified emplacements and a network of tunnels. Americans, British, Canadians, French, Indians, New Zealanders and Poles gave their lives clearing the slopes of Monte Cassino.*

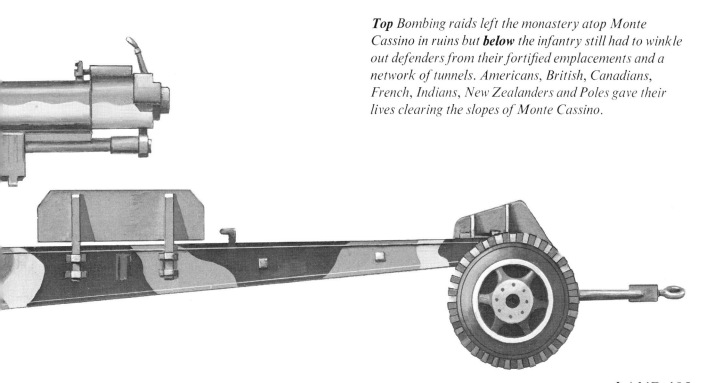

To shift Kesselring's Hitler Youth from their defensive positions around Cassino, the Allies had virtually to lay the area waste. Here the mountain looms over a destroyed bridge and a knocked out tank. Ironically the rubble proved a major obstacle to the Allied attack.

Landing at Anzio

Meanwhile, a seaborne landing behind the enemy's lines had moved from being one plan for Italy to being *the* new plan for taking Rome. Instead of smashing head on endlessly against the steep mountain, it seemed suddenly sensible to take him in the rear. As soon as enough landing craft were available, in the last days of January, 50,000 Allied troops with 5,000 vehicles went ashore on the gently graded beaches at Anzio, 80 miles north of Cassino and just 30 miles south of the eternal city. The immediate aim was to move east and cut the German supply routes, while the Fifth Army launched an all-out attack on Cassino. This would catch the bulk of the German forces in Italy in a nutcracker. There would be an attempted withdrawal in a panic from the mountains. The march on Rome could then proceed with haste, but with ease.

At first all went well at Anzio – too well. The landing was almost bloodless. Surprise was complete. The sad result was nobody tried to move ahead of schedule. Everyone waited through day one until day two brought the next scheduled moves. Meanwhile, Kesselring was rapidly moving troops down from Rome while reinforcing the Cassino area. Withdrawal apparently never entered his head.

Like their brothers at Cassino, the Allied troops at Anzio were overlooked – in their case from the Alban hills. Kesselring knew that observation was the key to any modern land battle. The Allies could have taken these hills on the first day. They were to suffer a long time for their lack of initiative.

Bloody stalemate

The bridgehead was soon surrounded; there was now no chance to break out and link with the Fifth Army. On both fronts it was a dreadful and bloody stalemate. All through the spring, Alexander tried everything. Eventually, he regrouped,

The American bridge head at Anzio, here 'Ducks' of the Fifth Army come ashore, was soon surrounded by the Germans and bloody stalemate descended on both fronts.

and drew from the best of the Eighth Army to buttress the Fifth for yet another 'decisive' attack on the Nazi mountain. Even when the bombing of the Monastery itself was sanctioned, after the monks had been advised on the radio to leave, no improvement was achieved.

Meanwhile, 80 miles to the north, an immense strain was put upon the Allied shipping which supplied and supported Anzio, and which was urgently wanted for the invasion of France. And over the beachhead, the Luftwaffe, with airfields galore nearby, had the edge over the RAF and the American Air Force.

With the 'Overlord' invasion scheduled for early June, it was imperative that Alexander should somehow succeed in Italy in May, and so release promised divisions for the main assault on Fortress Europe.

The final thrust

Early in May, the reinforced Allies had a two to one superiority in numbers over the Germans at Cassino, and could call on almost overwhelming air support. Heavy bombing of the strong areas immediately behind the mountain helped to isolate the German forces in the front of Cassino.

Alexander's imperative May attack went in, with immense weight, on the night of May 11. By sheer volume of artillery and air fire, and through the massed infantry of the Fifth and Eighth Armies, fairly rapid progress was made in the first hours; and, although enemy resistance stiffened, once surprise was over, the Allies superior fire power eventually prevailed.

By the third day, the two Allied armies had broken through to the main road to Rome, below Monte Cassino, and, early on May 18, Polish troops stormed the summit of the mountain to clear the last Nazi fanatics from around the ruined Monastery.

On May 25, nearly nine months after the first landing, the Fifth Army made contact with the Anzio invaders, and on June 4 the Allies entered Rome.

Two days later, Normandy was invaded.

Cassino blocked the Allied route through Italy, an out-flanking landing at Anzio got nowhere. Opening the road to Rome took massive reinforcements and overwhelming air bombardment.

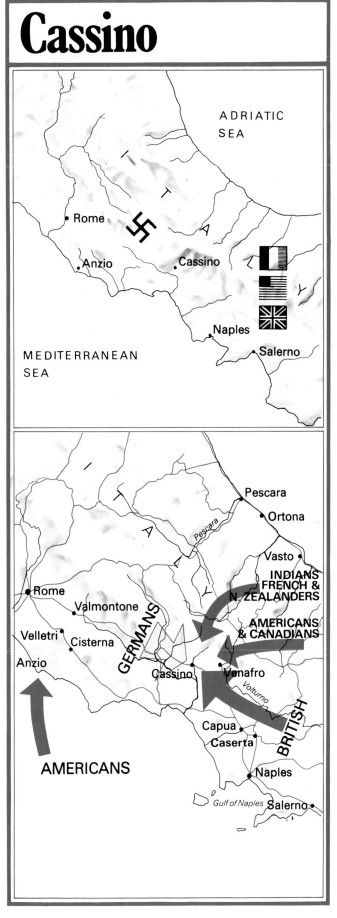

Cassino

BATTLE OF THE BULGE

Towards the end of 1944, Hitler tried for the ultimate grand slam with a Panzer drive through Luxembourg and the Ardennes. The counter-offensive, under Eisenhower, Montgomery and Patton, produced some of the toughest fighting of the war.

American Sherman tanks wait before going into action at the Battle of the Bulge.

Hitler was always a passionate advocate of the offensive as the only way to win, so it should have been obvious, when the Fuehrer had his back to the wall, in December, 1944, he would counter-attack.

But the Allies were flushed with success; their intelligence was misreading the German dispositions; and there were serious divisions between America and British opinion on how the war should be finished off quickly.

Field Marshal Montgomery maintained that his September, 1944 plan for moving forward in strength would have finished the Germans that autumn; General Dwight Eisenhower was intent on a slower strategy. Montgomery continued to believe that the Ardennes battle need never have happened had he had his way.

Madman or genius?

Hitler's grand-slam in December, 1944, was to be a forced drive across Belgium to Antwerp. At first glance it seemed mad; but, as in all Hitler's schemes, it contained elements of genius. Antwerp was vital to the Allies in that it had a capacity, as a seaport, of supporting 50 divisions on a continuing basis. Its loss could have set back Eisenhower's plans by a year. And in that year, Hitler would bring in his V-weapons in force, and possibly the A-bomb which was almost ready. There was real method in his madness.

There was an additional prong to the Fuehrer's counter-offensive thrust. He knew there was schism in the Allied backrooms; he believed his move would lead to the break up of the alliance – a situation he would know brilliantly how to exploit. There was also the fact that Hitler had succeeded – against the will of his advisors – in defeating the French across this same territory in May 1940.

His generals believed he was being over-ambitious. They favoured a smaller slam in which they would cut behind the First Army and drive northwards, east of the Meuse. But Hitler had been right so often before, against all the odds, that once more his will prevailed. That he almost proved to be correct is one of the breath-taking aspects of this incredible Battle of the Bulge in the worst winter weather of the century.

He still had brilliant generals in the field –

notably Rundstedt, who was commander in chief on the Western Front, Model, Kruger, Manteuffel and Luttwitz – and they were not only loyal to him; they also had searing experience of fighting in the wildness of the eastern front to throw into the Ardennes counter-offensive.

Unbeknown to the 'all-seeing' dictator, however, there was a joker in his pack. The comparatively inexperienced General Sepp Dietrich, who was to command the four crack SS Divisions which would carry the main effort of the great offensive, was flawed. There were many reasons why Hitler's target was not achieved, and not least of them was the fact that Dietrich's Sixth Panzer Army failed against the American 5 Corps in the swamps and forest of the Hohe Venne.

Hitler misleads the Allies

Eisenhower's policy, at this moment in the war, was that the Germans should be allowed no respite to build up during the winter. In fact, he had greatly underestimated the true German strength. And Hitler had again fooled the Allies by establishing an entirely new system of command, with the division of the bulk of his forces in two: Guderian commanding some 200 divisions in the east and Rundstedt some 60 to 70 in the west. Reserves were to be drawn from the German 'home guard' – the Volkssturm. In all, this meant that Hitler had reconstituted an army at least equal in size to that with which he had begun the war.

Against this, Eisenhower's armies were spread over a wide front – thinly at some points, in order that they could be thick on the ground at positions of attack potential. As Hitler well knew, the Ardennes segment was but lightly garrisoned; the Americans regarded it as merely an outpost for the important line of the Meuse.

Panthers and Tigers

Hitler had another trump up his sleeve the Allies

Hitler's thrust through the Ardennes took fire-power – **top** *the Tiger II or King Tiger provided the punch with its 88 mm. main gun – and mobility –* **below** *German troops make their way through Belgium.*

1 Turret, 360° traverse
2 Commander's seat
3 Commander's periscope
4 Anti-aircraft machine-gun, MG34: 7.92 mm. (2,925 rounds)
5 Rear hatch
6 Ammunition for 88 mm. gun: 22 rounds
7 Maybach HL 230 V-12 engine: 690 bhp. Gears: 8 forward, 4 reverse
8 Engine-driven blower. Impels clean air through radiator
9 Radiators (on either side)
10 Fuel tank (one of seven). Total fuel carried: 210 gal (864 litres)
11 Side ammunition racks for 88 mm. (24 rounds each side)

12 Steel-tyred wheels (eight each side)
13 Track, $31\frac{1}{2}$in (79 cm.) wide
14 Forward bulkhead
15 Side armour, $3\frac{1}{8}$in (80.65 mm.) thick
16 Machine-gunner's seat
17 Machine-gun, 7.92 mm. MG34 (2,925 rounds)
18 Front wheel sprockets
19 Frontal armor, $3\frac{15}{16}$in – $5\frac{9}{10}$in (100 mm./150 mm.) thick
20 Disc-brake drum
21 88 mm. main armament, muzzle velocity 3,280 ft./sec.
22 Muzzle brake to reduce recoil
23 Shock absorber
24 Driver's seat
25 Spare 88 mm. ammunition

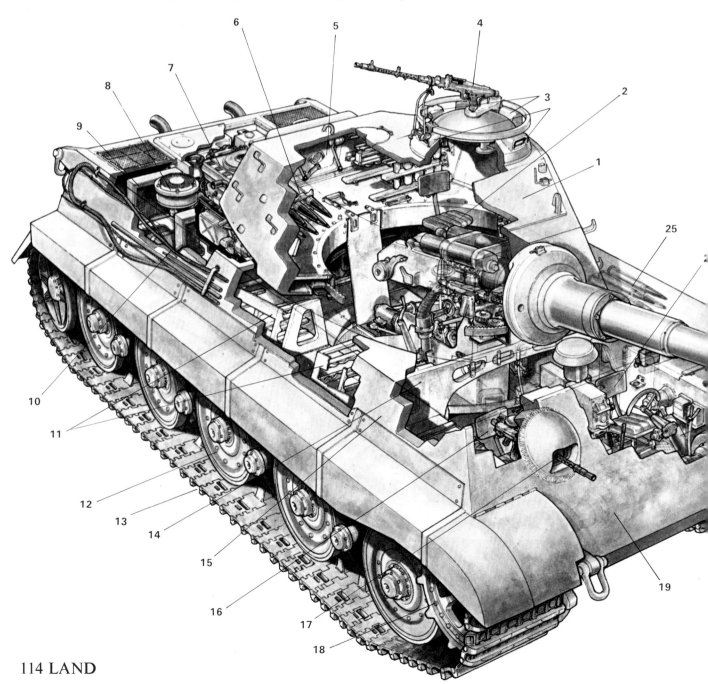

missed. The Sixth Panzer Army was being made ready for the counter-offensive so far from the front that Allied intelligence took it to be meant as a defensive reserve; and it was armed with the very latest heavy Panther and Tiger tanks.

This was the army Hitler believed could be driven straight through the Ardennes, across the Meuse, and across undefended country to Antwerp, cutting Eisenhower's forces in half on the way.

Rundstedt knew the way better than most. All his life he had studied the Ardennes, as one of the classic gateways into and out of Germany. And, in addition to the Sixth, Rundstedt planned also to commit the Fifth Panzer Army which was already in the line opposite Liege. These two would add up to the largest armoured spearhead the world had ever known, consisting of ten Panzer divisions, supported by 17 motorised divisions of the highest calibre, totalling at least 2,000 tanks and a quarter million men, in all.

Hitler had also ordered the use of two devices

The PzKw VI Tiger II – the Koenigstiger or King Tiger – commanded respect. The Americans thought it equivalent to four Shermans.

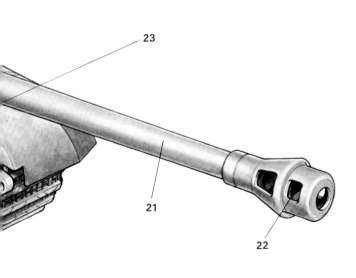

23

21

22

0

unheard of in modern warfare. One was a barrage of flying bombs; the other was an offensive recce brigade in American vehicles, some of its officers in American uniforms. These were 'suicide' troops whose do-or-die mission was to take and hold the Meuse bridges. The Luftwaffe had also regrouped, and was ordered to put up several thousand aircraft purely in tactical support.

The Allies hang fire

Eisenhower's winter offensive had got under way in November with a series of staggered attacks. There was to be no spearhead. One after another, the seven armies were to move on the Rhine in an endeavour to establish bridgeheads on the far side, and it was hoped that the Ruhr would be pierced. But, in most cases, the tanks were unable to follow the forward assault troops, and November's gains amounted to a few thousand yards at best. No bridgeheads were established. The Rhine continued to bar progress.

All Rundstedt needed now was a clear day, to begin the counter-offensive, followed immediately by the sort of bad weather that would keep the superior Allied air forces grounded.

Rundstedt strikes . . .

On the night of December 14 to 15, Rundstedt got what he wanted. The Fifth Panzer Army moved south to a point opposite Luxembourg; the Sixth took its place in the line. All was ready, and on December 16, in excellent conditions, both armies struck together on a front about 40 miles wide. The Bulge was about to be made.

Surprise was complete. The Allies were taken off balance. Half-a-dozen American divisions were rolled up, encircled, or over-run. Even army head-quarters were forced to pack up and run for it. Everyone had been thinking the war in Europe was virtually over and they had survived; now the situation was suddenly grave. Flying bombs were falling everywhere; German parachutists were landing in force behind the lines; for a few days chaos reigned. Not even SHAEF, supreme Allied head-quarters, had any clear idea of what was happening. A fog came to the aid of the Nazis, too, so that no Allied planes could take off for reconnaissance or defence.

... and Eisenhower counters

By December 18 things were totally out of control, and on December 19, with terrific rows going on among the Allies behind the scenes, Eisenhower – who had been made a five-star general three days before – took desperate measures.

He called in Montgomery to command all Allied land forces in the all-important northern shoulder, including the US First and Ninth Armies, and he moved Bradley to control the area south of a line from Givet to Prum, which gave him principally the Sixth Army Group. Bradley was to arrange a counter-attack through the so-called soft underbelly of the Bulge towards Houffalize; and Monty was to fight a defensive battle to hold the Germans away from the Meuse bridges at all costs.

There was little enough time for such counter-measures. It could not have been much more of a near thing. But the First American Army in the north had not panicked and was holding; and elsewhere – notably at Bastogne and St Vith – pockets or salients of American resistance were delaying German progress. Indeed this was perhaps Hitler's greatest miscalculation in planning his Ardennes drive. He had assumed the Americans would be easier to frighten than the British. He misread their 'sloppy' attitudes to discipline and their casual deportment.

Resourcefulness and stubborn bravery under attack were qualities he had not expected from the GIs. Their independence in 'going to business' for themselves, when out of touch with

headquarters upset Hitler's time-tables at several places in and around the Bulge. And these delays gave Montgomery and Bradley a few vital days to consolidate.

Montgomery quickly sent out 'spies' to gather information at all points of contact. In a matter of hours he was the only Allied officer 'in the picture'. He assessed the information and rightly guessed Rundstedt would attempt to wheel northwards and perform a left hook towards the Meuse near Liege. He set up a defensive corps in this path.

As the approach to the Meuse was held by the British and Americans, Eisenhower and Bradley hastily arranged a counter-attack from the south. They agreed there was only one man with the flexibility and charisma to get fresh troops into the line at Arlon. This was Eisenhower's long-time friend, the larger-than-life Lieutenant General George S. Patton Jnr., who tended to ride into battle on a cruiser tank like the US cavalryman he was at heart.

Patton steps in

Patton's Third Army had been poised for a major attack on the Saar just before Christmas. Asked on December 19 how quickly he could hand over and prepare to attack at the southern pimple of the bulge, he said 'Give me two days.'

'I'll agree to three or four, if that's possible,' said Eisenhower. 'Let's say not earlier than the 22nd and not later than the 23rd.'

'You're on!' said the irrepressible Patton, whose assessment of himself was that he was 'the ray of sunshine and the backslapper alike to superiors and to my men'.

It was no mean task to hand over, wheel his army through 90 degrees in a gigantic side-slip along wintry roads, and reorganize his elaborate communications system for the new attack all within 72 hours. But Patton did it. By December 22, he had three divisions fully prepared to take on the German Sixth Army – his 4th Armoured, with the 35th and 60th Infantry – as well as two more being readied, one armoured and one Infantry.

Left An American tank-destroyer with 105 mm. howitzer goes looking for a target. American resistance was the major factor in holding Hitler's first attacks.

The Bastards of Bastogne

The plan was to attack along a 30-mile front, with III Corps driving along the Arlon to Bastogne road to relieve the beleaguered 101st Airborne Division – symbol by that time of American toughness in battle – which had been holding on against all odds, in Bastogne supplied by air. Not without reasons these brave defenders called themselves the Battered Bastards of Bastogne.

This was in itself a swashbuckling mission in the Patton tradition. He reckoned he could pull it off in a couple of days and then push on up the bulge to link with the First Army.

But, for once, Patton's aims were beyond fulfilment. It should have gone well, for, on December 23, after 11 days in which all aircraft had been mainly grounded, the sun had come through, dispelling the milky fogs, and the combined fleets of the RAF and the Eighth

Below Lt.-Gen. Patton led the American counter-attack from the south. He visualized a grand drive through the Germans. The reality was tougher.

American Air Force were overhead with massive support.

Fighting was difficult and slow, with much close combat of the sort Patton liked least. And after two days of non-success on the ground, Patton had to tell Major General John Millicin, who was in charge of the III Corps thrust: 'There's too much piddling around. Press on and get the tanks through.' This was the 4th Armoured Division, the key to his plan for Bastogne.

On the afternoon of December 26, Christmas having been largely ignored, Patton's 4th Armoured broke through the minefields surrounding Bastogne and were greeted by General

Left Captured Germans in American uniforms, their job had been to hold the Meuse bridges.

Below The Sherman M4 with its 76 mm. armament became the main, well-liked Allied tank. Simple design and mass production put so many in the field that they over ran the technically superior King Tiger.

McAuliffe, commanding 101st Airborne with the laconic words: 'Gee, I am mighty glad to see you boys.'

At this moment, the Ardennes crisis could be said to have passed. Runsdtedt could no longer hope to plunge on to the Meuse and over it. He was being squeezed north and south. Progress was incredibly slow, with heavy losses in infantry. The weather closed in again and no longer could the Flying Fortresses be seen immensely high overhead, writing a message of hope in their contrails. Men froze to death where they crouched; petrol and anti-freeze solidified; villages changed hands several times.

Montgomery and Bradley

With the turn of the year, both Montgomery and Bradley turned on the counter-counter-offensive in full force, both pressing towards Houffalize. Deep snowdrifts, icebound roads, belts of minefields and flying bombs gave the two-pronged contest the style of a tortoise race, with even do-or-die Patton's now-strengthened Third Army making less than a mile a day's progress. He had hoped to push on quickly after Bastogne, and send another three divisions on the road to Bonn. But he had underestimated the difficulty in cutting through the German Sixth Army. This period featured some of the grimmest fighting of the entire war.

But as January went on, the tortoises squeezed the Germans back to the original starting line in Germany, to the very temporary shelter of the Siegfried Line.

The war had come to the crunch. Allied combat soldiers had stood toe-to-toe with the Wehrmacht in comparable strength on a battleground chosen by Hitler and had finally broken the back of the Nazi all-conquering machine. In the Ardennes, Allied casualties had been about 80,000 to the Germans' 110,000.

There was still much fighting and dying to be done. But the result of the war had hung on the Battle of the Bulge. With that won, the outcome in Europe was no longer in doubt.

Hitler's plan to swoop through the Ardennes to the Channel ports ran foul of American resistance. Patton from the south and Montgomery and Bradley from the north gradually pushed the Germans back.

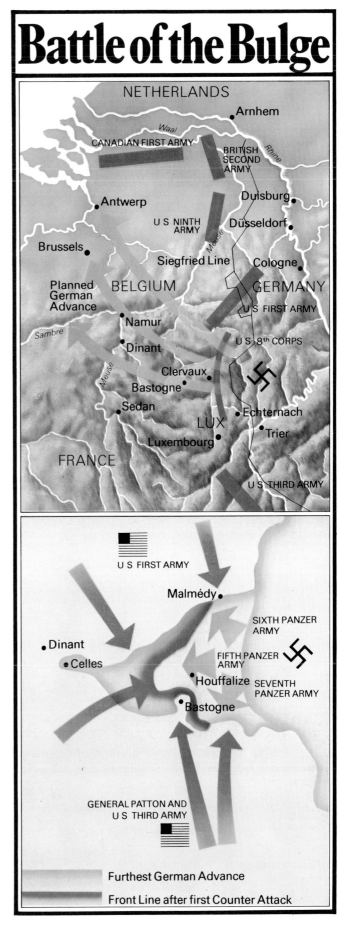

Battle of the Bulge

OPERATION COMMANDO

A true 'United Nations' took part in Operation Commando, an engagement in the Korean War during 1951 which involved bitter hand-to-hand-fighting against the Chinese by men from virtually every Commonwealth country supported by American tanks and aircraft.

Korea was the war with four million casualties and no victors. It went on for nearly three years, although the Communists began suing for peace before the first year's fighting was over.

The 38th parallel, which divided the totalitarian North Korean Democratic People's Republic from the West-orientated, free-wheeling, allegedly-democratic Republic of South Korea, was the Iron Curtain of the Far East.

The entire peninsula had been known historically as The Land of Morning Calm. But the morning of June 25, 1950 was pretty wild, as seven infantry divisions and one armoured division from the north invaded the comparatively-weak and defensive-minded south, using about 100 T34 Soviet tanks and 150 Yak fighters – supported by artillery and mortars in its aggressive probe.

More than a local war

But this was much more than a little local war. The country had been partitioned between the Russians and the Americans in 1945, as a military arrangement to facilitate the Japanese surrender. US occupation troops had been withdrawn for economic reasons, in 1949, but the Russians still ruled the northern roost.

NATO having blocked Soviet attempts to impose Marxist-Leninist beliefs on the countries of Europe, Stalin evidently thought that a swift take-over of South Korea, Hitler-fashion, might catch America looking the other way. He had no real faith in Mao and the Chinese Communists.

But President Truman responded swiftly, in a move he later described as 'my toughest decision'. Air and naval assistance was given at once, and the American-prodded UN Security Council recommended members to aid the southern Republic 'to repel the armed attack'. Led by America, 15 UN member countries would in due course send forces to the Republic of Korea, where a UN Command was set up. In due course, too, some incredible air battles would be fought there.

*Troops from all over the Commonwealth combined in the Commonwealth Division that spearheaded Operation Commando – and saw some of the toughest fighting of the war. **Top left** Canadians man a Vickers machine gun. **Left** A Sherman tank covers an infantry advance.*

As a kick-off, Truman ordered General Douglas MacArthur – then Supreme Allied Commander, based in Japan – to send US assault troops to South Korea. The American Eighth Army was assembled in record time and transported from Japan under General Walton Walker. Speed was of the essence, for by the first week in August, virtually all southern territory west of the Naktong River was in Communist hands.

MacArthur takes Inchon

MacArthur, now designated UN Commander, reacted with characteristic flamboyance. Napoleonically, he placed a US Marine division and an infantry division at Inchon, 200 miles behind the Communist lines, on September 15, 1950, whereupon the suddenly unsupported North Korean forces fled in disarray. Although the Russian tanks outgunned the American Shermans, the north's airforce could not last long against America's and Australia's flying power, while, around the peninsula, British and American warships tightened their stranglehold.

MacArthur then began a drive to Yalu, aimed at the 'liberation' of the north. At this point, Stalin considered intervention to save his 'satellite' state, but there was little doubt that this would have led to a Third World War. He dithered, and Communist China took over the situation instead.

Late in October, 1950, the first of 350,000 Chinese troops crossed the Yalu in support of North Korea, and these highly-trained, well-equipped and undeniably brave forces beat back MacArthur's 'home for Christmas' offensive towards the end of November. The Americans were pushed back from the Chongchong River, and the Chinese then moved freely south to the 38th parallel.

Riled at this set-back to his reputation as a fast positive operator, MacArthur wanted to reinforce and take the war offensively into Manchuria. But Truman met British prime minister Clement Atlee in Washington just before Christmas and they decided the best plan was to defend the parallel and forget about unifying the two halves of Korea. Apart from everything else, America had already suffered more than 60,000 casualties, and the war was unpopular.

MacArthur was recalled to Washington, where

General Bradley told a joint session of Congress: 'Frankly, in the opinion of the Joint Chiefs of Staff, the MacArthur strategy would involve us in the wrong war, at the wrong place, at the wrong time, and with the wrong enemy....'

General James Van Fleet took over as UN Commander in Korea. He had been a machine-gun captain in World War I, and had led an infantry regiment on D-day in the Second. Although he, too, was keen to push on to Manchuria, Van Fleet was bluntly told by General Ridgway – who had taken over from MacArthur in Tokyo – to carry out only 'limited offensives'.

Soon after this, the reinforced US forces were joined by a self-contained British brigade; Australia and New Zealand sent infantry and artillery; South Africa added a fighter squadron and Canada pledged to build up to a brigade. France, Belgium, Holland and India were also to play their parts.

The initial British forces – the 1st Middlesex and the 1st Argyll and Sutherland Highlanders – had arrived in August from Hong Kong, and were responsible for ten miles of the Allied line from the beginning of September. And when the redoubtable 3rd Royal Australian Regiment joined them, the three became the 27th British Commonwealth Brigade, under Brigadier B. A. Coad, fighting with the US 1st Cavalry Division.

The Chinese 'human wave'

Early in 1951, the front line moved up and down the peninsula as the weight of numbers engaged increased, first on one side and then on the other. In particular, the American and British forces just south of the 38th parallel inflicted incredibly heavy casualties on the fanatical Chinese motorized infantry which were attempting to break through to the south coast. Two later drives by the Chinese in April and May were halted by the superiority of American fire-power, on or near the parallel. The May battle was particularly bloody, and led to a Communist withdrawal for regrouping.

The Chinese had been blandly sacrificing themselves in apparently-endless waves – a bafflingly heartless technique in battle which became known as the 'human sea' or 'tidal wave' tactic. They had ceased publication of casualty figures, and whether these were ever made known to the Chinese people is doubtful.

Britain and America ...

In truth, the main spring offensive of 1951 from the north was largely fought and won by the 27th (Commonwealth) Brigade and the 29th British Brigade. These had worked out defensive drills, based on barbed wire, machine guns and dugouts, on which the Communists died like lemmings. This succeeded, in contrast to the American 'butt out' technique. But in due course, the Communists brought up bangalore torpedoes and pole charges to blast through the wire, so that the men of the two Commonwealth brigades had literally to wait till they saw the whites of the enemies' eyes.

... Australia and Canada

From these brigades, two battalions were singled out to receive a Presidential Citation from Truman. Only one other unit was so honoured at this stage of the Korean war – 'A' Company, 72 US Heavy Tank Battalion.

This was the beginning of the end for Communist ambitions in the area in that phase of the Cold War. From July, apparently interminable negotiations proceeded at Kaesong and Panmunjom.

At this period, the UN Line ran from a point on the west coast (about 20 miles south of the 38th parallel) north-eastwards to the east coast, approximately 20 miles north of the parallel, which it cut some 40 miles north-east of Seoul. It was to remain a stable line throughout the summer.

In July, 1951, the 27th Commonwealth Brigade became part of the 1st Commonwealth Division, when the American-trained 25th Canadian Brigade arrived at the front. The third segment of the division was Brigadier Tom Brodie's experienced 29th Brigade. This consisted of the 8th King's Royal Irish Hussars, the Belgian Battalion, the 16th and 45th Field Regiments, Royal New Zealand Artillery, and the 170th Mortar Battery. All were experienced in Korean fighting. The 60th Indian Field Ambulance was

A machine-gunner keeps watch over terrain typical of the hill country north of the River Imjin where Operation Commando took place.

also to be an important part of the division. The Argylls and the Middlesex had by now been relieved by the 1st King's Own Scottish Borderers, and the 1st King's Shropshire Light Infantry.

All in all, this was the first time in history that British, Australian, Canadian, Indian and New Zealand troops had been integrated in a combat division under a unified command.

The division also became, to a large measure, independent of the Americans. Up to this point the various Commonwealth units had been under American corps commanders, and the tendency had been to employ them as a sort of reliable stop-gap in an emergency.

The 1st Commonwealth Division was under the command of Major General A. J. H. 'Gentleman Jim' Cassells, a Seaforth Highlander and a highly experienced tactician who had commanded the 51st Highland Division in Europe in in World War II when in his thirties. Except for

Below A Bren gun team prepares to move out.

Opposite Australian troops 'brew up'. With the Scots, Australians saw one of the wildest day's fighting of the Korean War when they helped take Hill 355 and hold it against wild Chinese counter-attacks.

one Canadian, the divisional commanders were British. Regimental commanders included Lieutenant Colonel Hasset, an Australian, and Lieutenant Colonel Young, a New Zealander.

Lice and rats

There being no real fighting in August, the Commonwealth Division was exercised in the line by General Cassells. They were holding a sequence of cratered hills facing the Imjin River. These were infested by lice and by rats; they were hot by day and bitterly cold by night. But the 'men of Empire' made themselves as comfortable as they could by improvisation and 'kept their powder dry'.

The Commonwealth Division faced the 192nd Chinese Division, in their olive-green quilted uniforms, across the hills of what was known as the Kansas Line, south of the Widgeon Crossing on the Imjin River. Their neighbours were the US 1st Corps, and the Chinese 192nd had as their neighbours, their 190th and 191st Divisions.

The Chinese forward elements were about two miles north of the river. Their main defences were some 7,000 yards to the rear, which meant an unusually wide belt of no-man's-land.

In the quiet before the storm, the left of the

Commonwealth front was held by British infantry battalions and the right by Australian infantry. The 25th Canadians were held in reserve. To left and right of the Commonwealth troops were the 1st South Korean Division and the 1st US Cavalry Division respectively.

Early in September, spearheaded by the 3rd Battalion, Royal Australian Regiment (regarded by many as the finest fighting infantry in Korea), the Commonwealth force launched a probing raid across the Imjin against light opposition. A few Chinese prisoners were taken and interrogated, but little information about the enemy was obtained. When no counter-attack developed, a bridgehead was formed and within a few days the entire division was fed through to the far bank of the river without further fighting. This permitted a new defensive line to be established some 6,000 yards north of the river, in the Mison Myor area.

In the first week of October, General Van Fleet, commanding US Eighth Army, was given permission by Ridgway to launch a limited offensive. If successful, the advance was to be kept to about five miles, where the hills would offer better surveillance over the Chinese front and its supply lines. The Commonwealth Division was to be used, in its first ever major attack against defended positions, to facilitate the advance of the US 1st Corps.

The truce talks had been on and off several times. Now M. Malik, the Soviet UN representative, was apparently offering peace overtures but in such a double-talking way that a rap on Chinese knuckles was generally considered to be timely.

Operation Commando begins

The Commonwealth attack was given the code name Operation Commando. It was planned to

be carried out in three stages. The first was to be an attack on the right by the 28th Commonwealth Infantry Brigade (the new name of the original 27th) to secure the dominant feature known as Hill 355, together with adjoining hills. The second move was to be an advance on day two by the 25th Canadian Infantry Brigade on the left to capture and hold a line of high ground about two miles ahead of their position. Third move was to be the exploitation to the divisional line by the Canadian Brigade and the Commonwealth Brigade on the right.

First Battalion King's Own Scottish Borderers led the 28th into the attack at 3 a.m. on October 2, with the Australian infantrymen and the 1st King's Shropshire Light Infantry in support. The Royal Northumberland Fusiliers were also in attendance, having been brought in as specialists to carry out the separate task of capturing Hill 217, which adjoined Hill 355.

Yet a third hill in the neighbourhood, numbered 317, was to be assaulted by the 3rd Battalion Royal Australian Regiment.

Bayonets and bagpipes

Surprise was better than expected in the cold dark of the October morning. The KOSB had advanced nearly a mile, and had almost reached the first outposts before the Chinese had any inkling of what was afoot. Just before dawn, the Communists opened up with artillery, mortar and machine gun fire, and the Scots had to go to ground. They did this in the hillocks preceding the strong defensive positions the Chinese were holding along and atop steep hills in their forward positions.

The going then became extremely hard for the Borderers and the Shropshires who had joined them. But, meanwhile, the Australians had succeeded in storming and capturing a fortified elevation to the right of the divisional front and they were able to give covering fire as the KOSB again advanced.

On the second day, the Australians and the

Top A British Centurion tank lies in wait.

Bottom American infantry watch as UN troops drop white phosphorus on Communist-held areas. American support was essential to Operation Commando.

Scots crept forward, step by step, under withering Chinese fire. Using grenades and small-arms, with tenacious courage and flair, they took another Chinese strongpoint, going in with the bayonet in the final charge.

As the Australians again paused to give cover, the Border regiment advanced, led by a piper, on the afternoon of the second day and took the all-important Hill 355.

It was one of the wildest days of the entire Korean war. The Chinese now realized the scope and scale of the Commonwealth attack. They opened up barrage after barrage until the hills were pock-marked with shell-craters. Overhead Migs swarmed in, to be taken in combat by the Royal South African Air Force, while American fighter-bombers pounded the Communist positions with rockets a mere few hundred yards ahead of the British and Australian infantry.

A score or so of powerful T34 tanks then appeared on the right flank, where they were challenged to battle by the 75 mm guns of the American cavalry's Shermans, and by New Zealand anti-tank six-pounders.

The Communists then employed their latest weapon. This was a network of huge loudspeakers which roared out recorded messages in broken English, *à la* Goebbels, ludicrously interspersing such commands as 'Jocks go home!' with Communist 'home truths' on the decadence of the West.

By the time the Fusiliers had fought their way yard by yard up the steep slopes of Hill 217 and were engaged in hand-to-hand clearing operations on the top, at sundown on October 4, it was estimated that nearly 1,000 mortar bombs and 15,000 shells had fallen in the contested areas of no-man's land that day. And, in the same evening, a suicide regiment of Chinese commandos swarmed up the hill and re-took it from the Geordie fusiliers. Twice more that night Hill 217 changed hands and mounds of bodies littered its faces.

Hill 317, toughest of all

The next morning, just before dawn, the Australians went for Hill 317. This was the toughest of the three objectives physically, for it was a pyramid in shape and could only be climbed on hands and knees.

Nineteen Chinese machine-guns nests covered

Commando

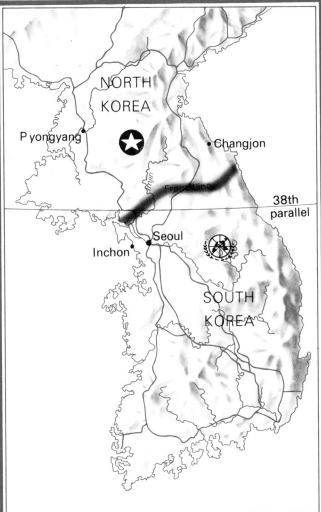

the Australian attack from the east. These were pounded by the RSAF and the American Air Force, but they were so well entrenched they survived. Australian progress was snail-slow. By dusk they were close enough to call up an artillery barrage and follow through with a bayonet attack. Thus they succeeded in mounting the lower defences of the hill, killing 58 Chinese in the process and taking 70 prisoners. There they remained for the night.

The following dawn saw the Australians moving on to a strong point higher up the feature, known as The Hinge. It was a key to the hill's conquest. Against deadly fire, they took The Hinge by 11 a.m. and held it all day despite a sequence of desperate counter-attacks.

In the late evening the feature was lit by a tremendous Chinese mortar and artillery bombardment. Even before the last shells had landed, wave after wave of Chinese assault troops had followed in, but the Aussies decimated them without faltering.

All night thereafter 'goon' patrols tried to creep up on the Allied positions, but flares and good marksmanship defeated each move. At 6 a.m., the Chinese retreated, taking with them some hundreds of their dead and wounded.

All three aims had been achieved. General Van Fleet sent unstinted congratulations to the Commonwealth Division which had welded itself so remarkably into a brave and efficient fighting unit in a very short time.

'Their sheer guts were beyond belief,' said Lt. Col. F. G. Hassett, who had commanded the Australians. He was speaking of the Scots and English as well as of his fellow-countrymen.

The Commonwealth had lost 58 killed and 262 wounded. Chinese casualties were five times as heavy but, more than that, they had suffered the equivalent of losing face. Thereafter stalemate prevailed, with but occasional flashes of cut-and-thrust until the much-delayed truce was signed on July 27, 1953. North and South Korea resumed the territories they had held three years before and settled down to lick unnecessary wounds, inflicted by the Great Powers, which would never entirely heal.

Operation Commando was a limited engagement in an indeterminate war. The aim was to stabilize the front line until Communists and UN reached a political settlement.

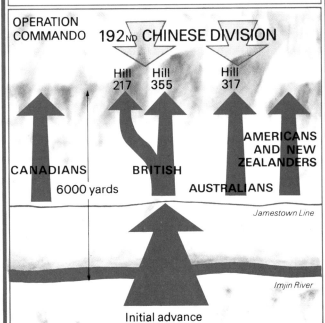

THE PICTORIAL HISTORY OF SEA BATTLES

THOMAS FOSTER

From Nelson's bravery at Cape St Vincent
to the death of the *Bismarck*, the pride of
Hitler's Navy, from galleys rowed by slaves to the
battleships and aircraft carriers the USA
and Japan threw against each other in
World War II, from the 32-pounder cannon
to the 16-inch guns at Jutland.
The Pictorial History of Sea Battles
is the story of conflict at sea.

The authoritative and highly-readable text
has all the information you require,
specially-drawn maps give you a clear guide
to the action, detailed diagrams flesh out the
technical specifications of ships and guns and
dozens of illustrations, many in full colour,
bring you the excitement, the danger—and
the sadness—of war.

The Pictorial History of Sea Battles
will take you right into the world of the great
admirals, the great heroes and the great fighting
ships. Once it is on your bookshelf you will
consult it again and again.

CONTENTS

SALAMIS

Galleys against galleys, mighty empire against city state — and victory went to the 'weaker' side. At Salamis on the Aegean Sea in 480 B.C., the vast and unwieldy Persian armada was beaten by half the number of sleek and better-crewed Greek Triremes.

'Master, remember the Athenians ... remember the Athenians' whispered the slave. His master was Xerxes, the warrior king of the Persian Empire and he had good cause to remember the Greeks. Years earlier the forces of the young and ambitious Persian Empire, under Xerxes's father Darius, had been smashed by the Athenians on the plains of Marathon. Xerxes was determined to gain revenge—and this led to one of the greatest sea battles in history, at Salamis in 480 B.C.

In two areas of the Mediterranean, then the centre of the known world, two young empires, the Greek and the Persian, were growing and spreading their influence. Greece possessed the most enlightened and free society of the ancient world and this was pitted against the expanding empire of the despotic Persians.

The seeds of war

Conflict between the two empires had started in a small way with fighting in the border towns of Greece and Persia. Persia was here flexing her muscles and trying her strength but as the years passed the fighting increased in ferocity, first on land, then on the sea. At times it appeared as if the fate of the whole of the then known world hung on the outcome of these small and petty battles.

The first recorded battle between the two empires was in the first half of the seventh century B.C., when the Persians attacked some

Top *Themistocles personified the vigorous Athenian spirit. He realized that Greek freedom depended on sea power and so persuaded the Athenians to expand the navy and train seamen.*

Below *Xerxes thought Greece would fall without struggle to the juggernaut of the Persian army and his ships were built to carry the maximum number of soldiers rather than for battle at sea.*

Left *When the two fleets met at Salamis, Themistocles' foresight paid off – and the Greeks, although heavily outnumbered, drove off the Persians.*

Greek cities on the border. The Greeks were quick to reply and, of course, the Persians replied again. Attacks and counter-attacks continued sporadically for the next few centuries. In the year 494 B.C., the Persians attacked Miletus and razed it to the ground. This was a terrible blow to the Greeks, for Miletus had been the richest and most brilliant of all the Ionian cities. The Athenian poet, Phrynichus, wrote the story of this tragedy—his play *The Capture of Miletus* was so overwhelming that the Athenian audience was moved to tears and wailing. Phrynichus was duly fined 1,000 drachmas for depressing his audience!

In the years that followed the Persians systematically nibbled at the borders of the Grecian Empire. City after city fell into Persian hands as they slowly got the better of their Greek adversaries. This could not continue much longer—if it did Greece would surely slip

Good training and highly-manoeuvrable ships were the key to Greek success at Salamis. Their fast-moving Triremes *left, driven by 170 slaves pulling on oars up to 14 feet long, were armed with metal-tipped, trident-shaped rams that ripped the Persian galleys apart. The much heavier Persian* Trieres *were really troop-carriers: although propelled by 200 oarsmen, they could not escape the darting Greek ships.*

under Persian domination. Then came the battle of Marathon.

Darius strikes at Greece

In the year 490 B.C., Darius I, who had succeeded to the Persian throne, struck at the Grecian Empire once more. A fleet of 600 ships sailed across the Aegean Sea towards the Bay of

Marathon. The Persians planned to land troops there to march on Athens and overrun it before the Greeks could muster any effective resistance. But the Persians sailed off course and had to revise their strategy. Their new plan was to sail round and attack Athens through the port of Phaleron. This manoeuvre took time though and the Athenians had warning of attack. In a hurried last minute plan they decided on their tactics.

The Persian and Greek armies met on the plains of Marathon. The Persians reeled under the violent Greek onslaught. The wings of the Greek army crushed their opposing forces and, wheeling inwards towards the centre, butchered the remaining troops. The Persians' army collapsed in disarray, huge numbers being slain or driven into the sea. A few fought a rearguard action and escaped in their ships but when the clamour

of battle died the grim toll was known—6,400 crack troops from the Persian army killed against the Greek loss of just 192 soldiers. Today the plain of Marathon has a high mound in the middle and legend tells that this is the spot where the ashes of the Greek dead were buried.

After the crushing victory of Marathon the Greeks had some ten years of respite. The Persians spent this time licking their wounds. Xerxes, the son of Darius, succeeded him to the throne of Persia in the year 485 B.C.

Xerxes avenges Marathon

Xerxes was determined to avenge the bitter ignominy of Marathon and prepared to strike at the Greeks once more. He gathered forces from far and wide, from India, Egypt, even Ethiopia and planned and trained a massive army. He also built the greatest battle fleet the world had ever seen. Persian pride demanded that the failure at Marathon must be erased from the minds of Persians.

Below *This carving of a Greek* Trireme *shows the three banks of sweeps that propelled the ship. Most of the oars were pulled by two men, some by three.*

Opposite *It was the desire to revenge the earlier Greek victory on the plains of Marathon that led Xerxes to strike at the Greeks once more.*

While Xerxes was planning the downfall of the Greek empire, the Athenians had been embroiled in internal political and military squabbles that could only weaken them in the face of a fresh Persian onslaught. Then one man, Themistocles, came to the forefront. Themistocles, in the coming years, was to personify the vigorous Athenian spirit of freewill. He was an impetuous man but a quick learner who became a very gifted politician with great foresight, for he alone realized that the future of Athens lay not in protecting its vast boundaries, but in sea power. Athens would flower only if the sea lanes were kept open and free from Persian aggression: Athens would wither and die if the Persians gained a strangle-hold on those sea lanes. This was Themistocles' simple, direct, reasoning.

So, in 483 B.C., Themistocles persuaded the Athenian Assembly to expand its navy. The old ships were replaced by warships of the latest design; men were trained and retrained in the arts of seaborne warfare; navigation, strategy, weaponry and all the other arts of war were drilled into the fighting men of Athens.

Three years after the Athenians had started to expand their navy Xerxes had completed the ten year task of building a mighty Persian force to do battle with the Greeks. The Persians now had a huge army of over two million men, 1,200 warships and 3,000 smaller vessels. A formidable force of disciplined warriors was now at Xerxes' command. The day was drawing near when he would seek vengeance for the humiliation of Marathon.

Three hundred Immortals

In 480 B.C., Xerxes moved against the Grecian Empire. Athens, thanks to Themistocles, was now far better prepared than she had ever been for the oncoming crisis. The Greeks had called on their allies and the Spartans, renowned for their brave and disciplined military prowess, now led the Greek army. Calling the combined military force *The League of the Greeks*, the Spartans massed the troops on the northern border near the narrow pass at Thermopylae. To attack Athens, Xerxes must lead his army through this pass.

Although the forces of the Persian empire suffered losses in a storm when several convoy supply ships grounded, the great juggernaut advanced, slowly but relentlessly and soon the Persian army was at the approaches to Thermopylae—once through the pass Athens, the centre of Greek culture, stood before them. But the narrow pass was now defended by a tiny but dedicated group of Spartan soldiers, remembered for their heroism as the 'Immortal 300'. The Greek defence held out against the huge power of Xerxes' army and gave Themistocles the breathing space he needed to organize the Greek fleet into battle stations. Thermopylae fell—but not before the gallant stand of the Immortal 300 had won valuable time for the Greeks.

After the fall of Thermopylae, the city of Athens was evacuated in preparation for the coming invasion. Themistocles ordered the women and children to the outlying cities of Salamis, Troezen and Aegina for safety. He then recruited all the remaining able-bodied men to fortify the Greek navy and set about the difficult tactical task of ensuring that the Greek navy went into combat with the Persian fleet on its own terms.

THE BATTLE OF MARATHON.

While Xerxes led his army forward from Thermopylae and into the empty city of Athens Themistocles finally shaped his tactics into a plan based on one very simple requirement—the Persian fleet had to be met in a restricted sea. So long as the battle was fought in a sea full of uncharted dangers and limited in space to

manoeuvre, the superior seamanship of the Greeks, rather than numbers, would win the day.

So with this plan in mind Themistocles re-grouped his fleet at Salamis ready to fight in the narrow channel between the island of Salamis and the mainland, not far from Athens. If the Persian fleet could be destroyed here Xerxes would be forced to retire from the city, his lines of supply and communication cut.

Battering rams versus . . .

Slowly the Greek fleet grouped itself. The spearheads of the Greek navy were *Triremes*, oar-driven timber warships, rowed into battle by 170 selected oarsmen. The ships were stoutly built with narrow hulls and streamlined looks which presented a very low profile in the water. The prow, designed for ramming, was built forward and outward as a battering ram with a metal cap shaped like a trident, the weapon of the Sea God, Poseidon. A trireme could be manoe-uvred quickly and skilfully into battle positions and the oarsmen could propel the ship forward at high speed to crush anything in its path. Archers

Above The unwieldy Persian galleys could not manoeuvre in the dangerous waters and many ran aground – or even smashed into each other.

Right Choosing the narrow channel at Salamis as the battle ground gave Themistocles and the light Greek ships the advantage they needed.

stood on the prow of each warship and from there rained down arrows into the enemies' ships. Themistocles had over 200 of these finely built, extremely efficient, 'battering ram' war-ships under his command.

. . . lumbering hulks

Xerxes' fleet, on the other hand, was not designed for combat at sea but for landing and boarding tactics, and for bringing ashore vast quantities of troops and munitions. The Persian warships, *Trieres*, were mighty looking vessels between 120 and 140 feet long. They rode high in the water and carried a towering stern and lofty decks, under which vast quantities of munitions,

Salamis

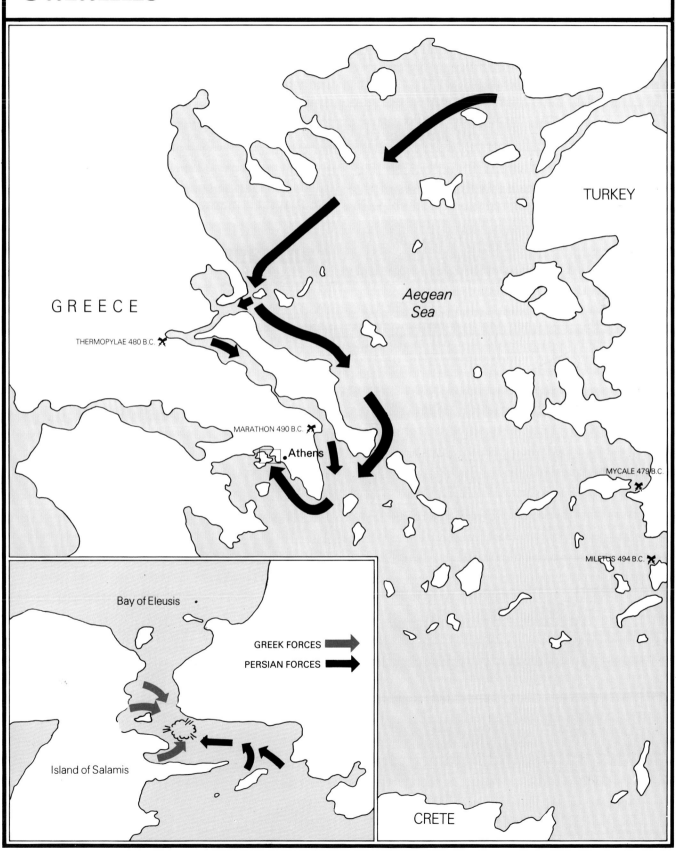

THERMOPYLAE 480 B.C.

GREECE

Aegean Sea

TURKEY

MARATHON 490 B.C.

Athens

MYCALE 479 B.C.

MILETUS 494 B.C.

Bay of Eleusis

GREEK FORCES

PERSIAN FORCES

Island of Salamis

CRETE

stores and marine soldiers could be kept. They were particularly noticeable, for, unlike the Greek warships, they carried rows of the marine soldiers' shields down the sides of the ship to give protection to the oarsmen. Because they had a very high profile, these warships were slow and lumbering in their movements and could not be turned quickly. Their effectiveness lay entirely in their brute force and power.

Themistocles had chosen exactly the right location to fight the battle that would decide whether the Greek empire would survive or die. The narrow Salamis strait would allow the Greek Triremes to move freely and quickly but hamper and restrict the lumbering Trieres of the Persians. But there were still some 800 ships in the Persian fleet to the 200 under Themistocles.

For days the rival navies grouped and re-grouped, scouting for the enemy. Then they caught sight of each other. The Persian fleet was massed outside the channel while the Greek warships formed up within the channel. Then, at sunrise on the day when the two fleets were to throw themselves into battle, a cruel misfortune befell the Persians. A violent storm blew up and sent many of the Persian ships, which were on the open sea and unsheltered, crashing on to the rocks. The Persian fleet was badly mauled—the Greek fleet, in the narrow and sheltered confines of the channel was barely touched.

As the storm died Xerxes received the bad news—over half of his ships had been lost. He was forced to withdraw his ships to regroup. Now he had just under 400 ships left but this was still over twice the number in the Greek fleet. Xerxes was still confident of victory. After two days he gave the order for his battle-fleet to move forward slowly and crush the Greek ships so that they could drive straight on to land. Then his marine soldiers would have the Greek lands at their mercy.

Panic among the Persians

Xerxes now brought his fleet through the narrow channel ready to smash through the 'lightweight' ships of Themistocles. But more problems befell the Persian battle plans. The narrow channel proved almost unnavigable for the high-sided

Persian warships. Lumbering out of line, they impeded each other. The Persian sailors started to panic and the loss of proper command spread throughout the Persian fleet. Xerxes now realized that the ships could not, in these conditions, navigate with the degree of accuracy that he wanted.

At this moment, while the commanders of the Persian warships were concentrating all their powers on navigating through the dangerously narrow waters, Themistocles struck. The Greek ships, fewer in number but far better manoeuvred and managed, moved easily through the narrow waters. Darting amongst the clumsy Persian warships, harrying them, driving them into each other, battering them with their massive rams the Greek Triremes wrought havoc. Persian warship after Persian warship foundered, crushed under the onslaught of the darting, ever-present Greek ships. Xerxes' mighty vessels collapsed like matchwood under the impact of the 'trident' rams. Their commanders were in complete disarray, unable to navigate the treacherous waters and unable to turn quickly. Their ships ran aground or smashed against the shallow reefs. Amid all the chaos, a relentless hail of arrows from the Greek archers rained down on the Persian warships.

The sea gives up its dead

Ship after ship turned over, foundered or ran aground. The sea changed colour from limpid blue to dark red as the waters ran thick with Persian blood. Trieres were crushed between land and battering ram. The marine soldiers, weighed down by their shields and armour, drowned without a hope of making the shore and without getting to grips with the enemy. Time and time again Themistocles regrouped his ships to drive them forward into the now completely disordered Persian navy. The sea became choked with the wreckage of ships and the bodies of slaughtered men. The straggling Persian ships, as they tried desperately and clumsily to turn about and make for the open sea, managed only to ram each other.

For 12 hours the Greek ships battered the Persian galleys, sinking more than 200 and turning the seas red with blood, until the Persians fled.

The blood-bath continued for over 12 hours. Xerxes had made a tragic mistake by trying to fight a battle on terms dictated by Themistocles. In the confined channel at Salamis the advantage had always been with the faster, lighter ships of the Greek navy. As the grey light of dusk closed in eye witnesses saw the Greek coast piled high with the carnage from the battle. The sea had returned the dead to the land, a land that for thousands of Persians once seemed to offer plunder and riches and now afforded only an unfriendly grave.

During the evening and the early hours of the morning the Greek ships withdrew to harbour, the warriors exultant in victory. The remains of Xerxes' Persian fleet limped into open waters to assess the damage. Exhausted, they counted their losses—of the 400 ships that had sailed proudly into battle at dawn, 200 had not returned. Half the battle fleet was lost. The Persians knew they could not continue the battle but more than that, they resolved, after the vicious defeat in the narrow channel of Salamis, never to send their ships against the Greek fleet again. Persian pride, bolstered during the long years waiting to avenge Marathon, had been crushed and their warrior king, Xerxes, went home defeated. He withdrew from Athens as Themistocles had expected, taking his troops and the remainder of his navy with him. The bloody battle was at an end.

By any standards the Greek victory at Salamis was an astonishing achievement. In view of the odds they overcame, the Greeks were rightfully filled with self-confidence, patriotism and pride and dramatists and poets recorded the noble deeds of Salamis.

Freedom!

After further years of small skirmishes on the borders, the Persians, now without a navy, and with a much depleted army, settled for a treaty of peace. This treaty recognized the liberty of the Greek states in Europe and Asia. The mighty sea battle of Salamis guaranteed the survival of the cultured Athenian state and crushed the ambitions of the autocratic Persian empire. The freedom of the individual in the most enlightened of all ancient empires had been safeguarded against the threat of harsh, unbending Persian rule and Greece lived on to deepen its influence on the civilization that followed it.

PREVEZA

At Preveza on the Ionian Sea in 1537, the ex-pirate Barbarossa drove his Turkish galleys against the Spanish galleons of Andrea Doria. After a day of cannon salvos, ramming and hand-to-hand-fighting. Doria fled, leaving Barbarossa 'King of the Seas'.

A pirate, known by friends and enemies alike as 'Redbeard' or Barbarossa, plied the Eastern waters of the Mediterranean in the early years of the sixteenth century. From very humble beginnings Barbarossa, together with his two brothers, rose from strength to strength. By example, courage and skulduggery this Barbary pirate, Khair-ed-Din Barbarossa, rose in stature in the eyes of the Sultan of the Ottoman Empire until, by the year 1533, he became, by the Sultan's command, the Grand Admiral of the Turkish Fleet.

Grand Admiral Khair-ed-Din Barbarossa proved himself to be a natural leader of the Ottoman Navy. At its helm he steered the Ottoman Empire into a massive Turkish-Ottoman alliance. He alone was mainly responsible for the upsurge of the Turkish and Moslem influence throughout the first half of the sixteenth century, an influence that slowly but surely spread across the Mediterranean.

In Barbarossa's Turkish Navy, slaves rowed galleys up to 150 feet long into action. The Spanish had huge sailing galleons as well as galleys – but these were a liability despite their heavy artillery. Unable to keep formation or make headway in light winds they fell easy prey to Barbarossa's oar-driven warships.

Barbarossa rose from Barbary pirate to Grand Admiral of the Turkish Fleet, but drew upon his pirate experience in defeating the Spanish Fleet at Preveza. He died in 1546, one of the major figures of the Ottoman empire.

Khair-ed-Din Barbarossa rapidly gained a reputation as the 'King' of the seas, the greatest Admiral that the Turks had ever known. He put the years of experience gained from piracy to good use and controlled the Eastern Mediterranean with a firm, but skilful, hand from his base at Constantinople.

The chief opponent of the increasing Moslem infiltration was Catholic Spain and the Spanish fought and fought again, in skirmishes and running fights, throughout the length and breadth of the Mediterranean, against the spread of what was to them the 'heathen' influence of the Ottoman Empire.

Spain, wishing to make alliances to combat the advance of their religious enemies courted the Italian states and Rome, the seat of the Catholic Empire. The courting proved successful and old and often bitter differences were forgotten in the common religious cause. An alliance was forged so that Spain might not only protect herself but also start to win back the sea power that she had already lost to the Turks. It was, or was called, a holy cause.

Spanish raids

The clash between Moslem Ottoman Empire and Catholic Spain came at last when the Spanish fleet, under the Genoese Admiral Andrea Doria, began the fight back. The religious war had started. The opening round was a Spanish raid which took the Turkish outpost of Coron, in Morea, in the southern part of Greece.

Barbarossa was perturbed for his plan for complete domination of the Mediterranean under the Moslem religion was under attack. He knew

he would have to confront the Spanish – and win. Slowly and steadily he devised the strategy and tactics that would bring victory.

One year and then two slipped by and still Barbarossa planned. He was loathe to move his complete navy, so, in the meantime, he maintained a policy of small violent confrontations at the outposts of the Empire. While these small engagements went on he designed plans for the greater kill.

By 1537 Barbarossa's plans were ready. His fleet, sailing from Constantinople, swept into the open Mediterranean. Coastal towns along the 'toe' of Italy were besieged while Barbarossa's ships played havoc with any Spanish or Italian craft that might fall into his path. The bait was being laid.

Week after week violent raids were carried out against outposts of the Catholic alliance. The raids continued throughout the summer. Would these skirmishes against the smaller fish entice the bigger fish? Barbarossa waited: then the news came. Andrea Doria had gathered together a massive fleet – the bait had been taken up.

Barbarossa's trap

Barbarossa's plans now began to unfold – the 'holy' battle was about to begin. He took his fleet through the winding channels of the many islands of southern Greece, into the Gulf of Arta. Here his fleet could lie in wait, in sheltered safety. He brought his fleet into a huge quadrant with the bows of the ships pointing towards the narrow entrance of the gulf. If Andrea Doria followed he would fall into a trap. Barbarossa, using his vast knowledge obtained by years of piracy, had chosen this anchorage with care – here he could do battle on his own terms.

Andrea Doria, unaware of the exact whereabouts of Barbarossa, brought his fleet into the Turkish-dominated waters and began to search. Through the early part of September, Andrea Doria hunted the Turkish Admiral and his fleet and then on finding him realized he would have to take the Gulf of Arta and flush out the enemy. But the channel leading into the Gulf was narrow and treacherous and the task would not be easy.

On September 25, the Spanish fleet lay off the entrance to the channel. The fleet, a mixture of oar-driven galleys and sailing galleons, vastly outnumbered the Turkish Navy, and Andrea

Doria thought that by sheer weight of numbers he could overwhelm Barbarossa's fleet.

But Barbarossa knew better. The heavier ships, the galleons, of the Spanish could navigate the channel only one at a time and as his fleet covered the entrance to the channel he could literally pick them off one at a time before they could take up battle formations. His light but extremely well-equipped galleys could fly forward and ram the massive Papal galleons as they spilled out through the channel.

Doria knew, as only an experienced Admiral could know, that under these conditions he could not hope for victory – his towering galleons could not safely navigate the channel. So he waited. The two navies were at either end of a long, tortuous and dangerous channel, each waiting for the other to venture through. Of the two positions, Barbarossa's was the happier in an enclosed gulf protected from the violent squalls prevalent at that time of year. Doria's fleet on the other hand, was exposed and a sudden squall would give him little time to seek shelter.

First blood

This appeared to favour Barbarossa – but he realized a potential danger. Doria, with his superior manpower, might seek to land his troops and his cannons, force-march them over the isthmus and lay seige to Barbarossa's fleet. If he did he could fire down at will upon the Turks and slowly bring their fleet to submission. But it was Barbarossa not Doria, who made the first move.

Taking the initiative, Barbarossa landed some soldiers and drove them hard over the isthmus with orders to set up a battery to bombard the enemy's fleet. But Doria spotted movement high on the shoreline and he brought his massive galleons as close as he dared to the shore. The Spanish gunners took steady aim and blasted Barbarossa's men before they had time to establish themselves. The cannons of the huge galleons ripped into the shoreline. Men fell

Opposite The Spanish Fleet had galleys as well as galleons and these too carried heavy artillery.

Right Andrea Doria, 1466–1560, was a great 'Freelance' admiral. Genoese by birth, he fought for several masters, usually with great success. Some rumours suggested he lost the battle of Preveza on purpose – because his fees had not been paid!

Overleaf The Battle of Lepanto in 1571 involved virtually the same forces as fought at Preveza. But Barbarossa and Doria were both dead and victory this time went to the Christian alliance.

without having the chance to reply and the rest fled in disarray. The short violent action ended when Andrea Doria withdrew his ships to deeper water, leaving Barbarossa's men to march their way back across the isthmus. Of those that had set out, less than half returned. Barbarossa had not yet fired a shot – and he had lost valuable men and armaments.

The quiet stalemate resumed, a cat and mouse game between two fleets. Then, after days of waiting, the Genoese Admiral made a move. He withdrew his fleet and headed south for the comparative shelter of the island of Levkas. His aim was to tempt Barbarossa into pursuit, out of the Gulf of Arta – would it work?

On the morning of September 27, Barbarossa responded as Doria had hoped. The Turkish

A Spanish galleass carried soldiers as well as sailors for boarding parties and hand-to-hand fighting. The broadside guns were mounted below the tiers of oars, which had to be raised so that the galleass could fire without crippling herself.

Admiral brought his fleet from their safe anchorage, through the narrow channel and out into open water. Driving his galleys as fast as he could he chased the fleeing Papal Fleet.

Andrea Doria was still trying to bring his massive fleet of many hundreds of royal and golden galleys and galleons into formation. At first the massive galleons under their huge canvasses appeared to come into position, but then the fickle wind dropped, leaving the canvasses hanging limply. Slaves, pulling at lengthy oars, tried to row the cumbersome galleys into formation but with scant success – the Papal fleet lost all coordination.

Into battle

Andrea Doria's fleet was strung out into a long, disorganized line – the Spanish Admiral could not afford to meet Barbarossa in this position. But to his dismay Barbarossa's fleet appeared over the

horizon. In perfect formation, the galleys, their blades flashing in the sun, bore down on the ragged line of the Papal fleet. The towering royal galleons of Spain could make little headway or escape from the powerful oar-driven warships. Barbarossa, in the leading galley, ploughed into the tail end of the straggling line while the galleons of the Spanish were almost unable to move forward.

The first shots rang out and cannons opened fire between the two closing enemies. Wave after wave of piercing attacks struck the straggling line of Doria's fleet. Driving the galleys on with every ounce of strength, the Turks slammed into the sides of the Spanish ships. With great crashing of timbers the galleons reeled under the impact as the Turkish galleys rammed, butted and bruised their way into the heart of the straggling fleet. The Papal ships fought back, blasting salvo after salvo into the waves of approaching galleys. Their cannons ripped gaping holes in the Turkish warships, smashing oars and men alike. The sides of the galleys were stove in and the oars, splintered and broken, fell from lifeless hands. Death and destruction were heaped on the heads of the galley slaves, as they strove to drive their ships onward, into the sides of the galleons.

The first attack was beaten off and the galleys withdrew. Barbarossa had suffered terrible losses, but had inflicted much damage. Ruined and wrecked ships littered the sea for the short violent action had ended with many hundreds of casualties on both sides. Barbarossa watched as his galleys limped back and regrouped. One of them, unable to bear its wounds any longer, slipped under the waves, taking with it screaming sailors and slaves.

A breathing space

The advantage was now with the Genoese Admiral. He ordered his guns to fire at will at the straggling galleys as they attempted to regroup and sweep forward into another attack. Andrea Doria ordered his ships to move in, do as much damage as they could in as short a time as possible and then withdraw before the Turks could respond. But the fickle winds made this manoeuvre impossible. Barbarossa was given a precious breathing space. His galleys regrouped and like angry hornets darted forward to deliver their sting.

The battle raged all day. Up and down the coastline the violent action raged until well into the afternoon. The light wind at last rose, filling the sails of the great Papal galleons, and Andrea Doria's fleet withdrew in a now fairly ordered formation, leaving Barbarossa's fleet to follow at will.

The 'pirate' Admiral would not allow the enemy to slip from his grasp so easily and he continued his harrying tactics with renewed vigour as the great sailing galleons endeavoured to get under way. His galleys swept in as fast as the slaves could be beaten into driving them. In such conditions the huge, lumbering galleons made little headway. Stragglers were picked off and crushed. Barbarossa steadily gained the advantage. Unable to make full use of the now

favourable winds, Doria was faced with mounting losses as Barbarossa's galleys crashed and smashed into the sides of the great galleons and violent hand-to-hand fighting broke out with the Turks swarming aboard the Spanish vessels. Oars crashed into the sides of the ships, as smoke and flame filled the air. The hornets were stinging hard and true.

Andrea Doria saw that Barbarossa's fleet had almost surrounded the Spanish fleet – but he could do nothing about it. The superior tactics of the Turkish 'pirate' were gaining the upper hand and the huge galleons were falling to the smaller galleys.

Victory and defeat

Sunset brought respite as Barbarossa ordered his fleet to withdraw. He had lost many men and he knew he could not continue these harrying tactics

much longer – the price of victory was mounting. But the prizes had been high also for he had accounted for five Spanish galleons. In the true pirate tradition of their Admiral, the Turkish ships were either sunk in action or destroyed by their crews – none had suffered the humiliation of capture.

That night Barbarossa slowly gathered his forces together, and with the captured galleons, waited for the dawn. The hours of darkness saw hasty repairs to the damaged galleys. Andrea Doria during the night, had decided to withdraw completely and as dawn broke his fleet was seen fast disappearing over the horizon, scurrying homewards. Barbarossa found himself without an enemy.

The Turks had won what became known as the Battle of Preveza, a holy battle. The 'pirate' Admiral, outnumbered and with smaller ships, had won the day. Here on September 28, 1537, Khair-ed-Din Barbarossa earned the title 'The King of the Seas'. On his return to Constantinople with his spoils he was feted and praised as only the victor of a mighty battle can be. His complete mastery and dominance of the Spanish and their allies, his ruggedness and ruthlessness in waiting for the right time and the ferocity with which he delivered his attacks made him a legend. Turkish-Moslem influence could now spread unchallenged through the Mediterranean. Thanks to Barbarossa a glorious future appeared assured for the Ottoman Empire.

Doria's fate was that of the vanquished servant of demanding masters. He had lost, he had run away when he should have fought to the death – so ran the thinking of the Papal dignitories, cosily removed from the cannon blasts and crashing timbers of the bloody conflict – and so he was charged with cowardice.

Above Victory at Preveza opened the way for the Turkish reconquest of Algeria and Tunis and established Moslem control of the Eastern Mediterranean.

Right Barbarossa lured Doria to the Gulf of Arta and then allowed himself to be 'tempted' out for a final battle on the open seas.

Preveza

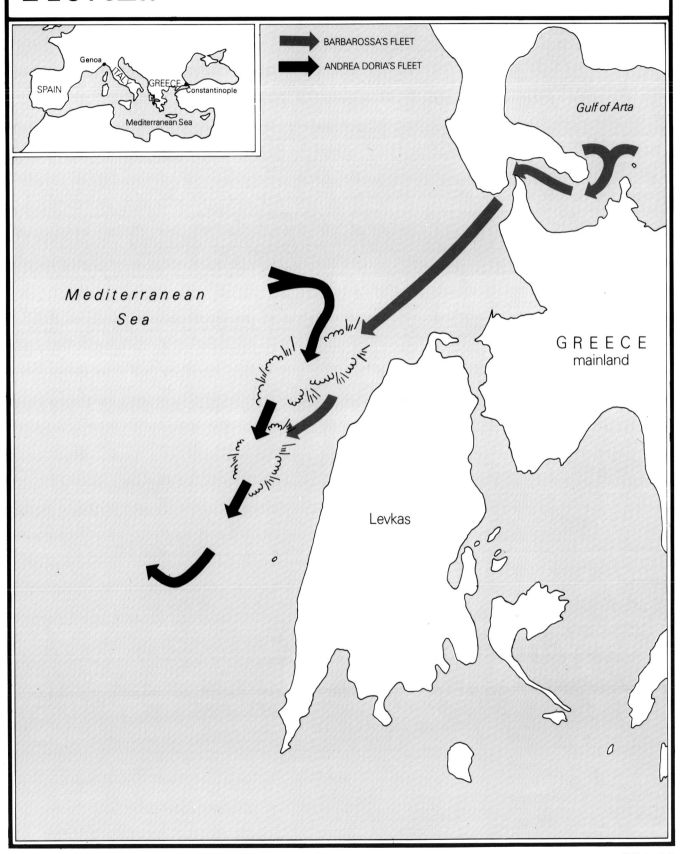

SPAIN

Genoa

ITALY

GREECE

Constantinople

Mediterranean Sea

BARBAROSSA'S FLEET

ANDREA DORIA'S FLEET

Gulf of Arta

Mediterranean Sea

G R E E C E
mainland

Levkas

THE SAINTS

British tactics and seamanship triumphed over an incompetently-crewed French fleet in the seas around the islands of the Saintes in the West Indies in 1782 and left the Royal Navy free to roam the Caribbean — the long experience of Admiral Rodney had paid off.

Fate sometimes reserves a man's greatest achievement for his later years, an achievement that surpasses all the other successes of his life. Such a man was George Brydges Rodney, who was born in February, 1718, and had to wait until his sixty-fifth year before reaching the pinnacle of his career. Already both a Knight Baron and an Admiral, his naval victory over the French in the Battle of the Saints, on April 12, 1782, allowed him the final accolade: an assured place in history.

His career in the Royal Navy started auspiciously when, as a young officer, he took part in Admiral Hawke's victory at the Battle of Ushant in 1747. He showed himself a ruthless man in his pursuit of 'prize money', chasing it with a single-mindedness that was not considered becoming for an officer and a gentleman of those times.

He seems to have used this same roughshod approach to his other career, that of a Member of Parliament. He was the elected member for Penryn, an officer of the Royal Navy, and something of a merchant, all at the same time. It is said he took advantage of his dual position as an officer and a Parliamentarian to advance the careers of his family and friends – but that is hardly remarkable in an age notorious for its political corruption. Against official objections, for example, he had a son drafted into the Navy and given the rank of 'post' Captain. The main objection was that the son was only 15 years old!

At the peak of the Battle of the Saints, with the 90-gun HMS Barfleur *firing into the French flagship, the 104-gun* Ville de Paris, *more than 60 men-of-war were engaged. French mistakes, and a change in the wind, allowed the British to bring them to battle although the French commander had planned only to exchange shots as he sailed by to escape into the Caribbean.*

Overleaf *The vigour of the British action, and their unorthodox tactics, scattered the French Fleet and as a result the British were able to sink many ships and capture others, including the* Ville de Paris.

Rodney sails

During his years as an active naval officer, he had fought against the greatest sea-powers of the day – the Spanish, the Dutch and the French. His year of destiny, 1782, saw him sailing from England towards the West Indies, where the French had been quietly assembling a fleet. With this fleet the French hoped to capture the main island of the West Indies, Jamaica. The French Fleet was commanded by Admiral Francois-Joseph-Paul Comte de Grasse, who, ironically, was attempting to set the seal on his own career.

Rodney had been sent to deal with this threat and had sailed from Plymouth on January 9, 1782. In just over a month his small fleet of 12 Royal Navy men-of-war were anchored in the harbour of the island of Barbados. The news that greeted him there was grim, for de Grasse was attacking the island of St. Kitts in his push northwards. The small British garrison on land and sea was holding out against tremendous odds. Supplies and ammunition were running out, and there was widespread disease amongst soldiers and sailors alike. It could only be a matter of time before de Grasse overwhelmed the island and continued his advance towards Jamaica.

A French success

Spending less than 48 hours in replenishing his stores from several merchant ships that happened to be in the port, Rodney sailed towards the beleaguered island. But it was too late – St. Kitts had fallen. Though the small naval force had managed to escape, de Grasse had finally succeeded in capturing the island. Rodney now joined the small escaping force and turned back to Barbados. Nothing could be done, so plans and tactics had to be reviewed.

Meanwhile, de Grasse swept on. The islands of Nevis and Monsarrat fell to him in quick succession. The French fleet was making tremendous inroads into the British-controlled territories. If the island of Jamaica fell to the French it would only be a matter of time before the Royal Navy was driven from the seas of the West Indies and the French would then have the rich undisputed mastery of Caribbean waters.

After the island of Monsarrat fell, Admiral de Grasse brought his fleet of 30 warships into Fort Royal, on the island of Martinique. There he planned his tactics for capturing the prize islands of Barbados and Antigua. His ships were replenished with stores and ammunition, and his hard-worked crews rested for the battle to come.

Sir George Brydges Rodney, who was now faced with the prospect of having to maintain a foothold for the British Empire in these waters, was also planning his strategy for a confrontation with de Grasse. He knew that de Grasse, lying at ease in the placid waters of Fort Royal, was planning his next move towards the final capture of his goal, Jamaica.

Waiting for a wind

Both men were impatient to start, but during those early spring weeks the weather was continually unsuitable. The ships of the line relied solely upon sail power, and therefore could not put to sea unless the winds were favourable.

Opposite Admiral George Brydges Rodney (1718-92), in a career that spanned the second half of the eighteenth century, fought the Spanish, the Dutch and the French, the major sea-powers of the day. His long experience gave him the advantage at the decisive Battle of the Saints.

Above Until this battle, Admiral Francois-Joseph-Paul, Comte de Grasse (1722-88) had had an equally distinguished career – but it ended with defeat.

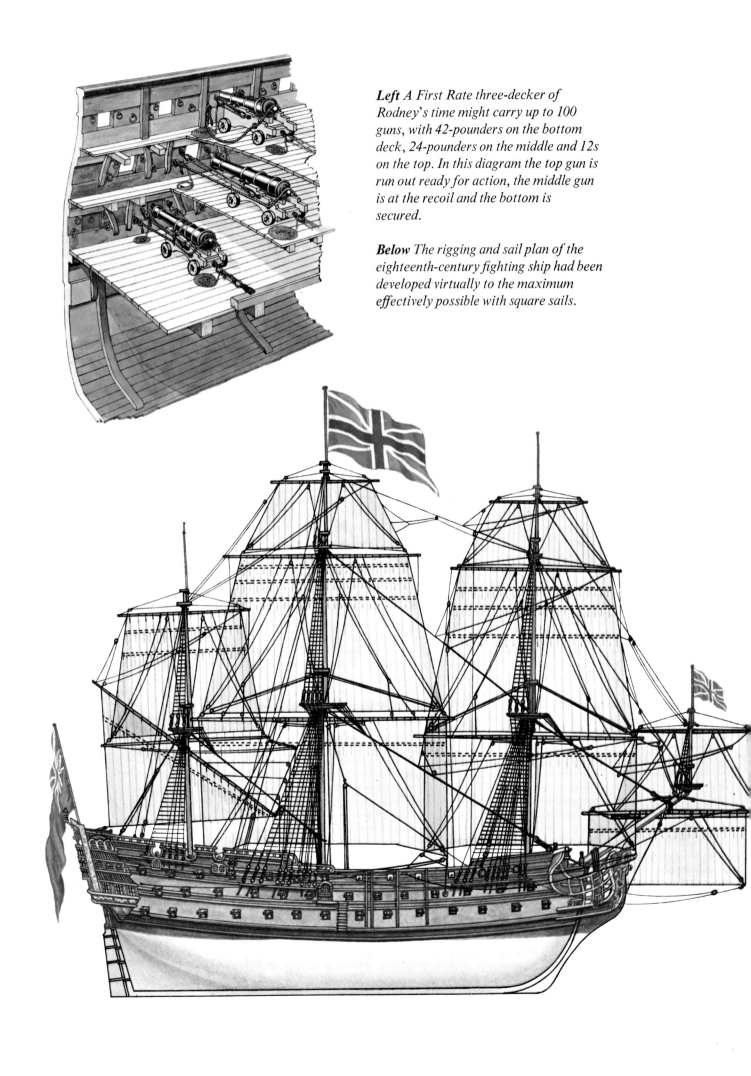

Left *A First Rate three-decker of Rodney's time might carry up to 100 guns, with 42-pounders on the bottom deck, 24-pounders on the middle and 12s on the top. In this diagram the top gun is run out ready for action, the middle gun is at the recoil and the bottom is secured.*

Below *The rigging and sail plan of the eighteenth-century fighting ship had been developed virtually to the maximum effectively possible with square sails.*

Week after week slipped by while the fleets anxiously waited for a break in the weather. Sometimes the winds were too light and sometimes too strong. With the light winds came heavy sea mists, and it was treacherous to put to sea in such conditions. If the winds were strong, manoeuvring the huge men-of-war became extremely difficult in the restricted passage-ways and channels.

So de Grasse and Rodney had no choice but to wait. They knew the weather would break with the coming of the late spring, and that suitable conditions would arrive. During these weeks of waiting, Rodney wrote home the following words: 'I'm of the opinion that the great events which must decide the Empire of the Ocean will be either off Jamaica or San Domingo.' Of this he was certain, his sense of strategy, and his years of experience telling him so. And, after all, he was a British Admiral, and would never be proved wrong. His vain nature told him that what he calculated would turn out to be true.

As the long wait drew on, news reached Rodney that must have jolted his confidence. French reinforcements had somehow slipped through his guard and had joined up with de Grasse. With these reinforcements of six men-of-war, and the 5,000 troops they were carrying, de Grasse now had a total of 36 ships. This was adequate for his rush northwards and the final phase of his operation, the capture of Jamaica itself.

Sir George Rodney had under his command 37 men-of-war. Some of them were from the force that had been stationed at St Kitts, some were from the West Indies' squadrons that had hastily been assembled, and some he had brought with him from England. It was a collection of warships of varying ages and varying degrees of reliability; men who had seen action rubbed shoulders with men who had never been in foreign waters before. But the weeks of waiting gave Sir George the opportunity to mould his forces and his age and experience enabled him to weld together the variety of ships and men into a fighting force.

The French fleet sails

The early summer of 1782 came to the Leeward Islands, bringing with it serene and fair weather. The winds moderated, and the sun shone brilliantly upon the clear blue waters. All was set for the battle. De Grasse gathered his fleet together and set sail. But they had been seen, for Rodney had positioned scouting frigates at strategic places in the channels and passages around Fort Royal. These ships had lain silently to watch for any French movements. On the night of April 6, the cruiser *Endymion* observed French activity within the port. The expected was happening, and the *Endymion* duly reported back to Rodney. As the *Endymion* scurried back with her news, the French fleet slid out of the port on a northerly course.

On hearing the news, Rodney immediately ordered his fleet to set sail in pursuit. The greater standard of discipline and seamanship that Rodney maintained now began to pay dividends. The great sailing warships, in perfect formation, slowly but surely made their way towards the French fleet – slowly, because the winds were now moderating and dropping. Offshore breezes, running from island to island, called for navigation and seamanship of the highest order so as to make the most profitable use of the light and airy conditions. Rodney had trained his crews well.

The strain begins to tell

Rodney's fleet closed with that of de Grasse. At times the two fleets could see one another in the perfect visibility, but yet little onward progress could be made. For several days, almost in slow motion, the fleets sailed on. The French were still heading northwards, with the British trying to overtake and stop them. In these extreme conditions frustration inevitably began to show itself in the French. Due to complete incompetence, the French warship *Zélé*, of 74-guns, collided with the 64-gun *Jason*.

Each ship had been endeavouring to catch the wind, and bad seamanship on the part of Lt. Gras-Préville, the Captain of the *Zélé*, brought about the collision. The *Jason* was so badly damaged that she hauled out of line and had to slowly make her way to Guadeloupe for repairs. De Grasse had lost a ship and not a shot had been fired yet. The *Zélé* had also been damaged, and on the morning of April 11, the 74-gunner was seen to be making very little headway, and was gradually slipping behind the rest of the French fleet. Rodney waited as the *Zélé* slowly came within his grasp.

Hour after hour in the airy conditions the ships

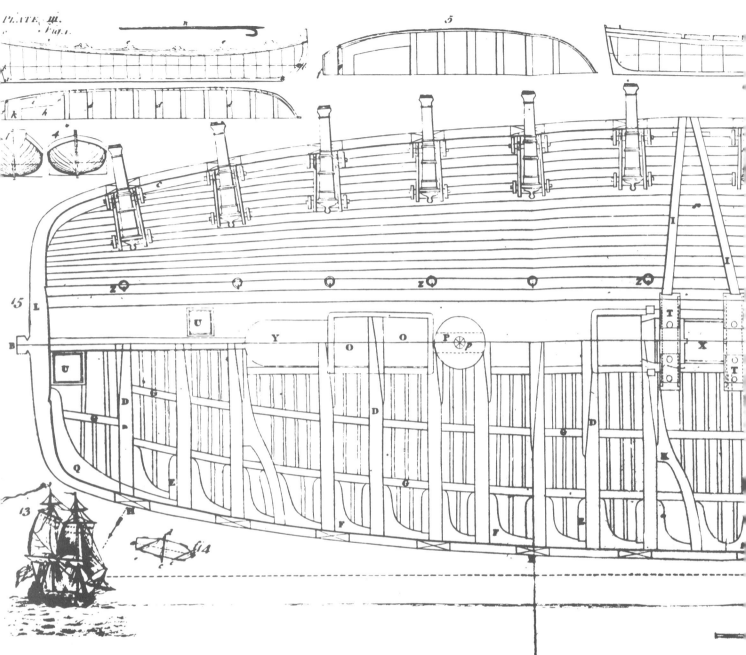

slipped towards one another. Hardly any winds filled their sails. For all the efforts of the crew of the *Zélé*, the distance between them and the oncoming British was steadily diminishing. Every yard of their canvas was aloft, but still she could not escape. Throughout that day the *Zélé*, at the very rear of the French fleet, strove to avoid the oncoming British. Night came and, with it, respite. The following morning the *Zélé* was nowhere to be found – rather than allow inevitable slaughter she had been abandoned.

Still the main fleets were within sight of one another, but were well outside artillery range. Then, in his anxiety to push forward de Grasse made a fatal error. The scarcity of wind left him

with two possible decisions, for behind him Rodney's fleet was slowly bearing down upon him. De Grasse's alternatives were either to turn to leeward, which would bring him face to face with the British fleet, or to turn southwards and try to run the gauntlet. Working up as much speed as possible, de Grasse started on the latter course.

Line ahead

Rodney knew what to expect of the French. On seeing de Grasse fly his signals he ordered, at first light, his ships into the classic battle station of ships of the Royal Navy: 'line ahead', was the

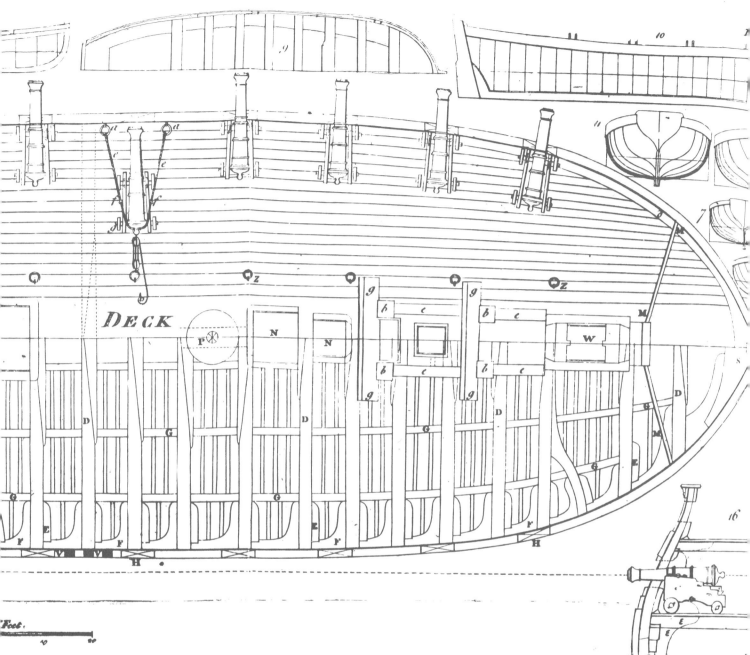

DECK

Feet.

order – line ahead at two cables (1,200 feet) distance. The sails strained to catch every breath of the light wind, as the mighty men-of-war approached the French. De Grasse watched the British manoeuvring into formation, and ordered his own fleet into battle stations. This was also the classic 'line ahead' – but poor seamanship left the line stretched, with several gaps in it. The French ships moved towards the confrontation with the British, and steadily the two lines advanced head-on.

From first light the respective manoeuvres had taken less than three hours. Captain Taylor Penny, leading the British line in the *Marlborough*, opened fire at a range of 400 yards at the leading

A First Rate ship of the line had a crew of 850 men: servicing the heavy guns in battle, and there could be up to 30 42-pounders on the 180-foot main gun-deck, made exhaustive demands on manpower. The guns were muzzle loaders and after each shot had to be cleaned out, a charge of gunpowder up to half the weight of the shot put in, a wad of rope-yarn rammed home and the cannon ball or grape shot loaded. After priming the touch-hole with powder the gun was run up and fired either individually or as part of a broadside. And under fire all this took place with cannon balls shattering the ship's timbers, splinters flying amidst the smoke and noise so loud that many gunners were deafened.

Although outnumbered at the Battle of the Saints, the
French theoretically held the advantage because their
ships were more heavily gunned and better designed than
those of the English – the English indeed tended to copy
French ship design. Tactically, however, the French erred.
Their tendency to aim at the rigging, hoping to cripple the
English ships while staying at long range, would do little
good in light airs when repairs were easy: the English
fired at the hulls – between wind and water – and their
better-served guns did far more damage.

French warship, the 74-gun *Hercule*. One by one the ships behind opened fire at their counterparts. The British *Arrogant*, the second in line, opened fire on the 74-gun *Neptune*, and the *Alcide*, of 74-guns, fired into the *Souverain*. Each ship attacked its opposite number as the lines passed each other.

Admiral Rodney opens fire

Rodney's own flagship, the mighty 90-gun *Formidable*, opened fire at a little after 8 a.m. It was actually impossible for Rodney to witness the whole scene, for with his ships in perfect line he was unable to see more than two or three ships either in front or behind. He was therefore un-

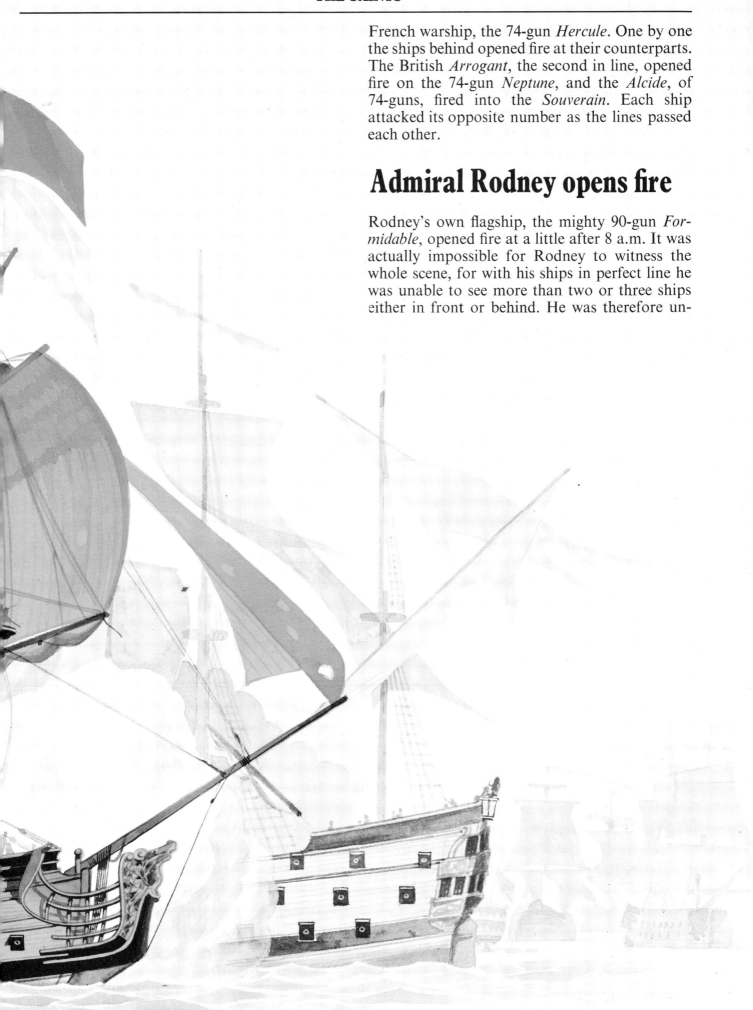

able to see precisely how the battle was faring at the head or stern of the great line.

Salvos ripped into the ships, as the distance between them was reduced to less than 100 feet. Shattered masts came tumbling down, to fall in disarray on the decks of the warships. Sails were torn from their shrouds, and the noise was deafening. Signals from ship to ship could not be made by loud-hailer, so they had to be made by hand. The massive barrage of the cannon ploughed into the French, and the French replied in kind. Smoke completely enveloped the ships. Records have it that Captain Savage, of the 74-gun *Hercules*, who had been wounded earlier on in the action, directed the operations of his ship from a chair. Unable to be heard above the tremendous noise, he was seen signalling frantically at the gunners to fire between wind and water to sink the French rascals.

An hour of this terrible exchange took place, an hour in which the lines came exactly head to tail. At this point Rodney's pre-arranged tactics came into play. Catching as much of the light winds as possible, the centre of the British line turned inwards by a pre-arranged order to break the straggling French line. The French ships were forced to bear away. Immediately a large gap opened up in the French line, and Rodney in the *Formidable* started the rout.

The rout begins

The French man-of-war *Glorieux* was singled out and came in for heavy punishment as the *Formidable* bore down upon her and at point-blank range fired withering broadsides into her. So lose did the ships pass that their spars became entangled for a second. The *Formidable* was pouring tremendous punishment into the side of the French man-of-war, and when she had passed the next in line, the 90-gun *Namur*, continued the uneven struggle. The *Namur* blasted round after round into the *Glorieux'* weeping side. The *Glorieux* ceased fire with smoke pouring from her gun ports, her masts askew, and her

De Grasse's flagship, the Ville de Paris *was the largest and most heavily-armed ship in the two fleets, and in de Grasse's eyes the key to the Caribbean. When he hauled down his colours, after ten hours of fighting, French power in the West Indies had been broken.*

sails torn to shreds. Slowly through the gaping wounds in her sides came the sound of cracking and crashing as her bulkheads gave way. Water poured into her and she settled into the water up to her ports.

The *Formidable* was still leading the attack: with five other men-of-war, she was ploughing into the disorganized French. The enemy was being scattered, and in the scattering became easy prey. But a lull now settled upon the battle. Every square yard of canvas was hoisted aloft, for the fickle winds had dropped, making manoeuvring impossible. It was as if the entire battle had been frozen. Ships could hardly make way, but there was at least the compensation that very quick repairs could be made. Sails that had been torn were hurriedly replaced, and the wounded were given hurried treatment.

After less than an hour, the sails began to fill as a light breeze returned. The ships once more commenced battle, and the French were by now in complete disarray. From the *Formidable* Rodney, together with his other ships, harried the disordered French. Ship after ship was attacked individually and laid bare, its masts brought down and its hulls rendered smoking pyres. Past noon and well into the afternoon the rout continued. As the battle progressed British colours were hoisted in the much-damaged *Glorieux;* the *Cesar* was captured, and later the *Hector* capitulated. De Grasse was indeed suffering a terrible defeat. His plan of French domination of the Caribbean, based on the capture of Jamaica, was being blasted to shreds before his eyes.

Rodney reaps his reward

At just after 6.30 p.m. de Grasse ordered his colours to be struck from the mast of his flagship, the *Ville de Paris*. Rodney then ordered the action to be broken off: the French had surrendered. That night the British fleet surrounded the French ships that had capitulated, and in the morning de Grasse came on board the *Formidable*, to remain there for two days as the 'guest' of Admiral Rodney. The British escorted, or towed, the captured vessels of the French fleet into Port Royal harbour, Jamaica. There they anchored on April 29.

The aging Admiral Rodney had gained a victory that had ensured the Royal Navy's domination of the seas of the Caribbean. Any threat of a

French invasion had been completely averted. Rodney himself had gained many prize ships, and was later to write of his career: 'Within two little years I have taken two Spanish, one Dutch, and one French Admiral.'

De Grasse, on being returned to his homeland, was virtually ordered to retire from the Navy. A sad man, he died in 1788, some six years after his defeat at the hands of Rodney. Ten years after the Battle of The Saints, Admiral Rodney died, safe in the knowledge that he had written his name for ever in the annals of the history of the sea. By supreme single-mindedness he had brought a rich conclusion to his life and saved the vast wealth of the West Indies for the British Empire.

Ships in the Battle of the Saints

BRITISH FLEET

Name	Guns	Name	Guns
Formidable (Flagship)	90	Marlborough	74
Agamemnon	64	Monarch	74
Ajax	74	Montagu	74
Alcide	74	Namur	90
Alfred	74	Nonsuch	64
America	64	Prince George	90
Anson	64	Prince William	64
Arrogant	74	Princessa	70
Barfleur	90	Prothee	64
Bedford	74	Repulse	64
Belliqueux	64	Resolution	74
Canada	74	Royal Oak	74
Centaur	74	Russell	74
Conqueror	74	St Albans	64
Duke	90	Torbay	74
Fame	74	Valiant	74
Hercules	74	Warrior	74
Magnificent	74	Yarmouth	64

FRENCH FLEET

Name	Guns	Name	Guns
Ville de Paris (Flagship)*	104	Hector*	74
Ardent*	64	Hercule	74
Auguste	80	Languedoc	80
Bourgogne	74	Magnanime	74
Brave	74	Magnifique	74
César*	74	Marseillais	74
Citoyen	74	Neptune	74
Conquerant	74	Northumberland	74
Couronne	80	Palmier	74
Dauphin Royal	70	Pluton	74
Destin	74	Réfléchi	74
Diadéme	74	Sceptre	74
Duc de Bourgogne	80	Scipion	74
Eveillé	64	Souverain	74
Glorieux*	74	Triomphant	80

Vessels captured.

Tactics decided the Battle of the Saints – so called because it took place in the Passage of the Saintes to the north of the island of Dominica. The two fleets were set to pass each other in line ahead when Rodney managed to turn the British ships in three sections into gaps in the French line – the first commander to use the technique. The French never recovered from their surprise at having to fight at close quarters and ultimately surrendered.

The Saints

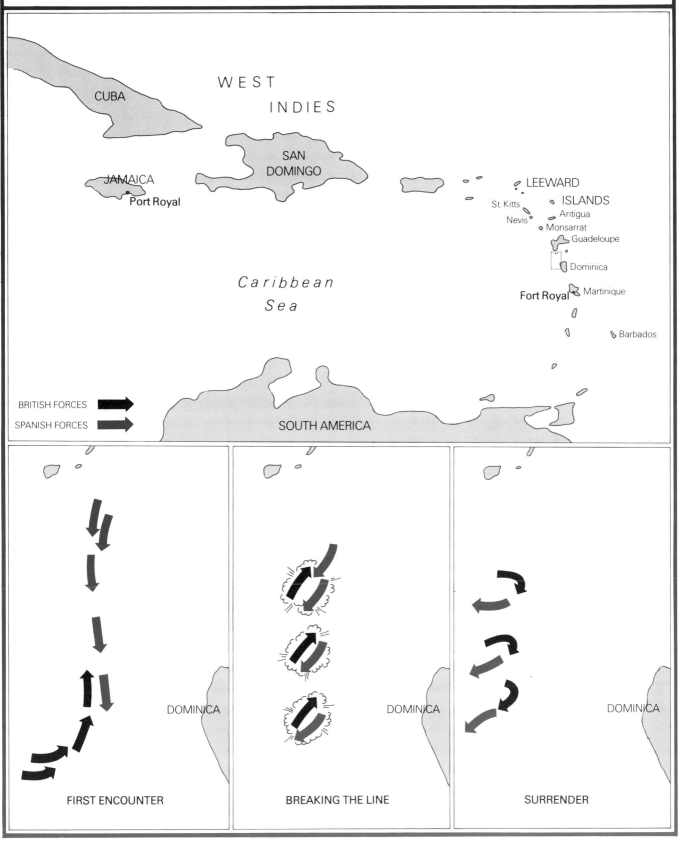

BRITISH FORCES
SPANISH FORCES

CUBA

JAMAICA
Port Royal

W E S T
I N D I E S

SAN
DOMINGO

LEEWARD
ISLANDS

St. Kitts
Antigua
Nevis
Monsarrat
Guadeloupe
Dominica
Fort Royal Martinique

Barbados

Caribbean
Sea

SOUTH AMERICA

FIRST ENCOUNTER

DOMINICA

BREAKING THE LINE

DOMINICA

SURRENDER

DOMINICA

CAPE ST VINCENT

One man's independent action gave Britain victory over the Spanish off Cadiz in 1797. That man was Horatio Nelson: as the Spanish fleet turned and ran virtually without fighting he swung his single ship across their path and by sheer audacity brought them to battle.

An embattled nation, Britain by 1797 was reeling under the hammer blows of France's greatest soldier, Napoleon Bonaparte. Disaster on disaster rained down as French troops swept into Italy, robbing Britain of its naval bases of Naples, Tuscany and Leghorn. The proud sea nation was being driven relentlessly from the Mediterranean. Then Spain allied with France and in October 1797 declared war on Britain who now stood alone against the might of Europe, isolated, dispirited and threatened with being driven from the shore of the continent.

The grim spectre of defeat stared Britain in the face. If she could not control the seas her natural defences counted for nothing. Napoleon's drive to European domination could not be halted.

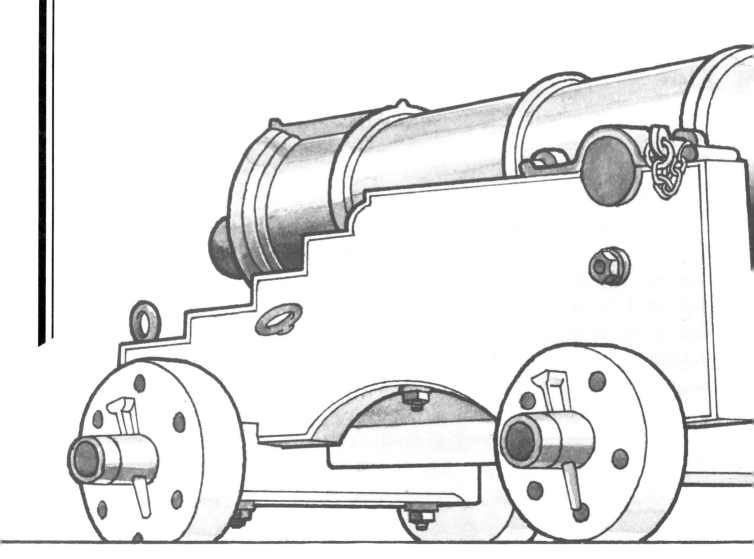

Then, with the last gasp of morale ebbing away, the man of the moment stepped forward to save the nation. That man was Horatio Nelson.

Born in 1758, in the tiny village of Burnham Thorpe in Norfolk, Horatio Nelson was the sixth child of the Reverend Edmund Nelson and his wife Catherine. Brought up in the strict atmosphere of a Christian household, the young Horatio was encouraged to fend for himself. In doing so he acquired his fascination with the sea. He spent hours watching the grey, foam-flecked waters of the stormy North Sea, seeing a whole spectrum of ships sail by. There were lumbering cargo ships, plying their trade along Britain's East coast, squadrons of warships, each magnificently bedecked and sailing by in perfect formation and ships of the line, mighty Royal ships.

There was no more romantic introduction to the prospect of a career on the high seas.

A Captain at 21

In 1770, at the tender age of 12 years, Horatio entered the service of the Royal Navy, as a midshipman on a Third Rate ship of the line, the 1,386 ton *Raisonnable*. In these early years Nelson learnt discipline above all else – discipline in handling a ship of the line and discipline in leading men. He spent many years learning the arts of true navigation, seamanship and the tactics of seaborne warfare.

Nelson progressed rapidly: in 1777 he became Second Lieutenant in the 32-gun *Lowestoffe*;

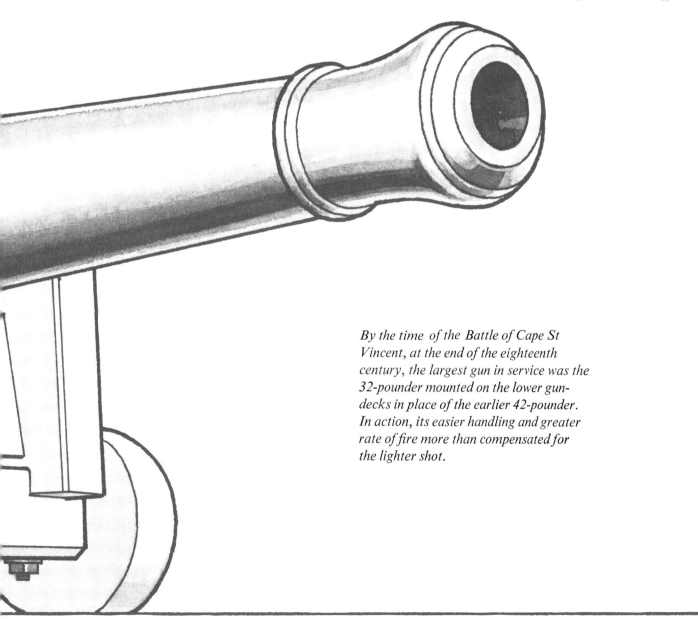

By the time of the Battle of Cape St Vincent, at the end of the eighteenth century, the largest gun in service was the 32-pounder mounted on the lower gun-decks in place of the earlier 42-pounder. In action, its easier handling and greater rate of fire more than compensated for the lighter shot.

Inset left Horatio Nelson (1758-1805) displayed the
initiative that made him one of the greatest naval
commanders of all time in turning his ship across the
Spanish line. His action allowed **inset right** Admiral John
Jervis, who had already smashed his way through the
Spanish line, to bring the Spaniards to battle and defeat
them. In the hotly-fought action the British captured four
ships and seriously damaged ten more without a single loss.

1778 saw him commander of the 138-ton brig
Badger; and within six months he was in command of the 557-ton 28-gun frigate *Hinchin-
brook*. Horatio Nelson had hoisted his Captain's
pennant before he was 21 years old. In the following years, Nelson served in North America,
Jamaica, Nicaragua, South America and the
West Indies.

Britain and France went to war in 1793 and
Nelson was shortly engaged in battle with the
French fleet. In 1794, on July 12, he was wounded
and lost the sight of his right eye. But this set-
back did not mar his progress, for Nelson was a
singleminded servant of his country. In 1795 he
fought at the Gulf of Genoa and at the Battle of
Hyéres. The French were becoming his constant
enemy.

In 1797 Nelson was despatched on a hazardous
mission in command of the frigate *Minerve*. His
aim was to raid deep into French dominated
waters and bring the small British garrison and
naval stores from the island of Elba. The *Minerve* ran into two Spanish frigates but Nelson's
brilliant seamanship outsmarted the Spanish
men-of-war and he fulfilled his task completely.

He then returned to join the English fleet under
its Admiral, Sir John Jervis.

Two fleets at Cadiz

Jervis had been sent to keep continuous watch
off the Spanish coast, near Cadiz, for any movements of the Spanish fleet commanded by its
admiral, Don José de Cordoba. The mighty
Spanish fleet of two divisions, totalling 27 ships,
had been stationed for some time at Cadiz. Jervis
was waiting for the Spanish fleet to move from
the harbour so that battle could be joined and,
he hoped, Spain's naval fighting force destroyed.
This would effectively drive the wedge for
Britain's re-entry into the Mediterranean, and
would also, because Spain was allied to France,

The 100-gun Victory, *flagship of the fleet commander at Cape St Vincent, Sir John Jervis, and largest ship in the British fleet, was herself overshadowed by the massive 130-gun Spanish flagship* Santisima Trinidad.

strike a blow directly against Bonaparte.

Jervis's small fleet numbered only 15 ships of the line. Six of these, including his flagship the *Victory*, had 100 guns, and a further eight had 74 guns each. The 1639-ton *Captain*, Horatio Nelson's ship, was one of these.

The flagship of Admiral Don José de Cordoba was an enormous 130-gun four-decked ship, the *Santisima Trinidad*. As well as this mighty flagship de Cordoba had six warships each carrying 112 guns, two carrying 80 guns and 18 other vessels carrying at least 74 guns. His was a mighty armada, a great fighting, battling force, but Admiral Jervis was not daunted. Although he

had only 15 ships, his men had been schooled in the highest standards of Royal Navy training.

The Spanish fleet, Jervis knew, was frail despite its appearance. The massive Spanish ships were under-crewed and the officers were poorly trained. Further, the guns were manned by soldiers, not seamen, for the seamen had not been instructed in the art of seaborne warfare! Anticipation riffled through the small English fleet stationed off Cadiz as it prepared for the coming battle with de Cordoba's armada.

The Spanish fleet was sighted on February 14, 1797 at 8.15 a.m. In perfect morning visibility, they were seen sailing in two divisions, line ahead. Admiral Jervis ordered his ships into close order, single line ahead. HMS *Captain*, Nelson's ship was placed three from the rear. The English plan was to steer between the two groups of Spanish men-o-war and then turn to destroy the large group with concentrated fire power. The English ships were no match in sheer size for the mighty Spanish warships – but Jervis accepted the risk.

The chase is on

Jervis's foresight and superior naval skill soon became apparent. The Spanish, on seeing the British Navy advance, failed to close their ranks; the Spanish seamen, so inexperienced, could not maintain good close order. Their ships started to straggle out into two vague groups and Jervis at once seized the initiative. The English bore down upon the disordered Spanish fleet like a hungry wolf pack. The Spanish panicked and tried vainly to regroup into one main defensive body. The English were in pursuit.

Belatedly the leading Spanish ships altered course to port in an attempt to fall back to their main body. Jervis responded with the dramatic signal to his ships. 'Pass through the enemy's line.' The bold approach gained the success it deserved because the Spanish could not close their ranks in time. Led by Captain Thomas Troubridge, in the 74-gun *Culloden*, the perfect line of British warships bore into the weak belly of the Spanish fleet. The British opened fire and a fusilade of shots ripped into the Spanish ships. The huge, three-decked flagship of the Spanish Vice Admiral, the 112-gun *Principe de Asturias*, was heavily raked. Her topmasts were shattered, her sails blown to shreds, her masts splintered

under the enormous fire power and flames started to lick her decks.

De Cordoba ordered the confused Spanish fleet to alter course to north in an attempt to shake off his pursuers. Jervis countered by tacking his ships about in succession. The enemy was now being raked with withering broadsides as cannon upon cannon was brought to bear on the lumbering Spanish warships.

Nelson makes his move

The battle, which had been a series of engagements between passing ships, reached its peak at 1 p.m. One after another, Admiral Jervis's warships had poured fire into the Spanish fleet, and had escaped virtually unscathed. But then an opportunity presented itself – the Spanish found themselves in a position where they could run for safety. Yet as they tried to flee from the clutches of the wolves, Horatio Nelson entered the scene.

Nelson had watched the battle from HMS *Captain* and his brilliant independent spirit now came into play. He quickly sized up the situation. Ignoring Jervis's orders of maintaining line and battle stations, Nelson took the *Captain* out to port, swinging away from the rear of the British fleet. He then reversed course through 180 degrees. This manoeuvre brought him face to face with the escaping enemy. The *Captain* then headed into the main Spanish body.

Ploughing forward with all the speed he could muster, Nelson produced a single-handed thrust into de Cordoba's fleet. The Spanish were amazed to see such audacity from a 74-gun ship: a small Third Rate vessel was challenging the massive 130-gun ships of the Spanish fleet. The *Captain* bore down upon the Spanish ships and once in range Nelson gave the order: 'Open fire!' The *Captain's* guns blazed at the enemy ships on the fringe of the main body. The Spanish were taken aback – and the immediate advantage fell to Nelson.

Seeing the *Captain* pull out of line, Captain Cuthbert Collingwood, in the 74-gun *Excellent*, Captain Thomas Elfrederick, in the 90-gun *Blenheim*, and several others swung out of line and rushed into support. The rout was now on. Nelson in the *Captain*, had closed upon the flagship, the *Santisima Trinidad*, and a tremendous bombardment was exchanged.

'*Raked her both ahead and stern*' *says the log of the*
Victory ***centre left*** *of one engagement during the battle.*
Victory's *guns sent 32-pound cannon balls into the sides of*
the Spanish ships, shattering timbers and creating great
confusion on deck.

Broadside after broadside

Still the *Captain* bore on, pouring broadside after broadside into the bemused enemy. The *Blenheim* and the *Excellent*, passing to windward, joined in. Masts came crashing down, sails were torn apart and smoke billowed, cloaking the Spanish fleet. Onlookers could barely see the British ships wrestling with the Spanish men-of-war. So violent and so intense was the action that the Third Rate 74-gun *Culloden* was crippled and the *Blenheim* beaten back.

The badly mauled *Captain*, after hauling away from the *Santisima Trinidad*, found herself alongside the damaged 80-gun *San Nicholas*. Nelson, in a remarkable feat of navigation, brought the battered *Captain* alongside the *San Nicholas*. At the head of a boarding party, Nelson swept on to the decks of the Spanish ship. A running hand-to-hand-fight developed. Sheer ferocity overwhelmed the Spanish in a brief, bloody battle. The Spanish ensign was hauled down and Nelson took possession of a prize Spanish man-of-war.

The *Excellent* engaged the *Salvador del Mundo*, then passed forward on to the *San Ysidro* which Captain Collingwood engaged at close quarters. Driving alongside he boarded the Spaniard, and again, after a very quick and one-sided action the Spanish flag was hauled down.

The *Santisima Trinidad* after some tremendous punishment struck her flag from the mast – she was capitulating. Jervis was overjoyed and he signalled his fleet to come to windward. But while he was re-positioning his fleet, the *Santisima*

A cross-section of the Victory, *the British flagship at Cape St Vincent and Nelson's ship 8 years later at Trafalgar. Designed by Sir Thomas Slade,* Victory *was launched on May 7, 1765 and became one of the greatest fighting ships of her time.*

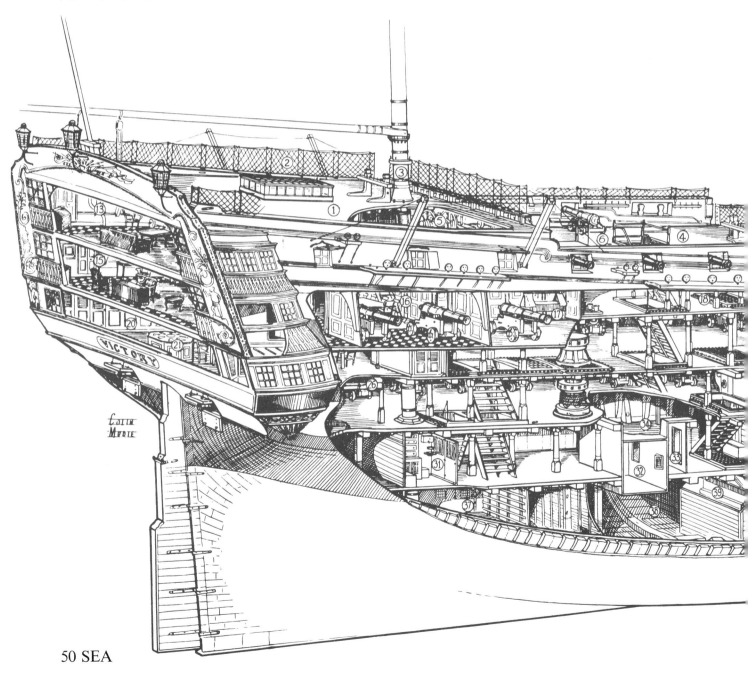

Key to diagram

1 *Poop*	12 *Foremast*	23 *Capstan head*	34 *(Nelson died in 1805)*
2 *Hammock nettings*	13 *Captain's cabin*	24 *Galley and Stove*	35 *Forward magazine*
3 *Mizzenmast*	14 *Upper deck*	25 *Lower deck*	36 *Powder store*
4 *Quarterdeck*	15 *Admiral's day-cabin*	26 *Tiller*	37 *Powder room*
5 *Steering wheels*	16 *Admiral's dining-cabin*	27 *Chain Pumps*	38 *Aft hold*
6 *(Nelson fell in 1805)*	17 *Admiral's sleeping-cabin*	28 *Mooring bitts*	39 *Shot locker*
7 *Pikes*	18 *Shot garlands*	29 *Manger*	40 *Well*
8 *Mainmast*	19 *Middle deck*	30 *Orlop*	41 *Main hold*
9 *Gangway*	20 *Wardroom*	31 *Sick-bay*	42 *Cable store*
10 *Foc's'le*	21 *Tiller head*	32 *Aft hanging magazine*	43 *Main magazine*
11 *Carronades*	22 *Entry port*	33 *Lamp room*	44 *Filling room*

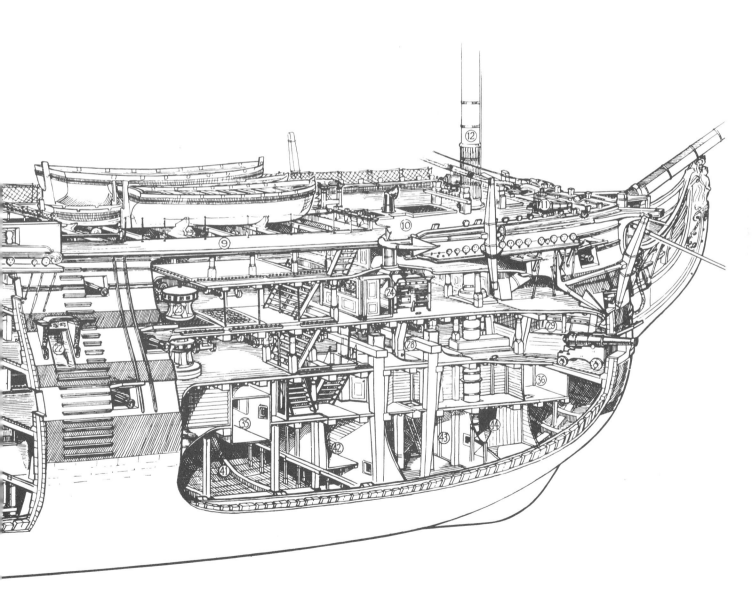

Above *Nelson's bold action in his ship the* Captain *brought him two personal prizes – the* San Josef *and the San* Nicholas, *both major Spanish ships. Here Nelson boards the* San Josef. *After a brief, bloody struggle the Spaniards surrendered.*

Below *Shredded sails and shattered timbers marked the ships that survived this hard-fought battle.*

Trinidad, taking a chance escaped. The largest war vessel then afloat escaped from the clutches of the Royal Navy; escaped to fight again eight years later at the Battle of Trafalgar.

A stunning victory

But Nelson's action, his fine initiative when all appeared to have been lost, enabled Admiral Jervis to claim four excellent prize vessels, the *San Josef*, the *Salvador del Mundo* (both of these ships were larger than most of the British First Rate ships), the *San Nicholas* and the *San Ysidro*. Admiral Jervis had not lost one ship and had suffered only 300 casualties.

Cape St Vincent was a stunning British victory. The Spanish had lost four ships, had suffered serious damage to ten more and their casualties were over 800. Jervis was pleased – but the prize, the *Santisima Trinidad*, had slipped through his fingers.

The following day the British shaped course for Lagos, while the remains of the Spanish fleet withdrew, under cover of night, to Cadiz.

When the news reached Britain of the tremendous victory, morale immediately rose; the joint threat of France and Spain together was dispelled. Britain's rulers richly rewarded their heroes. Jervis became an Earl and took the title Earl St Vincent from his victory. All the subordinate Admirals were made Baronets, and Nelson, promoted to the rank of Rear-Admiral, was created a Knight of the Bath. It was by his brilliant independent action and excellent judgement that victory had been won.

The gate to the Mediterranean had been reopened. Admiral Nelson's name now became a household word and from this time on his fellow countrymen were to heap honour upon honour on him. His decision on that St Valentine's Day in 1797, to turn the *Captain* out of line and prevent the Spanish fleet escaping, proved beyond doubt that the man of the moment had arrived. His action inspired the nation and the war against France and Spain was renewed with great vigour.

Nelson had cut his teeth in this violent battle, and proved he was a brilliant naval leader. He was to rise, in the years to come, to greater things, and greater honours. The culmination was the British naval victory of 1805 in the battle that was fought off Cape Trafalgar, when Horatio Nelson gave his life for his beloved country.

Ships in the Battle of Cape St Vincent

BRITISH FLEET

Name	Guns	Name	Guns
Victory	100	Diadem	64
(Flagship)		Egmont	74
Barfleur	98	Excellent	74
Blenheim	98	Goliath	74
Britannia	100	Irresistible	74
Captain	74	Namur	90
Colossus	74	Orion	74
Culloden	74	Prince George	98

SPANISH FLEET

Name	Guns	Name	Guns
Santisima Trinidad	130	Salvador del Mundo*	112
(Flagship)		San Antonio	74
Atlante	74	San Domingo	74
Bahama	74	San Formin	74
Concepcion	112	San Francisco de Paula	74
Conde de Regla	112	San Genaro	74
Conquistador	74	San Ildefonso	74
Firme	74	San Josef*	112
Glorioso	74	San Juan Nepomuceno	74
Mexicano	112	San Nicholas*	80
Neptuno	80	San Pablo	74
Oriente	74	San Ysidro*	74
Pèlayo	74	Soberano	74
Principe de Asturias	112	Terrible	74

Vessels captured

Right *The location of the battle of Cape St Vincent and the disposition of the opposing fleets came about because Admiral John Jervis saw the chance to cut off the Spanish fleet from its base at Cadiz and, by destroying it, open up the Mediterranean for the British.*

Cape St Vincent

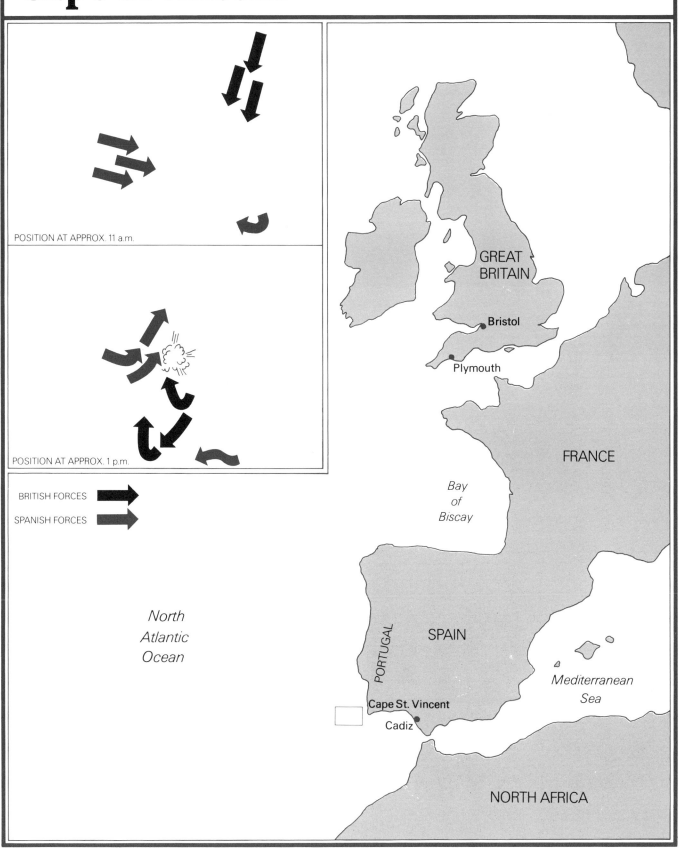

POSITION AT APPROX. 11 a.m.

POSITION AT APPROX. 1 p.m.

BRITISH FORCES

SPANISH FORCES

GREAT BRITAIN

Bristol

Plymouth

FRANCE

Bay
of
Biscay

North
Atlantic
Ocean

PORTUGAL

SPAIN

Mediterranean
Sea

Cape St. Vincent

Cadiz

NORTH AFRICA

Stark example of crushing defeat – a wrecked Russian battleship lies at anchor in Port Arthur. The defeat of the Imperial Russian fleet at Tsushima was total.

TSUSHIMA STRAIT

Halfway round the world for a rendezvous with disaster — that was the fate of the Russian fleet in 1905. As the pride of Russia set out the aim was vengeance against the Japanese, but at Tsushima Strait Admiral Togo annihilated the Russians and broke their power.

During the nineteenth century the European powers established almost complete dominion over the lands of the East. By the last quarter of the century, China and India had been reduced to the status of mere provinces of various European empires. Only Japan had managed to preserve its national sovereignty, maintaining her natural insular isolation until she realized that, to survive in the East, it was apparently necessary to use western methods and ideas.

Japan therefore 'westernized' her army, navy, industry and large sections of her whole society, in the space of 25 years. But in doing all this, she inevitably started to compete with some of the European powers she sought to emulate. In 1904, diplomatic relations with Tsarist Russia were near to breaking point. Both countries had long considered war an inevitable conclusion to their rivalry and the war that did finally break out between them is known as the Russo-Japanese war. It represents a turning point in the history of the modern world, for it was the first time an eastern nation successfully engaged a European power.

East against West

In preparing for this war, the Russians had steadily built up their fleets in the Far East. At Port Arthur (modern Lu-shun) in Manchuria, they had grouped seven battleships, seven cruisers, 20 destroyers and many gun-boats and smaller vessels. All were of modern construction, with well-drilled crews and efficient officers. In the port of Vladivostok they had gathered together a smaller force, consisting of three large cruisers and one small cruiser, together with many torpedo-boats.

The Japanese wanted above all to capture Port Arthur and at least part of the massive flotilla that was based there. By dealing the Tsarist forces such a damaging blow they would win control of the sea lanes of the Far East. This, then, was their ultimate objective, and a rich prize it was. The master-mind behind the Japanese plan was the brilliant tactician and naval strategist Vice-Admiral Heihachiro Togo.

In the early part of 1904 their plans were finally ready to be put into action. On February 6 Vice-Admiral Togo told his officers: 'The Russian fleet is massed at Port Arthur, prepare to sail at once. Annihilate the enemy and set His Majesty's heart at ease!' Diplomatic relations with Tsarist Russia were cut the following afternoon, and on the night of February 8, Togo despatched ten torpedo-boats to attack the Russian ships at anchor in Port Arthur. Togo realized that his moves had to bring quick and decisive victory before Russia was able to bring up her massive reserves.

A Japanese success

In the approaches to Port Arthur lay the unsuspecting Russian battle fleet. The Japanese torpedo-boats approached stealthily under the cover of night, only to find that the Tsarists appeared to be making their task even simpler. The cruiser *Pallada* was making half-hearted attempts to patrol the entrance to the port, and in doing so, had all of her powerful searchlights switched on. This meant that the Japanese torpedo-boats could pick their targets almost at leisure. They steamed past the Russians in two groups of five, and each boat then discharged her torpedoes into the heart of the Russian ships. Having delivered their deadly weapons they turned away sharply at full speed.

In all, of the 18 torpedoes fired only three were effective – but effective these three certainly were. The cruiser *Pallada* was struck amidships and her coal bunkers set on fire. The First Class battleship *Retvizan* was hit on the port side, having a hole 220 feet square torn in her. Another battleship, the *Tsarvitch*, was struck in the aft magazine. This hit shattered her bulkheads and flooded the steering compartment.

The action was quickly over and had been a brilliant initial success for the Japanese. They themselves suffered neither hits nor casualties. The Russians had been foolishly complacent and they had paid the price. The Japanese, on the other hand, had struck just as Togo had intended, quickly and accurately.

On the morning after the attack, Togo brought up his heavy guns and, at long range, poured fire into the rest of the Tsarist fleet. Having thrown the Russians into confusion by the speed of his first thrust, he now pressed home his advantage. Within a few hours the Russian fleet had taken severe damage. The cost to Togo this time was only six Japanese lives. In the space of just 24 hours, the complete balance of naval power in the Far East had been reversed.

After this successful opening, Togo put the second stage of his plan into operation. Port Arthur was put under blockade by the Japanese fleet. Admiral Togo blockaded the naval base and was content to keep the crippled Russian ships bottled up. He knew that this effectively rendered the Russian ships powerless and he had only to wait until the Japanese troops encircled Port Arthur on the landward side for the port to be his for the taking.

The Russians fight back

Total victory, however, was not to come quite so easily, because now the Russians produced their most brilliant tactician and naval officer, Admiral Stephan Ossipovich Makarov and ordered him to command the remains of the beleaguered

fleet penned up in Port Arthur. His orders were simply to bring the remains of the fleet into top fighting condition and then to crush the Imperial forces. This was indeed a commission to tax all Makarov's skill as a commander, and he did not shrink from it.

Togo and Makarov were admirable adversaries: Togo attempting to strangle Makarov into submission and Makarov endeavouring to break Togo's grip. But fate was again on the side of the Imperial Japanese. After more than a month of continually harassing the Japanese blockaders, Makarov's flagship struck a Japanese mine while returning from a raid and blew up. Makarov was killed, and his loss was a terrible blow to the besieged Russians at Port Arthur. Despondency now set in amongst the Tsarist troops, as the scales tipped again in favour of Togo's forces.

All was not well with the Imperial Japanese Navy, however. The damage inflicted by Admiral Makarov in his daring raids, added to the enormous resources needed to keep up the blockade, were taking their toll. The drain on Togo's strength involved in applying a death grip to the Tsarist Navy was considerable. He realized that he had to bring about the complete destruction of Port Arthur quickly, or the Tsarist fish would get off his hook.

Half round the world

In St Petersburg (modern Leningrad), the news from Port Arthur had been received with consternation. A decision was quickly taken to send reinforcements to the Tsarist fleet. But this was where the heart of the Russians' problem lay, for they could only be sent from St Petersburg, and that was half-way around the world.

So it was on October 9, 1904, that Tsar Nicholas II despatched the reinforcements for Port Arthur from the naval base of Reval. The Tsar was sending the newly-completed battleship *Kniaz Suvarov* along with her sister-ships, the *Orel*, *Vorodino*, and *Imperator Alexander III*. These battleships were the backbone of a mighty fleet which the Russians regarded as invincible: Admiral Togo would surely be crushed by this force. The main problem was that of speed – the Russian reinforcements had to reach Port Arthur as quickly as possible. All the while, Togo had virtually a free hand to bring up his own reserves and make his own plans

for the inevitable battle that would decide the issue.

The vast Russian armada that set sail for the Far East consisted of 42 vessels, and the man chosen to command was one of the most senior officers in the Tsar's Navy, Vice-Admiral Zinovy Petrovich Rozhdestvensky. Rozhdestvensky, devoted to the Navy, to his Tsar and to his country, was a man of great intelligence who had reached the high rank of Vice Admiral strictly on his merits. A brilliant commander and tactician, he spared himself even less than he spared his men. He demanded the best of himself and his men, and he usually obtained both.

Soon after the fleet started on its 18,000 mile voyage to Port Arthur, an incident occurred that demonstrated to Rozhdestvensky just how great was the need to spend the voyage in training his inexperienced crews. On October 22, as the Russian fleet was passing through the southern reaches of the North Sea, the nervous and obviously frightened Russian gunners mistook a fleet of British trawlers for Japanese

Opposite In line ahead formation and with battle ensigns hoisted, Admiral Togo's fleet steams confidently towards the Russian adversary.

Above left Given command of the Russian Baltic fleet, Vice-Admiral Rozhdestvensky had the unenviable task of sailing 18,000 miles to the Pacific to do battle with the Japanese. The battle was lost and just three years later Rozhdestvensky died, a sad and embittered man.

Above right Admiral Heimachoro Togo was a ruthless and resourceful commander of the Imperial Japanese fleet.

destroyers! On seeing these trawlers in the half-light, they immediately opened fire, sinking one and damaging many others. Rozhdestvensky was wild with rage, but was wise enough to take the lesson of this debacle. He reprimanded those responsible and then ordered intensive battle training for all his crews. The best possible must be achieved, and that was the least Rozhdestvensky demanded. The majority of the Tsar's more seasoned officers and men might well be blockaded at Port Arthur, but he was determined that his crews would be every bit as battle-ready by the time they arrived.

To add to his difficulties Rozhdestvensky also had the problem of refuelling his armada in the months before it reached its destination. Only after much diplomatic wrangling could re-fuelling take place at Dakar on November 16. But by mid-December the fleet was rounding The Cape of Good Hope and ploughing forward into the Indian Ocean.

Russia decides on battle

News was received towards the end of the year that Port Arthur was falling to the besieging Japanese land forces. The Russian ships there were being slowly destroyed by Admiral Togo's fleet. Relief was not possible any more, for Port Arthur could not last out long enough for it to arrive. Rozhdestvensky therefore analysed and revised his orders. As Port Arthur could not now be relieved, the enemy must be faced in the open sea and the issue decided there.

By March 1905, as he prepared to leave the refuelling port at Madagascar, Rozhdestvensky had decided on this new course of action. He was eager to do battle with Togo now, but, as the

Russian battleships steam towards Tsushima Strait – and disaster. Four new battleships, the flagship Suvarov, Alexander III, Borodino *and* Orel *formed the core of the fleet. All but* Orel *were destroyed.*

fleet was about to set sail, another order was received from St Petersburg. The order instructed Rozhdestvensky to join the Third Pacific Squadron, as this would give him yet more ships for his striking force. What, on the face of it, appeared to be extra help Rozhdestvensky knew to be potentially disastrous. For the Third Pacific Squadron was nothing more than a group of rusting old ships, led mostly by passed-over officers. They would weigh down his fast-moving modern fleet. The ships were not nearly so fast, nor so heavily armed and the men were even less experienced than his own battle fleet.

Rozhdestvensky, however, had no choice, and set sail for Port Arthur in mid-March to rendezvous with his promised reinforcements at Cam Ranh Bay. He pushed his fleet at full speed across the Indian Ocean, through the Malacca Strait, around Singapore, and on to Cam Ranh Bay, arriving on April 14 to join with the squadron of ancient war vessels that awaited him there. The Tsarist fleet now numbered 52 ships.

Admiral Togo was well aware of the coming Tsarist armada. He knew that if he could destroy it, the seas would be wiped completely clear of Russian influence. Imperial Japan would win a momentous victory, and the Divine Navy would reign supreme throughout the waters of the Far East. After the fall of Port Arthur, therefore, Togo rushed his fleet back to Japan for a badly needed overhaul and a complete refitting.

Togo's foresight in doing this now proved its value. Patrols were ordered to scour Tsushima Strait, for Togo was certain that Rozhdestvensky would make his way there. This was because Tsushima Strait lay between Korea and Japan, and Togo was certain that Rozhdestvensky's only possible course was to make for the one remaining port held by the Russians, Vladivostok. The Japanese patrols were to search for the oncoming Tsarist fleet – if the fleet could be sighted soon enough, Admiral Togo could meet it on his own terms, he would have time to place his fleet strategically and, if the divine guidance he sought was with him, annihilate the Russian armada.

First contact

On May 27, 1905, at first light, the Japanese cruiser *Shinano Maru* of the advance patrol sighted a Russian vessel. The cruiser shadowed for nearly two hours until the light improved sufficiently for it positively to identify at least ten Russian warships. They were sailing in formation into Tsushima Strait, just as Togo had expected. A message was quickly despatched informing the Admiral. Togo knew that the first part of his plans could now be put into action. Admiral Rozhdestvensky was running his armada of 52 vessels right down the Japanese throats!

But the *Shinano Maru* had been spotted, and for his part Rozhdestvensky knew that his own plans had to be revised. He could no longer hope to slip through Tsushima Strait unobserved, so he prepared his fleet for action, and issued the signal 'ammunition not to be wasted' to all of his ships. Manoeuvring his ships into battle formation, he steamed on into the Strait. The Russians had sailed half-way round the world and had waited from October 9, 1904, until now, May 27 of the following year, for this action. Rozhdestvensky was determined to avenge the defeat of Port Arthur and to restore Russian honour. Togo was equally determined to blast the remains of the Russian fleet from the seas.

Shortly after noon on May 27, the battle forces approached one another. On paper both fleets were formidable, but in practice they were poles apart. There was, however, one obvious similarity between them: they both contained a large proportion of old ships. The Tsarist fleet consisted of Rozhdestvensky's flagship, the *Kniaz Suvarov*, plus 11 battleships, some of which were very old, four large cruisers, four light cruisers, two of which acted as flotilla leaders and two as escorts, nine destroyers, several transport repair ships, hospital ships, and an auxiliary cruiser, the *Ural*. Admiral Togo had at his disposal his flagship, the *Mikasa*, plus 27 capital ships, many gun-boats, 21 destroyers, over 70 torpedo-boats and several torpedo gunboats.

Although the Japanese possessed a marked superiority in numbers, the mighty Russian battleships were equipped with heavy armaments that might possibly carry the day in the teeth of the greater Japanese numbers. It was a bringing together of two of the greatest sea powers of the time. Such a clash between two mighty imperial warriors, each with an iron resolution to slay the other, would indeed exact a terrible toll in both lives and material.

Admiral Togo attacks

As the forces slowly closed, the Tsarist fleet was in two columns, in line ahead formation. The Imperial fleet took up a single line ahead disposition. The first move was to fall to Admiral Togo. He decided to attack the Tsarist port column, as this was nearest to the course to Vladivostok and was therefore a possible escape route for the Russians. He also realized that this column contained the weaker, slower ships. He increased speed and crossed the Russian bows five miles in front as he was anxious to prevent the battle developing into a chase which could lead to the escape of a few Russian ships. Togo was confident enough to play for the highest stakes and was determined that the Russians would be staking all or nothing as well.

During the 15 minutes it took the Japanese fleet to complete its manoeuvre, Rozhdestvensky opened fire. Shells ripped into the Japanese armoured cruisers *Yakumo* and *Asama*. The *Asama's* steering gear was badly damaged and she was sent wallowing out of line. In all, three Japanese ships had been seriously damaged in the opening salvo. It appeared that Rozhdestvensky had won a first crucial advantage, but it now slowly slipped from him. The old vessels at the tail of the Russian columns were falling behind, unable to keep up with the headlong pace.

The U-turn completed, Togo's gamble at last began to pay off. The first Japanese broadsides crashed into the fore-funnel of the flagship *Kniaz Suvarov* and more salvos followed, slamming into its conning-tower and breaking communications with the rest of the fleet. Fire blazed everywhere as smoke and flame belched from her decks. Admiral Rozhdestvensky was wounded. The speed of the *Kniaz Suvarov* had been severely reduced and there was smouldering debris everywhere: the ship was in complete disarray.

The Russian flagship sinks

The ships astern, the *Imperator Alexander III* and *Borodino*, were already being engaged by the Japanese. The Imperial Japanese battleships were firing armour-piercing shells, and pulverizing blasts on the *Kniaz Suvarov* tore into her hull. The grey sea poured in through the breaches, the main mast was hurled over and a

Japanese warships open fire on the Russian fleet at the start of the battle. At Tsushima the Russian guns fired first while the Japanese fleet manoeuvred into positions that would ensure a complete victory.

funnel collapsed across the deck, exploding as it crashed down. All authority disappeared from the maimed flagship; and she listed out of control wreathed in smoke and flame.

At a little past seven in the evening, having been reduced to a blazing wreck, the vessel was violently attacked by the Japanese torpedo boats. The wounded Admiral Rozhdestvensky was transferred to the destroyer *Buiny*, which had run alongside the stricken battleship to take off a number of the wounded sailors. The *Kniaz Suvarov* now came in for a tremendous onslaught. As shells poured into her she staggered, rolled on her side and sank.

Of the five new battleships the *Orel* was the only one now left afloat. The remainder of the Russian fleet was fairing slightly better and, though they had been battered, they were intact. At sundown Togo signalled his triumphant battleships to withdraw leaving the night free for torpedo-boat attacks. Throughout the night these fast little ships dogged the heels of the battered fleet as it made what speed it could for the haven of Vladivostok.

The Divine Wind was indeed blowing for Togo, and he could do no wrong now. Even a parting shot from the battleship *Fuji* found its mark in the *Borodino*. An eye-witness account stated that the *Borodino* immediately burst into flame, and immense clouds of smoke poured from her funnel tops. Her boilers exploded with an ear-shattering roar as dense clouds of smoke and steam billowed high into the air. The *Borodino* went to the bottom with a series of tremendous explosions.

The Japanese torpedo-boats lunged their parry-and-thrust attacks time and time again at the limping Tsarist fleet. So daring were these torpedo-boats' raids that they came at times to within 20 yards of the Russian ships before despatching their cargoes of death and destruction.

As dawn broke on May 28 the remains of the Russian fleet found themselves surrounded by Japanese cruisers. The torpedo-boats had completed their task admirably. Admiral Togo now ordered the cruisers to open fire. They started to pour in rounds of fire while they themselves kept out of range of the remaining old Russian guns.

'We surrender' . . .

Due to the wounds Rozhdestvensky had received, and his subsequent transfer to the destroyer *Buiny*, an underling, Admiral Nebogatov had assumed command of what was left of the Russian fleet. In the conditions in which he now found himself Nebogatov decided to surrender, being convinced that no more useful purpose would be gained by the sacrifice of the 2,000 men left under his command. They still had 300 miles to go to Vladivostok, and in the circumstances could not possibly make it.

Over 25 Japanese vessels now surrounded the remnants of the once proud Tsarist fleet, and leading them was Admiral Togo's flagship, the *Mikasa*. Admiral Togo had the Russian fleet within his grasp. From the bridge of his flagship Togo slowly savoured the scene. His eyes, scanning every Russian ship in turn, told him all he needed to know. Victory was his. The Russians could not possibly escape.

Admiral Nebogatov's decision weighed heavily. Admiral Rozhdestvensky was lying

Opposite Japanese gunners in action at Tsushima.

Above The 13,500 ton Russian flagship, Suvarov, *starts to sink (foreground). The* Alexander III *blazes in the background before sinking. Both were new battleships.*

unconscious and all his fleet, after so long a journey, were tired and worn out. The Russian ships hauled down their colours and Nebogatov ordered the flag 'XGE', the international code flag for 'we surrender', to be raised. But Admiral Togo was amazed. 'We surrender' was not a message a Japanese officer would ever make and he was deeply worried lest this was a last minute ploy. One of Togo's maxims had always been 'Never fear a strong enemy, and never despise a weak one'.

. . . but Togo continues fire

What was Togo to do? Let the Tsarist fleet off the hook and 'surrender'? Or do as he had always done, and make completely sure of victory? Togo thought for a few moments and then ordered the big guns of his fleet to blast the Russian ships out of the water. But when the Japanese started bombarding the Russian fleet, and Togo saw the helpless Russian ships with surrender flags at their masts being inevitably battered to death, he took pity on them. He soon had had enough of this obviously one-sided action. With the Russian ships at a stand-still he ordered the cease-fire. Togo was to recall, years later, that the Russian decision to surrender was 'utterly beyond our expectations'.

The final reckoning

The Russians had lost all of their battleships, four of their eight cruisers, seven of their nine destroyers, as well as 4,830 officers and men, with over 10,000 wounded or captured. The Japanese had lost only 117 men, with less than a thousand wounded, and two torpedo-boats.

Of the Russian ships that entered Tsushima Strait, all but three had been sunk, captured or interned. These three finally limped out of the clutches of the Imperial Japanese Navy and staggered, miraculously, into Vladisvostok. The captured Russian ships were escorted or towed back to Japan, and the wounded Rozhdestvensky put into a naval hospital. Togo was heaped with honours from his delighted Emperor and was hailed as the greatest sea warrior Japan had ever known. The prize he had won for Japan was nothing less than the foundation of an Empire.

As the weeks slipped by, Admiral Rozhdestvensky slowly recovered his health but time could not restore his spirit. The once proud

Major ships in the Battle of Tsushima Strait

RUSSIAN FLEET

Name	Tonnage	Main Armament		Speed
Kniaz Suvarov* (Flagship)	13,516	4 12in.,	12 6in.	17.6 Knots
Imperator Alexander III*	13,516	4 12in.,	12 6in.	17.6 Knots
Borodino*	13,516	4 12in.,	12 6in.	17.8 Knots
Orel	13,516	4 12in.,	12 6in.	17.6 Knots
Osslyabya*	12,674	4 10in.,	11 6in.	18.3 Knots
Sissoi Veliki*	10,400	4 12in.,	6 6in.	15.7 Knots
Navarin*	10,200	4 12in.,	8 6in.	15.7 Knots
Imperator Nikolai I	9,672	2 12in.,	4 9in.	14.0 Knots
Admiral Nakimov*	8,524	8 8in.,	10 6in.	16.6 Knots
Oleg	6,645	12 6in.		23.0 Knots
Aurora	6,731	8 6in.		20.0 Knots
Dimitri Donskoi*	6,200	6 6in.,	10 4.7in.	16.5 Knots
Vladimir Monomach*	5,593	5 6in.,	6 4.7in.	17.5 Knots
Admiral Senyavin	4,960	4 9.4in.,	4 6in.	16.1 Knots
General Admiral Apraxin	4,126	3 10in.,	4 4.7in.	16.0 Knots
Admiral Ushakov*	4,126	4 9.4in.,	4 6in.	16.1 Knots
Jemtchug	3,103	6 4.7in.		24.0 Knots
Izumrud	3,103	6 4.7in.		24.0 Knots
Almaz	3,285			
Svietlana*	3,828			

* Vessels known to have been sunk

JAPANESE FLEET

Name	Tonnage	Main Armament		Speed
Mikasa (Flagship)	15,140	4 12in.,	14 6in.	18.0 Knots
Asahi	15,200	4 12in.,	14 6in.	18.0 Knots
Shikishima	14,850	4 12in.,	14 6in.	18.0 Knots
Fuji	12,450	4 12in.,	10 6in.	18.0 Knots
Idzumo	9,750	4 8in.,	14 6in.	21.0 Knots
Iwate	9,750	4 8in.,	14 6in.	21.0 Knots
Tokiwa	9,750	4 8in.,	14 6in.	21.5 Knots
Asama	9,700	4 8in.,	14 6in.	21.5 Knots
Yakumo	9,646	4 8in.,	12 6in.	20.0 Knots
Adzuma	9,307	4 8in.,	12 6in.	20.0 Knots
Nisshin	7,628	4 8in.,	14 6in.	20.0 Knots
Kasuga	7,628	1 10in.,	2 8in. 14 6in.	20.0 Knots
Chin-Yen	7,220	4 12in.,	4 6in.	15.0 Knots
Kasagi	4,862	2 8in.,	10 4.7in.	22.5 Knots
Chitose	4,760	2 8in.,	10 4.7in.	22.5 Knots
Itsukushima	4,210	1 12.5in.,	11 4.7in.	16.0 Knots
Hashidate	4,210	1 12.5in.,	11 4.7in.	16.0 Knots
Matsushima	4,210	1 12.5in.,	11 4.7in.	16.0 Knots
Naniwa	3,650	8 6in.,		18.0 Knots
Takichiho	3,650	2 10in.,	6 6in.,	18.0 Knots
Tsushima	3,365	6 6in.		20.0 Knots
Nitaka	3,365	6 6in.		20.0 Knots
Fuso	3,718	4 10in.,	4 6in.	13.0 Knots
Akitsushima	3,150	4 6in.,	6 4.7in.	19.0 Knots
Otawa	3,000	2 6in.,	6 4.7in.	21.0 Knots
Izumi	2,950	2 6in.,	6 4.7in.	17.0 Knots
Akushi	2,657	2 6in.,	6 4.7in.	20.0 Knots
Suma	2,657	2 6in.,	6 4.7in.	20.0 Knots
Chiyoda	2,450	10 4.7in.		19.0 Knots

Masampo Bay in South Korea was Togo's base and from here the attack on the Russians was mounted.

Inset *The Baltic fleet's long voyage to destruction involved a farcical attack on British trawlers.*

Tsushima Strait

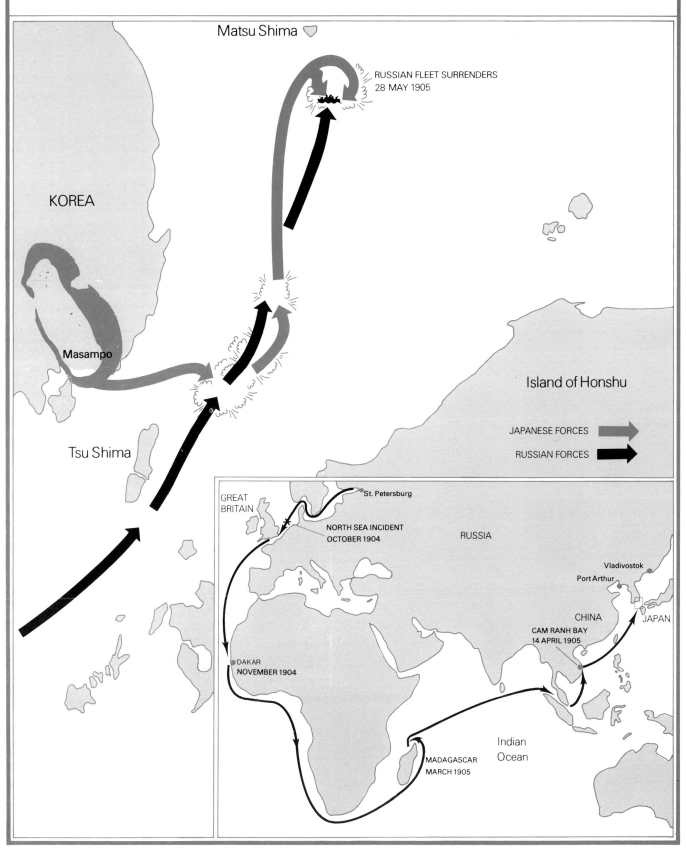

Matsu Shima

RUSSIAN FLEET SURRENDERS
28 MAY 1905

KOREA

Masampo

Island of Honshu

JAPANESE FORCES

RUSSIAN FORCES

Tsu Shima

GREAT
BRITAIN

St. Petersburg

NORTH SEA INCIDENT
OCTOBER 1904

RUSSIA

Vladivostok

Port Arthur

CHINA

CAM RANH BAY
14 APRIL 1905

JAPAN

DAKAR
NOVEMBER 1904

Indian
Ocean

MADAGASCAR
MARCH 1905

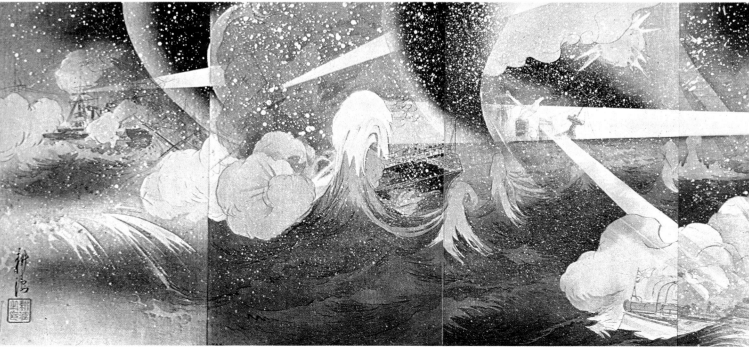

Tsarist naval officer was now a broken man. Although Tsar Nicholas II sent him a letter, which thanked him for his services to Russia, he was not to be consoled. Even the now renowned Togo visited him but could not remove the cloud of despair, although he could order that the best medical treatment be given to his adversary. Rozhdestvensky alone realised the gravity of the great disaster that had befallen the once great Russian Navy. The balance of sea power had now swung away from the Tsar and towards Imperial Japan.

Eventually Rozhdestvensky, together with other officers, was allowed to return to St. Petersburg and there the inevitable happened, for a head had to be found on which the blame could be placed. A court martial was held and the verdicts soon reached: Admiral Nebogatov was given the death sentence for surrendering the fleet. Admiral Rozhdetsvensky while not sentenced to death, because he was unconscious at the time, received, for him, an almost equal punishment. He was dismissed from the Service. The Tsar intervened and commuted the death sentence on Nebogatov to life imprisonment. Rozhdestvensky did not live to old age. He died within three years, in 1909, a sad and embittered man.

When Admiral Togo achieved his remarkable victory in Tsushima Strait he had, at one stroke, brought about the emergence of Japan as a massive sea power. This island race was now emerging from its sheltered past into a great future.

Left above A Japanese print showing a Russian warship sinking during the battle of Tsushima.

Left Another print depicts night fighting at Tsushima. Russian searchlights sweep the sea – and light up Russian targets for Japanese torpedo boats.

JUTLAND

Two mighty fleets met at Jutland in the North Sea in 1916 in what should have been the greatest battle of all time, a test of the British faith in guns and of the German confidence in their new tactics. But both sides were too wary for a decisive engagement.

When war broke out between the British and German Empires in 1914, the world had been in a state of uneasy peace for many years. The all-powerful British Empire had seen with mounting alarm how the confident young German Empire was growing in power and ambition. As the interests of these two great powers clashed in one place after another, it became obvious that the traditional way of settling rivalries between empires would soon be called for. Events following in the wake of the assassination of the Archduke Ferdinand in Sarajevo brought these tensions to a head, and war was declared.

A bloody and dogged struggle for supremacy developed. Germany tried new and often daring tactics on both the land and the sea, whereas the more traditionally-oriented Allies preferred their own well-tried methods.

One such confrontation between the young and venturesome and the old and tried took place in May 1916, around an area known as the Jutland Bank, in the North Sea. The navies amassed by the two Empires were vastly different in character and design. The tactics employed by the Royal Navy were those that had stood the test of time. They were, in fact, similar to those employed by brilliant commanders like Nelson and Rodney in bygone days. The 'single line ahead' battle formation, which relied for its success on accurate and heavy gunfire, was that adopted by the conservative strategists of the Royal Navy.

Guns to smash any enemy

Their ships were all powerfully armed, but carried weak armour. This meant that they were still capable of sustained high speed under battle conditions. It was thought, as it had always been thought, that the powerful armament could completely overwhelm any enemy. The single line ahead formation was considered an arrow flying through the seas, capable of delivering its fire to left or right at an enemy and piercing his set battle lines. The plan was to drive an attack direct straight at the heart of the enemy's fleet.

The German Navy, for its part, had developed its own types of naval strategy. A modern, independent plan of campaign had been devised in the privacy of secret naval exercises in the Baltic

Sea. This relied upon the fleet being broken into small and extremely manoeuvrable squadrons. These squadrons were trained to adopt independent action, in place of the rigid patterns of the massed fleets of the Royal Navy. Individual small fighting squadrons were to carry out raids with lightning speed and precision. These then were the tactics to be employed by the antagonists.

Jellicoe and von Scheer

The British Fleet, known as the Grand Fleet, was led by Commander-in-Chief Admiral Sir John Jellicoe. His opponent was Admiral Reinhard von Scheer. The two men were as different in character and temperament as were their respective fleets. Jellicoe, a trained gunnery officer, placed his faith in the trusted methods of the Royal Navy. He was a man who could bear great burdens with bulldog-like tenacity, a man who was as solid and dependable as the Empire he served.

Von Scheer was a man young in ideas, willing to experiment and even to take risks in order that new methods and inventions might be tried. He realized that his enemy was formidable, and respected that enemy enough to learn from him. He realized, too, that the tactics of the Royal Navy had changed little over the last few decades, and was therefore willing to consider

Top Admiral Sir John Jellicoe, Commander-in-Chief of Britain's Grand Fleet believed in rigid, regimented tactics. **Above** *His opponent, Admiral von Scheer, Commander-in-Chief of the German High Sea Fleet, was daring and inventive. At Jutland their fleets waged a bloody struggle. The outcome was inconclusive and the naval balance between the two warring empires remained unchanged.* **Below and overleaf** *British warships in action.*

daring and sometimes foolhardy innovations in battle training. By constantly experimenting with new ideas, he hoped to arrive at a brand of naval warfare that the British Fleet could not counter.

The full-scale confrontation of the two navies was not long in coming. The German Fleet, in a series of brilliantly conceived raids upon the coast of Great Britain, had considerably wounded the pride of the Royal Navy. One such raid, on April 24, 1916, consisted of part of the German complement of battle-cruisers drawing in close to the British coast near Lowestoft and there, for a short while, bombarding the town before retiring at great speed. It took audacity, stemming from the ideas of Admiral von Scheer, to come in so close to the shores of Great Britain and deal such a blow to morale.

Battle Fleets gather

Admiral Jellicoe had gathered his Battle Fleet together at three stations in Scotland: the Firth of Forth, the Moray Forth and Scapa Flow. Shortly after the daring raid on Lowestoft, on May 30, he received a signal that the German High Seas Fleet was massing in strength off Wilhelmshaven. That news was enough to spur Jellicoe into action. He arranged with Vice-Admiral Beatty, the commander of the British battle-cruisers in the Firth of Forth, to rendezvous with him in a position to the south of Norway, near the entrance to the Skagerrak, latitude 57° 45′ North, longitude 04° 15′ East, at 1400 on May 31. After despatching the message to Vice-Admiral Beatty the two halves of the main British Fleet sailed from Scapa Flow and the Moray Forth, linking up at noon to continue their journey together.

About to gather together was one of the biggest fleets of heavily-armed ships that the world had ever seen. There were four Battle Squadrons, the 1st Squadron having as its flagship the Fleet flagship HMS *Iron Duke*, a 25,000-ton battleship

of which the armament consisted of ten $13\frac{1}{2}$-inch guns and 12 six-inch guns. In this 1st Battle Squadron were seven other battleships of equal or comparable size. The 2nd Battle Squadron had as its flagship HMS *King George V*, a 23,000-ton battleship, also with ten $13\frac{1}{2}$-inch guns, and 16 four-inch guns. As well as the *King George V*, the Battle Squadron boasted seven other huge 23,000-ton battleships. The 4th Battle Squadron had at its head HMS *Royal Oak*, a 27,500-ton battleship with eight 14-inch guns and 12 six-inch guns. She was supported by six other similar battleships. The smallest Battle Squadron, the 5th, was led by one of the heaviest battleships in the entire Fleet, HMS *Valiant*, a 27,500-ton vessel with eight 15-inch guns and eight six-inch guns. She was supported by three 27,000-ton battleships.

Admiral Beatty's Battle-cruiser Fleet, which was to join up with Jellicoe's, was a much more flexible array. It consisted of nine battle-cruiser and light cruiser squadrons. HMS *Lion* was Vice-Admiral Beatty's flagship, and also led the 1st Battle-cruiser Squadron. The 26,350-ton *Lion* sported heavy armaments of eight 13.5-inch guns and sixteen four-inch guns. All told, the Battle-cruiser Squadrons and Light-cruiser Squadrons totalled 35 warships. Attached to the massing Fleet was five light-cruisers, three leading flotilla cruisers and over six destroyer flotillas. One seaplane carrier acted as a support.

The German Fleet

The German Fleet was not nearly as large, but all its ships were of fairly recent construction. The Fleet flagship, which headed the 1st German Battle Squadron, was the *Friedrich der Grosse*. This 24,700-ton ship had ten 12-inch guns and fourteen six-inch guns. The 1st Battle Squadron consisted of eight other comparable battleships. The 2nd Battle Squadron was headed by the

Deutschland, a 13,200-ton pre-Dreadnought battleship, with armament of four 11-inch guns and 14 6.7-inch guns. She was joined by five other pre-Dreadnought battleships of the same type. The 3rd Squadron was led by the *Konig*, a 25,390-ton battleship, which was armed with 12-inch guns and 14 six-inch guns. She in turn was supported by six other battleships of the same description. Supplementing these were one Battle-cruiser Squadron of five warships, a Light-cruiser Squadron of nine warships, two cruisers and over six flotilla destroyer squadrons.

These two enormous Fleets covered a huge area of sea. The British Grand Fleet now ranged from horizon to horizon, a vast armada ready to destroy the enemy. The German Fleet had also assembled, and was moving out into the North

Above Part of the massive firepower that the British Grand Fleet brought to Jutland.

Below The Hercules, *20,000 tons, and the* Invincible, *17,250 tons.* Invincible *was sunk at Jutland.*

Sea with Admiral von Scheer in command. Slowly, and as yet unknown to one another, the two antagonists closed. Surprise was a vital part of Jellicoe's plan, which was to sweep into the Skagerrak and Kattegat with his light-cruisers hoping to flush out the enemy into the jaws of his massed battleships lying in wait outside.

First contacts

HMS *Galatea*, of the 1st Light-cruiser Squadron, made the first sighting of a German ship at 1420 on May 31 and immediately sent signals to Vice-Admiral Beatty and Admiral Jellicoe to inform them. The German warship was the *Elbing*, one of the light cruisers of an advance scouting group. Naturally the *Elbing* also signalled her superiors, and Vice Admiral von Hipper, who commanded the light-cruisers, and Admiral von Scheer were duly informed of the Royal Navy's presence. Slowly the two mighty Fleets manoeuvred into their battle formations.

At 1547, in perfect visibility, the battle cruisers of both Fleets opened fire simultaneously at a range of approximately 16,000 yards. Because of a missed signal, British fire upon the German Fleet was at first uncoordinated. After ten minutes this mistake was rectified, and the British and German Fleets exchanged even fire, ship for ship, blow for blow. But the first advantage had already gone to von Scheer: the British had manoeuvred themselves into a position where they were clearly defined against a western sky. This meant that the German gunners could pick their targets at will. The German commanders, bringing their modern tactics into play, now adopted a less regimented form of attack against the inflexible British formation. No major hits had yet been scored, however, despite the thousands of rounds of ammunition that had been poured into both armadas. Like two heavyweight boxers trading punch for punch, they continued to slog out the battle.

A thousand men go down

At this point the German cruiser *Von der Tann* was engaging her opposite number, HMS *Indefatigable*. The *Indefatigable* was struck by two accurate salvos in quick succession, both of which burst upon her upper deck-work. She exploded in a sheet of flame and sank immediately. Over 1,000 men perished.

At 1625, the Royal Navy suffered another blow: after sinking the *Indefatigable*, the *Von der Tann* had turned her attentions to the 26,000-ton cruiser *Queen Mary*. The precision of the gunners on the German battle-cruiser was demonstrated a second time. An accurate salvo hit the *Queen Mary* and she too immediately exploded and sank, taking with her over 1,250 men.

The 5th Battle Squadron finally managed to come within firing range. Closing at a rate of some 25 knots, they started a bombardment of the German ships. The initial advantage was slowly slipping from von Scheer, and he thought about breaking off the action and retiring quickly after his two successes. The 5th Battle Squadron had other ideas and the battle went on as furiously as ever.

The German squadrons were now independently attacking the massive Grand Fleet. During one of these sallies Admiral von Hipper directed his fire against the weaker destroyer flotillas and the destroyers *Nestor* and *Nomad* were severely mauled and left almost awash, wallowing helplessly. Von Scheer ordered his battleships to finish them off and the destroyers were sunk by gunfire delivered at point-blank range.

Battle-cruiser Lion, *Admiral Beatty's flagship and leader of the 1st Battle-cruiser Squadron. The 26,350-ton* Lion, *which carried eight 13.5-inch guns and 16 four-inch guns, took a heavy pounding in the battle despite its nine-inch armour.*

The Grand Fleet attempted to maintain its rigid disciplined lines, with von Scheer trying as many shifts of tactics as he could. The two battle-ships HMS *Barham* and HMS *Malaya* were now in disarray after suffering several concentrated attacks. On the German side, the *Konig* had received a severe battering and was almost put out of action.

Smoke blots out the sun

Fighting was taking place over a wide area of sea. By this time, the smoke had almost blotted out the light of the sun. For miles and miles around the air was thick with the smell of cordite. But still the battle raged. Concentrated fire upon the German Second Scouting Group was rewarded when the Royal Navy's battle-cruisers sank the

Below Smoke billows from the 26,000 ton cruiser Queen Mary *as she sinks with her 1000 strong crew. She carried eight 15-inch guns. Her killer, the* Von der Tann *also sank the* Indefatigable.

Right *The 24,600 ton German cruiser* Seydlitz *shrouded in smoke after scuttling at Jutland.*

4,900-ton light-cruiser *Wiesbaden*, but the British lost the destroyer *Shark*. The armoured-cruiser HMS *Defence*, after being attacked by German battle-cruisers, exploded and sank immediately with her complement of 900 men. The cruiser HMS *Warrior*, astern of the *Defence*, also came in for heavy punishment and was extensively damaged. She rode out the attack, but could not be of any further use to Jellicoe that day. Two of the German battle-cruisers hauled out of their line, so fierce was one particular engagement with the British 3rd Battle-cruiser Squadron. The *Konig* was completely aflame by now, but on the British side, the *Invincible* was hit near her magazines and exploded in a sheet of blinding flame, sinking with the loss of 1,000 men.

The battle was now approaching its final phase: the British had, as far as possible, maintained their stations, but had taken enormous punishment. The advantage swayed to and fro. First von Scheer, then Jellicoe appeared to take a lead. At about 1900, as the mist began to come up and reduce the already deteriorating visibility even further, von Scheer started his last attack. He knew he had gained more than he had lost, and was ready to withdraw gracefully as soon as he had delivered one more blow. He was determined, in the failing light, to deliver a body blow

to the very heart of the British Grand Fleet. He ordered his battle-cruisers to charge at will the highly disciplined formation of the British Fleet. But what was to be a body blow turned out to be a near disaster.

The German 'death ride'

As soon as the German battle-cruisers came into range, Jellicoe's guns delivered a highly concentrated and efficient barrage which von Scheer's battle-cruisers had no choice but to run. This charge became known later as the 'death ride'. The accuracy of the British fire brought the German warships to a virtual halt and seeing that the body blow could not be delivered, von Scheer ordered his battered cruisers to turn away under the cover of a smoke screen. They soon disappeared from Jellicoe's sight into the fading light. Jellicoe would not be drawn into following the fleeing German ships. He was later to say that he had thought von Scheer's intention was to draw the British over strategically-laid mines. He declined to risk his ships in such a pursuit.

With the disappearance of the German cruisers the main engagements came to an end. A sudden silence came upon the battered Fleets which were shrouded in smoke and mist as well as the darkness of night. The cloak of darkness, however, was to prove a mixed blessing to both sides. Admiral Jellicoe ordered his ships back into line, but not to show too many lights lest these should give away their positions to any lurking or stray German warship. Von Scheer gave the same order: the two battle fleets were both trying to regroup, groping their way sightlessly in an inky darkness. Chance meetings were bound to happen, and they were not long in coming.

The first disaster came to the cruiser HMS *Black Prince*. While endeavouring to rejoin her squadron, she blundered into the retreating German warships. The *Black Prince* was recognized, fired upon and sunk in one swift action before she had any chance of escape. She took over 850 men to a watery grave. The German battleship *Pommern* was caught without guard and attacked by the Royal Navy's 12th Destroyer Flotilla. She was sunk by torpedo, 'blown to atoms' according to eye-witness accounts.

The battle peters out

Admiral Jellicoe re-grouped throughout the night in an attempt to manoeuvre his vast Fleet into a

position between the German coastline and where he calculated the German Fleet to be. When daylight broke he was convinced that his ships now lay ready to catch the retreating von Scheer as he slipped back to port. Hour after hour Jellicoe waited, scanning the horizon for the remains of von Scheer's squadrons. Shortly after 1430, after some ten hours of waiting, he received a signal from the Admiralty informing him that the German Fleet had evaded him, and was now back in its own ports. Admiral Jellicoe turned his fleet homeward to Scapa Flow. The Battle of Jutland had come to an end.

The battle itself was indecisive, for neither side suffered complete defeat. This did not stop it being considered a severe blow to morale by both nations. Although Jellicoe earned considerable respect for the discipline that had been apparent throughout his Fleet, he came in for criticism. He had lost three battle-cruisers, three cruisers and seven destroyers, against the German loss of one battleship, one cruiser, two destroyers and four light-cruisers. Over 6,000 men of the Royal Navy had been lost, as against the German casualties of 3,000. Jellicoe was forced in the days to come to ask himself why the battle had not been decisive, and why his rigid, regimented tactics had not won the day. It was later accepted that a 'strategic' victory had, in fact, been achieved, for the German Fleet was never again to put to sea in such large numbers. For von Scheer, the battle had valuable lessons. He had endeavoured to use modern and untried tactics, but these had only been partially successful. He in turn was to re-think his battle strategy.

The slogging heavyweight contest had proved little, other than that the combatants had lost 21 ships and 9,823 men. This was a tremendous price to pay for an indecisive outcome: the naval balance of power between the two nations remained unchanged. Indeed, the lesson of Jutland can virtually serve as the lesson of World War I. For all the heroism and suffering of both sides, in the end too many men had perished for very little.

Major ships in the Battle of Jutland

BRITISH FLEET:

1st Battle Squadron:

Name	Tonnage	Main Armament		Speed
Iron Duke (Flagship)	25,000	10 13.5in.,	12 6in.	21 Knots
Agincourt	27,500	14 12in.,	20 6in.	22 Knots
Colossus	20,000	10 12in.,	16 4in.	21 Knots
Hercules	20,000	10 12in.,	16 4in.	21 Knots
Marlborough	25,000	10 13.5in.,	12 6in.	21 Knots
Neptune	19,900	10 12in.,	16 4in.	21 Knots
Revenge	25,750	8 15in.,	12 6in.	22 Knots
St Vincent	19,250	10 12in.,	16 4in.	21 Knots

2nd Battle Squadron:

Name	Tonnage	Main Armament		Speed
King George V	23,000	10 13.5in.,	16 4in.	22 Knots
Ajax	23,000	10 13.5in.,	16 4in.	22 Knots
Centurion	23,000	10 13.5in.,	16 4in.	22 Knots
Conqueror	22,500	10 13.5in.,	16 4in.	21 Knots
Erin	23,000	10 13.5in.,	16 6in.	21 Knots
Monarch	22,500	10 13.5in.,	16 4in.	21 Knots
Orion	22,500	10 13.5in.,	16 4in.	21 Knots
Thunderer	22,500	10 13.5in.,	16 4in.	21 Knots

4th Battle Squadron:

Name	Tonnage	Main Armament		Speed
Royal Oak	25,750	8 15in.,	12 6in.	22 Knots
Bellerophon	18,600	10 12in.,	16 4in.	21 Knots
Benbow	25,000	10 13.5in.,	12 6in.	21 Knots
Canada	28,000	10 14in.,	16 6in.	23 Knots
Superb	18,600	10 12in.,	16 4in.	21 Knots
Temeraire	18,600	10 12in.,	16 4in.	21 Knots
Vanguard	19,250	10 12in.,	18 4in.	21 Knots

5th Battle Squadron:

Name	Tonnage	Main Armament		Speed
Valiant	27,500	8 15in.,	8 6in.	25 Knots
Barham	27,500	8 15in.,	12 6in.	25 Knots
Malaya	27,500	8 15in.,	12 6in.	25 Knots
Warspite	27,500	8 15in.,	8 6in.	25 Knots

1st Battle-cruiser Squadron:

Name	Tonnage	Main Armament		Speed
Lion (Flagship)	26,350	8 15in.,	16 4in.	28 Knots
Princess Royal	26,350	8 15in.,	16 4in.	28 Knots
Queen Mary*	26,350	8 15in.,	16 4in.	28 Knots
Tiger	27,000	8 15in.,	12 6in.	28 Knots

2nd Battle-cruiser Squadron:

Name	Tonnage	Main Armament		Speed
Indefatigable*	18,750	8 12in.,	16 4in.	26 Knots
New Zealand	18,750	8 12in.,	16 4in.	27 Knots

3rd Battle-cruiser Squadron:

Name	Tonnage	Main Armament		Speed
Indomitable	17,250	8 12in.,	16 4in.	28 Knots
Inflexible	17,250	8 12in.,	16 4in.	28 Knots
Invincible*	17,250	8 12in.,	16 4in.	28 Knots

1st Cruiser Squadron:

Name	Tonnage	Main Armament		Speed
Black Prince*	13,550	6 9.2in.,	10 6in.	22 Knots
Defence*	14,600	4 9.2in.,	10 7.5in.	21 Knots
Duke of Edinburgh	13,550	6 9.2in.,	10 6in.	22 Knots
Warrior*	13,550	6 9.2in.,	4 7.5in.	22 Knots

The 27,500 ton Warspite *at Jutland.* Warspite *and her sister ships of the Queen Elizabeth class were super-dreadnoughts, the finest capital ships of their day.*

2nd Cruiser Squadron:

Name	Tonnage	Main Armament		Speed
Cochrane	13,550	6 9.2in.,	4 7.5in.	22 Knots
Hampshire	10,850	4 7.5in.,	6 6in.	22 Knots
Minotaur	14,600	4 9.2in.,	10 .75in.	21 Knots
Shannon	14,600	4 9.2in.,	10 7.5in.	21 Knots

Light Cruisers:

Name	Tonnage	Main Armament		Speed
Active	3,440	10 6in.,		25 Knots
Bellona	3,300	6 4in.		25 Knots
Birmingham	5,400	9 6in.		25 Knots
Birkenhead	5,250	10 5.5in.		25 Knots
Blanche	3,350	10 6in.		25 Knots
Boadicea	3,300	6 4in.		25 Knots
Calliope	3,800	2 6in.,	8 4in.	30 Knots
Canterbury	3,750	5 6in.,		29 Knots
Caroline	3,800	2 6in.,	8 4in.	30 Knots
Castor	3,750	5 6in.,		29 Knots
Champion	3,520	2 6in.,	6 4in.	30 Knots
Chester	5,250	10 5.5in.		26 Knots
Comus	3,800	2 6in.,	8 4in.	30 Knots
Constance	3,800	2 6in.,	8 4in.	30 Knots
Cordelia	3,800	2 6in.,	8 4in.	30 Knots
Dublin	5,400	8 6in.,		25 Knots
Falmouth	5,250	8 6in.		25 Knots
Fearless	3,440	10 4in.		25 Knots
Galatea	3,520	2 6in.,	6 4in.	30 Knots
Gloucester	4,800	2 6in.,	10 4in.	25 Knots
Inconstant	3,520	2 6in.,	6 4in.	30 Knots
Nottingham	5,400	9 6in.		25 Knots
Phaeton	3,520	2 6in.,	6 4in.	30 Knots
Royalist	3,520	2 6in.,	6 4in.	30 Knots
Southampton	5,400	8 6in.		25 Knots
Yarmouth	5,250	8 6in.		25 Knots

Destroyer Flotillas: 1st, 4th, 9th, 10th, 11th, 12th, 13th

(7 Destroyers lost)

GERMAN FLEET:

1st Battle Squadron:

Name	Tonnage	Main Armament		Speed
Friedrich der Grosse (Flagship)	24,700	10 12in.,	14 6in.	20 Knots
Heligoland	22,800	12 12in.,	14 5.9in.	21 Knots
Nassau	18,900	12 11in.,	12 5.9in.	20 Knots
Oldenburg	22,800	12 12in.,	14 5.9in.	21 Knots
Ostfriesland	22,800	12 12in.,	14 5.9in.	21 Knots
Posen	18,900	12 11in.,	12 5.9in.	20 Knots
Rheinland	18,900	12 11in.,	12 5.9in.	20 Knots
Thuringen	22,800	12 12in.,	14 5.9in.	21 Knots
Westfalen	18,900	12 11in.,	12 5.9in.	20 Knots

2nd Battle Squadron:

Name	Tonnage	Main Armament		Speed
Deutschland	13,200	4 11in.,	14 6.7in.	18 Knots
Hannover	13,200	4 11in.,	14 6.7in.	18 Knots
Hessen	13,200	4 11in.,	14 6.7in.	18 Knots

2nd Battle Squadron: (continued)

Name	Tonnage	Main Armament		Speed
Pommern*	13,200	4 11in.,	14 6.7in.	18 Knots
Schlesen	13,200	4 11in.,	14 6.7in.	18 Knots
Schleswig-Holstein	13,200	4 11in.,	14 6.7in.	18 Knots

3rd Battle Squadron:

Name	Tonnage	Main Armament		Speed
König	25,390	10 12in.,	14 5.9in.	22 Knots
Grosser Kurfurst	25,390	10 12in.,	14 5.9in.	22 Knots
Kaiser	24,380	10 12in.,	14 5.9in.	21 Knots
Kaiserin	24,380	10 12in.,	14 5.9in.	21 Knots
Kronprinz Wilhelm	25,390	10 12in.,	14 5.9in.	22 Knots
Markgraf	25,390	10 12in.,	14 5.9in.	22 Knots
Prinzregent Luitpold	24,380	10 12in.,	14 5.9in.	21 Knots

Battle-Cruiser Squadron:

Name	Tonnage	Main Armament		Speed
Derfelinger	26,600	8 12in.,	12 5.9in.	28 Knots
Lutzow*	26,600	8 12in.,	12 5.9in.	28 Knots
Moltke	22,640	10 11in.,	12 5.9in.	27 Knots
Seydlitz	24,610	10 11in.,	12 5.9in.	27 Knots
Von der Tann	19,400	8 11in.,	10 5.9in.	25 Knots

Light Cruisers

Name	Tonnage	Main Armament	Speed
Elbing*	4,320	8 5.9in.	28 Knots
Frankfurt	4,900	7 5.9in.	28 Knots
Frauenlob*	2,715	10 4.1in.	22 Knots
Hamburg	3,250	10 4.1in.	23 Knots
Muenchen	3,250	10 4.1in.	23 Knots
Pillau	4,320	8 5.9in.	28 Knots
Regensburg	4,900	12 4.1in.	28 Knots
Rostock*	4,900	12 4.1in.	28 Knots
Stettin	3,450	10 4.1in.	24 Knots
Stuttgart	3,450	10 4.1in.	24 Knots
Wiesbaden*	4,900	7 5.9in.	28 Knots

Destroyer Flotillas: 1st, 2nd, 3rd, 5th, 6th, 7th, 9th

(2 destroyers lost)

Vessels known to have been lost.

Leading up to the Battle of Jutland, Beatty's Battle-cruisers sailed from the Firth of Forth, Jellicoe's Battleships from the Moray Firth and Scapa Flow. The engagement was indecisive because neither commander could take the risk of fully committing his ships. During the night the German fleet slipped past Jellicoe to regain the safety of their own ports.

Jutland

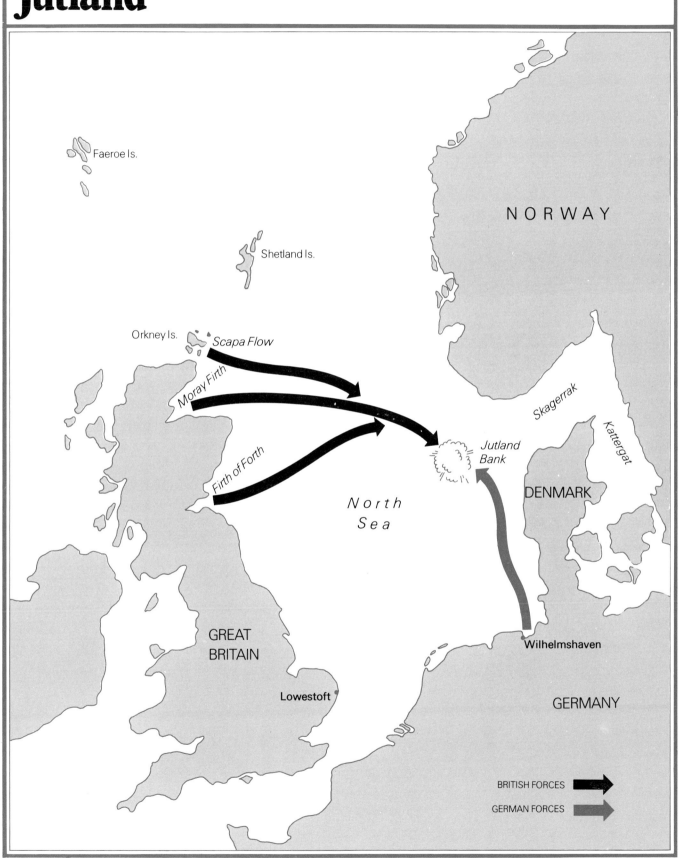

Faeroe Is.

NORWAY

Shetland Is.

Orkney Is. *Scapa Flow*

Moray Firth

Skagerrak

Kattergat

Jutland Bank

DENMARK

Firth of Forth

North
Sea

GREAT
BRITAIN

Wilhelmshaven

Lowestoft

GERMANY

BRITISH FORCES

GERMAN FORCES

MERCHANT CRUISER AT BAY

Against the odds was an understatement when the merchant cruiser Rawalpindi, *armed with six-inch guns, met the* Scharnhorst *and* Gneisenau, *Hitler's most up to date battleships, with their 11-inch guns. But bravery defiantly did what it could . . . .*

Silent and deadly, the single torpedo streaked through the dark Atlantic waters towards its unsuspecting prey, the 13,500 ton passenger ship, *Athenia*. Seconds later the torpedo ripped into the port side of the ship, giving the startled passengers and crew the first horrible realization of disaster and announcing to the world that the desperate struggle for mastery of the seas in World War II had begun.

The *Athenia*, a passenger liner of the Donald-

Merchant cruiser at bay

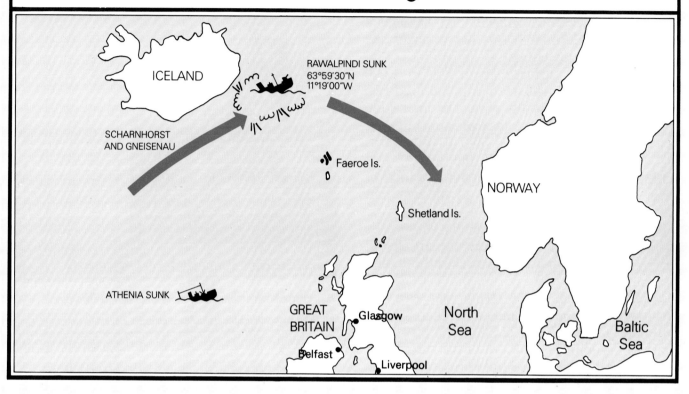

ICELAND

SCHARNHORST
AND GNEISENAU

RAWALPINDI SUNK
63°59'30"N
11°19'00"W

Faeroe Is.

NORWAY

Shetland Is.

ATHENIA SUNK

GREAT
BRITAIN

Glasgow

North
Sea

Baltic
Sea

Belfast

Liverpool

Above The Rawalpindi's *gallant stand against the pride of Hitler's Kriegsmarine occured as the German battleships headed for the Baltic.*

Below The Scharnhorst's *huge guns fire on the* Rawalpindi. Scharnhorst *and her sister ship* Gneisenau *were fast 26,000 ton battle-cruisers, each armed with nine 11-inch guns.* Rawalpindi, *a 17,000 ton merchant ship hastily armed with eight six-inch guns to counter the U-boat threat, was no match for the German warships.*

son Atlantic Line, had left Glasgow on Friday September 1, 1939 at about noon on a voyage, via Liverpool and Belfast, to Montreal. On the evening of September 3, the liner was some 250 miles west of Ireland when, at 1945 the torpedo crashed into her. The *Athenia* had become a victim of the German Navy, her attacker the deadly predator, the U-boat.

The submarine surfaced about 800 to 1,000 yards from the maimed steamship and fired two shells at the ship's wireless gear. The liner soon began to list, making the task of launching the lifeboats extremely difficult. Shortly afterwards the *Athenia* slipped beneath the waves. Her death toll was announced as 128 out of a total of 1,418. The first merchant ship of the war had been lost.

The aftermath was a propaganda battle. The Germans, it seemed had broken the articles of war by sinking a merchant vessel without first ensuring the safety of the passengers. They denied this, claiming that the *Athenia* was carrying arms and ammunition and was, therefore, a legitimate target. The Germans claimed that Winston Churchill, First Lord of the Admiralty, was seeking to draw the United States into the war by provoking an attack on a merchant ship carrying arms, and then claiming that no arms were aboard. Churchill denied this.

Against the odds

The sinking soon highlighted the fact that German submarines had now declared a war of attrition against any British vessel, be it merchant ship or warship. The merchant ships on their peaceful errands had now come under the

Above Hero of the Rawalpindi *was Captain E. C. Kennedy RN. When the German warships fired a warning shot at the* Rawalpindi *Kennedy ordered his meagre six-inch guns to open fire. They blazed in magnificent but futile defiance. Shells from the German warships' massive guns thundered a reply and the brave merchant ship sank. Kennedy and all but 37 of the 302-strong crew were killed.*

Below Rawalpindi *in dock before her fateful voyage. One of her six-inch guns is visible before the bridge.*

The prodigious guns of the Scharnhorst. *The lower guns are 11-inchers and the upper guns are part of the ship's battery of 12 5.9-inch weapons.*

scourge of the Swastika. So devastating was the onslaught against British merchant ships, that 21 vessels were lost in the first couple of weeks of the war. Germany was openly violating international law with these violent acts. 'Sink at sight' with no warning was now common German policy and practice.

By November 1939 the British merchant fleet was starting to be equipped with meagre anti-submarine and anti-aircraft guns for protection. The German press immediately claimed that this 'heavy' armament meant that merchant ships were now auxiliary cruisers. If not before, the German naval forces could now sink them without fear of recrimination!

The beautiful liner *Rawalpindi* was one of the ships converted into an armed merchant cruiser. This 16,700 tons gross steamship was one of four sister ships requisitioned by the Admiralty from their owners, the Peninsular and Oriental Steam Navigation Company, the P & O, for war service. The *Rawalpindi*, launched in 1925, was one of the most elegant liners afloat and the pride of her owners.

Captain E. C. Kennedy commanded the *Rawalpindi*, and the crew was drawn from the ranks of the Royal Navy Reserve, the Royal Naval Volunteer Reserve and Reservists of the Royal Navy. These men were excellent and enthusiastic seamen, but they were given neither the arms nor the type of ship in which to be an effective fighting force.

At the beginning of November 1939 the Admiralty had ordered the *Rawalpindi* to be attached to the Northern patrol, south-east of Iceland. The patrol acted as a lookout and reported the movements of the German Navy in that area. As the elegant *Rawalpindi* first patrolled the cold dark waters of Iceland they were empty – but only for a time. Into the dark seas came an even darker enemy.

Sink at sight

Two German battleships slithered into the liner's view, modern 26,000 ton fighting machines with tremendous armaments, capable of delivering

Death hangs over the Rawalpindi *as smoke and flame billow from her decks. Her crew kept fighting until every gun was out of action and the ship ablaze.*

violent destruction from their 11-inch guns. They were the *Scharnhorst* and the *Gneisenau*, the prize battleships of the German fleet and the most up-to-date fighting machines of their class in the world.

After carrying out unrestricted warfare in the Atlantic Ocean the mighty battleships were returning to the Baltic, and home. Passing south-east of Iceland on the afternoon of November 3 they came into view of the *Rawalpindi* and were sighted at 1530.

The armament allocated to the *Rawalpindi* – eight meagre six-inch guns – was no match for

The 11-inch guns of the Gneisenau *thunder out a salvo, photographed from her sister ship, the* Scharnhorst.

the 11-inch guns of the German battleships. Immediately Captain Kennedy realized that the lamb had strayed into the path of the tigers. Not only was he facing vessels built for war, but the odds were two-to-one against him.

On identifying his adversaries, Captain Kennedy ordered that a smoke screen be put up. The smoke screen was laid as quickly as possible to cover an escape he hoped to achieve into a fog bank on the *Rawalpindi*'s port bow. But the lamb had been seen. The *Scharnhorst*, anticipating a possible escape, increased speed and intercepted the *Rawalpindi*'s escape route. A signal ordering Captain Kennedy to stop was sent from the *Scharnhorst* and a shot fired across her bows in warning. This action was followed at 1545 by a salvo from the 11-inch guns at a range of approximately 10,000 yards, for the *Rawalpindi* had ignored the warning.

A lamb to the slaughter

Captain Kennedy quickly ordered open fire and the *Rawalpindi*'s four starboard six-inch guns burst into splendid defiant action. Amazed that a liner, armed with such meagre weapons, should defy the might of the German Navy, the battleships quickly replied. Their third and fourth salvos burst open the *Rawalpindi*. The lamb was being slaughtered. The electric winches of the ammunition supply were destroyed and all the lights put out, the bridge was shot away and the wireless room destroyed, killing nearly everyone stationed there. Death now hung over the proud liner. The *Gneisenau* scored a hit on the starboard battery and immediately put it out of action. Smoke and flame billowed from the *Rawalpindi*'s decks. The enemy battleships had the once majestic liner at their mercy, but the gallant *Rawalpindi* continued to fight until every gun was out of action and the ship ablaze. A pall of fire and smoke cloaked the great and once beautiful liner.

The enemy ceased fire to allow lifeboats to be lowered. The fire had now taken a massive grip and the liner was ablaze from bow to stern. The action had lasted approximately 40 minutes. In that short time the battle of completely unequal adversaries and of tremendous gallantry and bravery by Captain Kennedy and his crew was over. Two of the three boats which were lowered were picked up by the Germans, and the third was picked up later by the *Chitral*, another auxiliary cruiser and also a P & O liner.

The end of the Rawalpindi

Slowly, as if reluctant to die, the *Rawalpindi* slipped under the waves and the seas closed over her. Her 39 officers, including Captain Kennedy, and 226 ratings perished along with their ship. Only 37 seamen survived. The *Scharnhorst* and *Gneisenau* had completed their grim task and continued their broken journey homeward, homeward to the Baltic.

The *Rawalpindi* was the first armed merchant cruiser to be sunk during the war. It was clear that merchant ships with meagre armaments were no match for powerful warships and if the tenuously stretched life-supporting convoys from the Americans were to be maintained something more positive had to be done. A scheme was devised to patrol the break-out areas for the German warships from their home ports, in the Baltic, into the North Atlantic by the warships of the Royal Navy and the aircraft of Coastal Command and not by the poorly equipped armed merchant ships. Then fire could be met with fire.

But the gallant spirit of Captain Kennedy and his crew was not forgotten. Captain Kennedy was himself awarded, posthumously, the Victoria Cross, the nation's highest award for bravery, a fitting reward for an inspiring act of defiance.

Ships in the Merchant cruiser action

Rawalpindi (Armed merchant cruiser)		
Launched:	March 26, 1925
Tonnage:	16,697 gross
Dimensions:	length 548ft. beam 71ft. draught 28ft.
Speed:	17 knots
Main armament:	8 6in.
Complement:	302

Scharnhorst (Battleship)		
Launched:	October 3, 1936
Tonnage:	26,000 displacement
Dimensions:	length 741ft. beam 98ft. draught 25ft.
Speed:	(designed) 27 knots, (actual) 29 knots
Main armament:	9 11in. 12 5.9in.
Complement:	1,461

Gneisenau (Battleship)		
Launched:	8.12.1936
Other details identical to Scharnhorst	

DEATH OF THE BISMARCK

A single German ship attempting to reach the open spaces of the Atlantic in 1941 took on the British Navy — and only just lost. In her dash for freedom, the Bismarck *sank the* Hood, *fought many others and almost slipped clear before she was finally caught.*

During April and May of 1941 Grand Admiral Raeder, the outstanding strategist for the German Third Reich, conceived a plan to destroy the convoy system that was keeping Britain alive – and bring Britain nearer to capitulation. The plan consisted of a simultaneous breakout from the Baltic ports and from Brest of the capital ships of German Navy which would then rendezvous in the North Atlantic and, at will, destroy the convoys one by one. The plan also involved five tankers with two supply ships and two reconnaissance ships to support this force. The breakout was code named 'Exercise Rhine' or 'Rheinubung' and was originally planned to take place in the second half of April when the new moon would

Bismarck, *the newest of Germany's capital ships, threatened to sever Britain's convoy lifeline. In a deadly game of hide-and-seek the older ships of the Royal Navy scoured the northern waters for the* Bismarck – *and sank the pride of the German Navy.*

give dark nights for the breakout.

The Royal Navy was well aware of the tenuous life lines that brought food, oil, munitions; vital materials all needed to keep Britain alive. Realizing the real danger of letting these convoy routes fall to the mercy of the enemy, the British Admiralty made plans to counteract any such act. The Denmark Strait, the main highway into the North Atlantic for any protagonist, was patrolled by the limited forces of the Royal Navy.

Germany's mighty warship

The stage was set for drama. Would the sword of Damocles, in the shape of the new and mighty warships of the German Navy, fall? In falling, would it crush the older and weaker forces of the Royal Navy – put to death the vital, weakly armed, cargo ships – and cut the main life arteries to Britain?

Fate, however, was nibbling at Admiral Raeder's plans. Of the capital ships at his disposal, the modern 10,000 ton heavy cruiser *Prinz Eugen* had been partially damaged by a magnetic mine

in the Baltic. The 26,000 ton battleship *Gneisenau*, built in 1936, was torpedoed by Coastal Command aircraft and extensively damaged. And her sister ship the *Scharnhorst*, also built in 1936, was having an untimely refit which was taking longer than estimated and she had to be ruled out for any immediate plans. The *Bismarck*, however, launched in 1939 and the most powerful warship under Raeder's control, the deadly weapon that bore the name of the founder and First Chancellor of the German Empire, was ready.

Because of these unexpected events the whole breakout operation had to be postponed until the middle of May. Admiral Raeder had set his heart on Exercise Rhine and was determined to see it through. A stranglehold had to be put on Britain if Germany was to emerge victorious.

Bismarck sets out

The damage to the *Prinz Eugen* was repaired as quickly as possible; so she sailed together with Admiral Lutjens in the *Bismarck* after dark on May 18 from the Baltic port of Gdynia to start Exercise Rhine. But fate was against Admiral Raeder. On May 21 a pilot in a Coastal Command photo-reconnaissance Spitfire searching the Norwegian coastline, sighted and photographed, while on routine patrol, two warships in a secluded fiord. One of the warships was identified as the *Bismarck* the other as a cruiser, which later was discovered to be the *Prinz Eugen*. British Intelligence realized from this photograph that the breakout had begun. Sir John Tovey, the Commander in Chief of the Home Fleet, at once sent the battle cruiser HMS *Hood* and her squadron to try and locate and destroy these ships.

Though *Hood* had been built in 1918 her eight 15-inch guns were thought to be the right instruments for inflicting destruction upon the modern German warships. Might would prove right was the British Admiralty's thought.

On May 22 Admiral Tovey received further aerial reconnaissance reports that the *Bismarck* and *Prinz Eugen* were no longer in the fiord. Action had to be taken immediately. The 13-year-old cruiser HMS *Norfolk*, which was already on patrol in the Denmark Strait, was reinforced by sending an older cruiser, the 15-year-old HMS *Suffolk*.

Captain R. M. Ellis, Commanding Officer of the *Suffolk*, had had a very exhausting 48 hours

Opposite 'I shall have to sacrifice myself sooner or later . . . I am determined to execute the task which has been entrusted to me in an honourable manner.' Thus Admiral Gunther Lutjens, commander of Exercise Rhine, summed up his task. Lutjens had hoped to postpone the operation until other German capital ships were ready.

Below The 50,000 ton Bismarck, as seen from the Prinz Eugen, 17,000 tons. Exercise Rhine was ill-fated from the start since neither Gneisenau nor Scharnhorst was ready in time for the operation.

for, on the evening of May 23, he had been on duty all that day, the night before and the night before that. The atmospheric conditions where *Suffolk* was searching were unusual; for in the Denmark Strait at this time the visibility was clear over and close to the ice but misty between the ice and the land. *Suffolk* was taking advantage of this, keeping close to the edge of the mist so as to be close to cover if the *Bismarck* were sighted at close range.

Suffolk sights Bismarck

At 1922 a look-out from the *Suffolk* sighted the *Bismarck* closely followed by the *Prinz Eugen* seven miles on the starboard quarter steaming the same course as herself. Captain Ellis immediately forgot his fatigue and made an enemy report signal to Admiral Holland in *Hood*. He then increased the speed of *Suffolk* and altered course to take cover in the mist. Manoeuvring with extreme skill in the mist, and keeping the *Bismarck* under constant radar contact he allowed

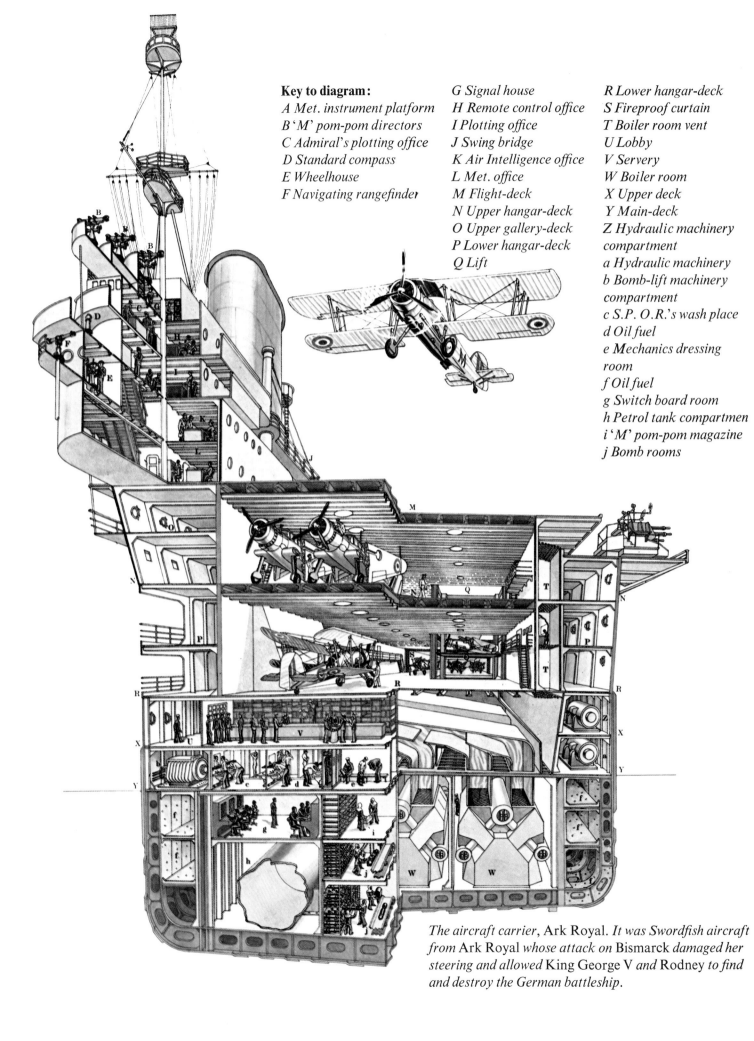

Key to diagram:
A Met. instrument platform
B 'M' pom-pom directors
C Admiral's plotting office
D Standard compass
E Wheelhouse
F Navigating rangefinder

G Signal house
H Remote control office
I Plotting office
J Swing bridge
K Air Intelligence office
L Met. office
M Flight-deck
N Upper hangar-deck
O Upper gallery-deck
P Lower hangar-deck
Q Lift

R Lower hangar-deck
S Fireproof curtain
T Boiler room vent
U Lobby
V Servery
W Boiler room
X Upper deck
Y Main-deck
Z Hydraulic machinery compartment
a Hydraulic machinery
b Bomb-lift machinery compartment
c S.P. O.R.'s wash place
d Oil fuel
e Mechanics dressing room
f Oil fuel
g Switch board room
h Petrol tank compartmen
i 'M' pom-pom magazine
j Bomb rooms

The aircraft carrier, Ark Royal. *It was* Swordfish *aircraft from* Ark Royal *whose attack on* Bismarck *damaged her steering and allowed* King George V *and* Rodney *to find and destroy the German battleship.*

her to pass. At 2028 the *Suffolk* again made visual contact with the enemy, again reported their positions and once more retired into the gathering mists. At the same time *Norfolk* had been closing towards *Suffolk* and also made contact with the *Bismarck*. This time *Bismarck* was on the alert and the very first exchanges of the running battle took place. *Bismarck's* salvos were fairly accurate but *Norfolk* retired unscathed under a smoke screen. So accurate had been the opening salvos from *Bismarck* that large splinters were thrown on board from the shells exploding in the water.

The engagement had been short; *Norfolk* with *Suffolk* had now sought the sanctuary of the mist and were shadowing well behind the enemy. The weather was deteriorating but the pursuit continued. *Norfolk* and *Suffolk* continued the shadowing; awaiting the arrival of the heavy guns of *Hood* in order to try and stop the *Bismarck* and *Prinz Eugen* attempting the break out into the North Atlantic. Through the half-light of the Arctic night, through the mists, through the snow squalls and rain, the pursuit continued.

Hood had not been idle since she received the first enemy report from *Norfolk*. Vice-Admiral Hollands had brought his ship, together with the *Prince of Wales* and six destroyers, at full speed to try and cut the enemy off in the Denmark Strait. All the crews of the ships were put on battle stations shortly after midnight and after five and a half hours of waiting the prey came into sight at 0535. At 0553 firing opened up simultaneously at a range of 25,000 yards, the *Hood* and *Prince of Wales* firing on the *Bismarck* and *Bismarck* and *Prinz Eugen* at once replying. Following discreetly astern, the crews of *Norfolk* and *Suffolk* watched with anticipation; their guns could not cope with the enormous fire power now being used. Could the *Hood* and *Prince of Wales* outgun the pride of the German Navy?

HMS Hood blows up

The first hit went to the *Prinz Eugen* in little under a minute starting a fire on *Hood* which spread rapidly forward and set the whole ship ablaze. The range between the ships was decreasing rapidly and several times the *Bismarck* just missed the *Hood*. Then, suddenly, the British were horror-struck to see a vast flame leap upwards between the *Hood's* masts. A direct hit

had been scored. There was a huge explosion between the after funnel and the main mast and the *Hood* sank within three to four minutes; she had fired only five or six salvos in the whole action. The *Hood* had gone. Only then was it realized what had happened. *Bismarck* had fired a salvo and scored a hit upon *Hood*. The battle cruiser had been struck in the neighbourhood of a magazine. The *Hood*, one of the oldest British warships afloat, had met with sudden and complete destruction. There were to be only 3 survivors out of a total complement of 1,419 officers and men. 44,600 tons of battleship and 1,416 people had been lost at a single stroke.

Now it was the *Prince of Wales'* turn for the enemy's ferocity. So much water was being thrown up around the *Prince of Wales* by exploding shells that onlookers thought that she in turn was doomed. The range was about 18,000 yards. Within a very few minutes she was hit by four 15-inch shells and probably three smaller 8-inch shells. The bridge received a direct hit and instantly became a shambles. Every officer and man on the bridge was killed or wounded except Captain J. C. Leach, the Commanding Officer, and the Chief Yeoman. In the plotting room just below the wrecked bridge, blood began to drip off the end of the bridge voice-pipe onto the plot.

Prince of Wales withdraws

As well as the direct shell damage, small mechanical breakdowns were now seriously affecting the efficiency of the *Prince of Wales*. Captain Leach decided that the time had come to withdraw. Still more shells poured into her, two piercing her side at the waterline and flooding a number of compartments. Captain Leach had moved during the chaos to the lower bridge to command his ship, the wheel was put over and *Prince of Wales* retired from the engagement with all the speed she could muster. In pure arrogance *Bismarck* and *Prinz Eugen* made no attempt to follow but let the wounded ship limp away to lick its wounds. Theirs was the greater prize ahead,

Overleaf Bismarck *engages the 44,600 ton* Hood, *an early victim of the battle. A shell from the German ship struck the* Hood *near the magazine, which exploded. 1,416 men died on the* Hood *and only three survived.*

the rich pickings of the North Atlantic. They thought that now the way was clear, for they had sunk the *Hood*, the best and the biggest warship of the British Fleet, and they had sunk her decisively in a short swift action. The *Bismarck* may have been extremely lucky in penetrating the *Hood's* armour to explode her the way she did, but the fact remains that the *Hood* sank after a very short action.

Vice-Admiral Sir James Sommerville received the news of the sinking of *Hood* and the damage to the *Prince of Wales* with some dismay. Force H, which was under his command, consisted of the battle cruiser *Renown*, the aircraft carrier *Ark Royal*, the cruiser *Sheffield* and six destroyers, was stationed at Gibraltar, 1,500 miles away. Its normal duty had been to seal the western exit of the Mediterranean – now it was decided to throw Force H into play against *Bismarck*.

The *Bismarck*, too, had suffered injury in the action. Three times she had been hit, a glancing blow across the deck, one just forward of the port boiler room, this immobilizing one of her main dynamos, and a shell which passed through her bows, piercing two oil tanks. It was this shot that

eventually sealed her fate. At the time the loss of oil was considered quite insignificant, for still the greater prizes of the North Atlantic lured the *Bismarck* and *Prinz Eugen* on. These three bruises were nothing compared to the pride they felt after sinking one capital ship and damaging another.

Keeping in touch

Norfolk and *Suffolk* had gone on shadowing after the *Hood* was sunk. After some hours the weather cleared and the cruisers kept the *Bismarck* and the *Prinz Eugen* at a range of 15 to 18 miles. At 1100, however, the weather quickly deteriorated, mist rising rapidly. The cruisers closed in as much as they dared but about noon they lost sight and radar contact became intermittent. Shadowing continued until at 1830 *Suffolk* reported that the range by radar was rapidly decreasing. Captain Ellis was alert against such an ambush, he turned the ship hard away and increased to full speed. *Bismarck* was now on the *Suffolk's* port quarter and opening fire at long range. A few salvos were

Opposite above Hood *at anchor in Scapa Flow. Built in 1911, she was Britain's oldest warship.*

Above Hood *explodes – a shell hit her magazine.* Prince of Wales, *to the left, looks on.*

exchanged. The brief action took both ships towards the *Norfolk* and *Prince of Wales*. The *Prince of Wales* opened fire in support of *Suffolk* and *Bismarck* turned away.

This rather aimless ploy of the *Bismarck* – going into action again so quickly – was a cover for what was really happening. During the early afternoon, Admiral Lutjens had decided *Prinz Eugen* was to carry out warfare independently in the North Atlantic while the *Bismarck* was to make full speed for one of the ports on the Biscay coast so that the slight damage to the oil tanks might be repaired. Then she could join the *Prinz Eugen* in their plunderings.

Lutjens now hoped to shake off his pursuers, but they clung more desperately than ever to his tail worried lest by a sudden increase of speed the *Bismarck* might give them the slip and realizing

that the only way to prevent this was to launch attack after attack as quickly and as often as possible in order to maim the prey.

Aircraft attack

The first way this could be done, in fact the only way at this particular point, was for the aircraft from HMS *Victorious* to enter the attack and so, for the first time in the history of naval warfare, a battleship at sea was attacked by aircraft launched from their mother carrier. Number 825 Squadron, stationed on *Victorious*, of the Fleet Air Arm consisted of nine Fairey Swordfish bi-planes and six Fulmar monoplanes but unprepared as it was, only nine aircraft could be made ready in haste to be launched against the might of the Bismarck. Each of the seven Swordfish and the two Fulmars were armed with one deadly torpedo.

The untrained flight crews gallantly pressed home their attack, all the torpedoes being dropped – but only one was seen to strike the ship. The single hit was on the *Bismarck* amidships. All the

Above Sheffield, *one of the ships that shadowed the* Bismarck. *She had the misfortune to be attacked by British aircraft who mistook her for the German ship but fortunately was not damaged.*

Below Bismarck, *under attack, fires a salvo from her 15-inch guns. She had eight such guns as well as 12 5·9-inch guns, 16 4·1-inch and 16 20mm anti-aircraft guns.*

Swordfish aircraft returned to the *Victorious* and landed successfully. The two Fulmars stayed in the air, shadowing the prey.

So the day ended, the pursuers demoralized and annoyed for they had suffered heavily, and *Bismarck*, the object of their hoped-for revenge, appeared to be slipping slowly but surely away from them. The escorting destroyers had had to break off for the long high-speed pursuit had run their fuel levels dangerously low for them to remain in the chase. The bruised *Prince of Wales*, the *Norfolk* and *Suffolk*, continued to follow the *Bismarck* throughout that night, reporting her course and speed, at intervals, to the Commander in Chief.

Where is the Bismarck?

Still the *Bismarck* played with her pursuers. At about 0100 on May 25, she mockingly exchanged shots with the *Prince of Wales* at maximum range.

All the shells fell wide. Although this was a somewhat pointless gesture it had the effect of making the *Suffolk*'s shadowing even more difficult. The *Suffolk* was on extreme radar range and at the same time zig-zagging to avoid U-boats which were believed to be in the area. But worse fortune was to befall the pursuers. At 0306 on May 25 at a nominal radar range of 20,900 yards she lost contact with the *Bismarck* through a mixture of bad luck and over confidence. The enemy had altered course sharply to starboard while the *Suffolk* was moving to port and by the time the *Suffolk* returned on the dog leg of the zig-zag the *Bismarck* had gone. She was to stay lost for $31\frac{1}{2}$ hours.

Where was the *Bismarck*? What was her course? Had the killer of the mighty *Hood* escaped? *Suffolk* searched towards the enemy's last bearing during the morning of May 25 but it became obvious that the enemy had evaded her pursuers. Aircraft from *Victorious* were put into action this time to search, but the attempt proved

negative. *Norfolk* and *Suffolk* had searched to the south-east of the last reported position but they too drew a blank. There was no sign of *Bismarck*, she had gone. Then came a stroke of luck – at 1030 on May 26 a Royal Air Force Catalina Flying Boat of Coastal Command, flying on patrol, sighted the *Bismarck*. The hunt was on again. Within a few minutes of the Catalina sighting, the *Ark Royal*, together with Force H, drew close to the reported position. This time they would never lose sight of her until full vengeance had been extracted. The *Bismarck* had to be pegged back, she had crept a lead of over 50 miles and if this increase were to continue, she would soon be within German bomber range and therefore become almost untouchable. She must, above all else be stopped – the prey could not be allowed to slide from their grasp again.

A British error

The only real hope lay in the *Ark Royal*'s aircraft. A force of 15 Swordfish aircraft flew off at 1450 to strike at the *Bismarck*. The weather was particularly bad in the vicinity of the target, but the crews had been told that no other ship was anywhere nearby. Meanwhile, Vice-Admiral Sommerville had ordered the cruiser *Sheffield* to find and shadow the *Bismarck*. The order was flashed by signal searchlight and went only to the *Sheffield*; the *Ark Royal* never noticed her departure. The flying crews in the rain and mist and virtually nil visibility, picked up a ship on their radar in roughly the expected position. Assuming it to be the *Bismarck* they pressed home their attack – on the *Sheffield*.

Eleven torpedoes were fired at the *Sheffield* – two exploded on hitting the water, three more exploded when crossing the wake of the cruiser and the remainder were successfully avoided by the *Sheffield*. With great forebearance she did not fire a single round in reply!

Luck, however, was now swinging away from the *Bismarck*, the hunted, and towards the Royal Navy, the hunters. A second striking force of 15 aircraft was launched at 1915. Because the number of serviceable aircraft was limited, most of the aircraft which had flown in the first misplaced attack were re-armed and refuelled for the second attack. Heavy rain swept across the flight deck as the planes took off. The feeling on *Ark Royal* was that this striking force must succeed – it was the

last chance. This time the Swordfish found their true prey and the attack was pressed home.

Bismarck at bay

In face of intense and accurate fire from *Bismarck* the aircraft swung in pairs and attacked with gallantry and determination. At least two hits were scored on the *Bismarck*, one damaged the rudders and this was to be the Achilles heel. When the aircraft returned five had been severely damaged by gunfire. In one, 127 holes were counted, the pilot and the gunner having both been wounded, but despite all this only one aircraft crashed.

Reports now poured in from the other pursuers that *Bismarck* had drastically altered course. Why was she behaving so strangely? The damage to the rudders must be serious. Straggling aircraft landing on the *Ark Royal* reported that immediately after the attack *Bismarck*, trailing oil, had made two complete circles and apparently come to a stop heading north. She was lying wallowing in the seas. One of the two hits, the one which damaged the rudders, had been so accurate that the steering mechanisms had been virtually destroyed.

The Royal Navy, who had suffered much, now knew their chance was coming. *Bismarck* was lying helpless. The pursuers gathered their strength for the final confrontation, but *Bismarck* was not done yet and she fired six accurate salvos at her persistent chasers as if in defiance to try and keep alive her hopes. The escorting destroyers *Cossack*, *Maori*, *Sikh* and *Zulu* together with the Polish destroyer *Piorun* approached the stricken *Bismarck* and started to harass the enemy. Soon it was clear that the destroyers' main objective was to keep in touch with the enemy and the secondary objective to attack if an opportunity arose. Orders were therefore despatched that the destroyers were to attack independently as opportunity offered and not to risk their ships. Throughout the night and until 0845 on May 27 when the main battle fleet gathered, these destroyers maintained constant touch in spite of heavy rain squalls and low visibility.

The final kill

At 0847 the mighty warships *Rodney* and *King*

George V moved into action. *Rodney*, a 33,900 ton battleship, built in 1925, opened the account with a salvo from her nine 16-inch guns. This was immediately followed by a salvo from the ten 14-inch guns from the 2-year-old, 35,000 ton, battleship *King George V*. The *Bismarck* quickly replied. The battle to the death was on. At 0854 the *Norfolk* opened fire at 20,000 yards. At 0904 the cruiser *Dorsetshire* joined in the action. In order to concentrate their fire power, the battleships continued to close on their target, coming in to 3,300 yards. By 1015 the *Bismarck* was a wreck, without a gun firing, on fire fore and aft and wallowing more heavily every moment. Men could be seen jumping overboard, preferring death by drowning to the appalling effects of the fires which were now raging over her decks. *Bismarck*'s masts were down, the funnel had disappeared and smoke and flames were rising from the middle of the ship. But her flag still flew ostentatiously; she remained defiant though powerless. In the midst of her death throes the

Below *Aircraft aboard* Victorious *await orders to attack the* Bismarck. Victorious *had nine Swordfish biplanes and six Fulmar monoplanes. Only nine, each armed with one torpedo, were ready when the order came.*

vultures moved in for the kill.

Dorsetshire torpedoed the *Bismarck* on both sides at close range. The proud battleship of the Third Reich was now a battered hulk. The torpedoes exploded right under the remains of the bridge; heeling over to port, then turning upside down, the *Bismarck* shuddered and disappeared beneath the waves. The hunters had finally caught their prey.

Longest chase in history

The destruction of the *Bismarck* had been one of the longest chases in naval history. For Grand Admiral Raeder, Exercise Rhine was at an end. What would have happened if his plan had succeeded and *Bismarck*, *Prinz Eugen* and others had broken out into the North Atlantic to run amok amongst the life supporting convoys that were reaching Britain from the Americas? As it was, thanks to the tenacity, the courage, the forbearance of many officers and men of the Royal Navy during the period from May 18 when the *Bismarck* and *Prinz Eugen* sailed from Gdynia to the time *Bismarck* slid beneath the waves on May 27, the convoys were still able to continue their life-supporting efforts. Exercise Rhine had been

Major ships in the *Bismarck* action

BRITISH SHIPS

Hood (Battle-cruiser)	*Tonnage:*	44,600
	Speed:	32 knots
	Armament:	8 15in., 12 5.5in., 8 4in. AA, 24 2in. guns, 4 21in. torpedoes
Prince of Wales (Battleship)	*Tonnage:*	35,000
	Speed:	32 knots
	Armament:	10 14in., 16 5.25in., 4 pom-pom. Carried four aircraft launched by catapult
Norfolk (Cruiser)	*Tonnage:*	9,925
	Speed:	32.8 knots
	Armament:	8 8in., 8 4in. AA, 4 3-pounder, 16 smaller arms, 8 21in. torpedo tubes. Carried one aircraft launched by catapult
Suffolk (Cruiser)	*Tonnage:*	10,000
	Speed:	31.5 knots
	Armament:	8 8in., 8 4in. AA, 20 smaller arms. Carried one aircraft launched by catapult
Dorsetshire (Cruiser)	*Tonnage:*	9,975
	Speed:	32 knots
	Armament:	8 8in., 8 4in. AA, 4 3-pounder, 16 smaller arms, 8 21in. torpedo tubes. Carried one aircraft launched by catapult.

GERMAN SHIPS

Bismarck (Battleship)	*Tonnage:*	50,000
	Speed:	29 knots
	Armament:	8 15in., 12 5.9in., 16 4.1in. AA, 16 20mm guns. Carried two aircraft launched by catapult
Prinz Eugen (Cruiser)	*Tonnage:*	17,000
	Speed:	32 knots
	Armament:	8 8in., 12 4.1in., 12 37mm AA guns. 12 21 in. torpedo tubes. Carried three aircraft launched by catapult

brilliantly conceived but failed hopelessly in its objectives and the convoy lanes, the life lines of Britain, had been kept open.

The battle had been waged by the older ships of the Royal Navy against the faster and more up to date ships of the German Navy. The Germans had expected to make an easy passage to dominance of the seas, but they had not bargained for bulldog-like tenacity. Once the Royal Navy caught the scent of battle then nothing could shake the belief that victory was the only course of action; and victory was achieved.

There were to be many more confrontations between the Navies of Germany and Britain during World War II. Some were great and some were small, but always, from this action onwards, the German Navy respected her enemy. She was not the tired old lady that they had been led to believe. If Germany wanted dominance of the seas it could only be achieved at a terrible cost. Events were to prove that the cost was too great.

Above Bismarck's *huge guns thunder a salvo at the doomed* Hood. *But Britain had her revenge.*

Right *Voyage to oblivion. The course of the battle was mainly a chase with sporadic and ill-coordinated attacks. But at the end* **inset** *the British ships closed in for the kill.*

Death of the Bismarck

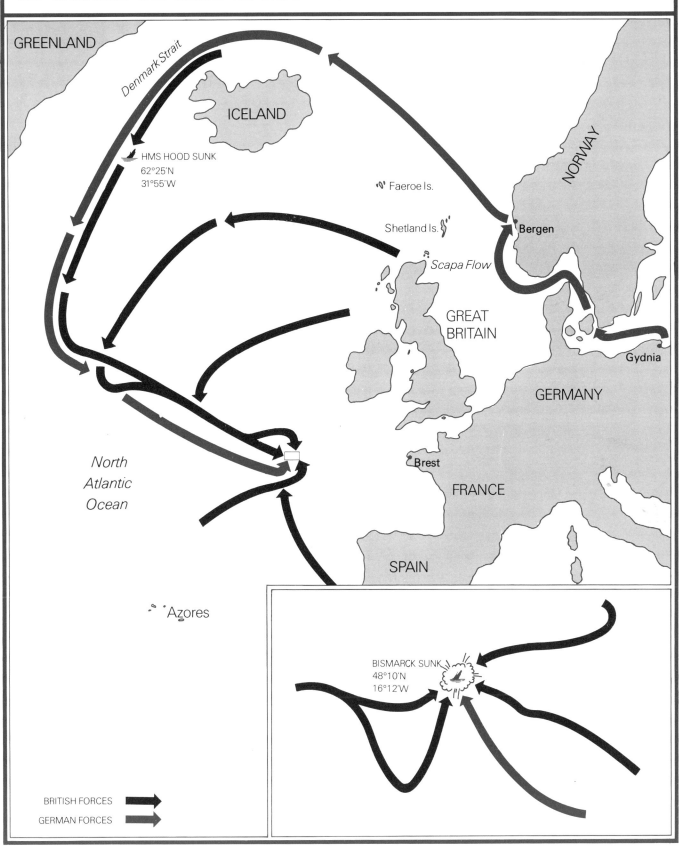

GREENLAND

Denmark Strait

ICELAND

HMS HOOD SUNK
62°25'N
31°55'W

Faeroe Is.

Shetland Is.

Scapa Flow

NORWAY

Bergen

Gydnia

GREAT
BRITAIN

GERMANY

Brest

FRANCE

North
Atlantic
Ocean

SPAIN

Azores

BISMARCK SUNK
48°10'N
16°12'W

BRITISH FORCES

GERMAN FORCES

SUBS v. TIRPITZ

Lurking in the Norwegian fiords, the Tirpitz, *Hitler's greatest battleship, threatened convoys supplying the Russians — until, in 1943, small submarines, the X craft, crept bravely through the dark and well-defended waters to plant explosives beneath the mighty ship.*

Tirpitz, *sister ship of the* Bismarck, *was a threat to the Russian convoys until severely damaged by bombs laid by X craft, the Allies' midget submarines. Her eight 15-inch guns were never again to fire in action.*

Like minnows in search of a shark, three tiny submarines swam through the hazards of Norway's Altenfiord towards the *Tirpitz*, proud battleship of the German Third Reich. The mission of the submarines was to cripple the mighty fighting ship and prevent her ever again venturing from her icy lair to savage the straggling convoys that were the supplies life line to the hard-pressed Russian ally. The odds were immense – and so was the achievement.

When Russia entered the Second World War in 1941 vast quantities of war materials had to be transported from the embattled Allied forces to the Russian war effort on the Eastern front. The Allies established convoy routes from Great Britain northwards round the North Cape into the White Sea, landing at the Russian port of Archangel.

The Germans had to strangle this life line. They had made the mistake of fighting on two fronts and in both the East and the West the war was taking its toll. But the Russian assault in the East depended on a flow of munitions from the other allies and Hitler and his naval aides soon came to the conclusion that the munitions lifeline, stretching tenuously round the North Cape and into Archangel, must be broken. If the munitions flow could be halted then the sting of Russian aggression on the Eastern front would be blunted, and would eventually cease. So plans already made to move the capital ships of the German Navy into such a position that they could spring out and crush the convoys, were brought into play.

Cats and mice

The plans involved moving the capital ships of the Reich into the naval anchorages of Trondheim, Narvik, and Altenfiord (Altafjord), along the pitted coastline of occupied Norway. These anchorages were natural, deep and winding fiords that cut far into the coastline, dark and dank sanctuaries that were ideal places to hide the capital ships of the German Navy. There the 'cat' would wait, in comparative safety, for the convoys to pass. Then, so the plans had it, the cat could spring from its lair and kill the 'mice', the Allied munitions ships. The munitions lifeline would be severed.

The most northerly and most tortuous harbour chosen by the Third Reich was that at Altenfiord, and here the modern 42,000-ton battleship *Tirpitz* lay. The presence of this warship, the most highly efficient and deadly weapon of the German Navy, played havoc with the already greatly stretched convoys. One convoy, number PQ17, was virtually wiped out after it scattered thinking the *Tirpitz* was out; others were strafed so that very few ships reached their destination, Archangel. If the Russian war effort was to be sustained something had to be done to counter the menace of the predators.

The British Admiralty decided that the only way to safeguard the convoys was the elimination of the German capital ships. But how? Several

methods had been tried – all had failed. RAF bombers were sent to blast the ships while at anchor deep in the fiords, but the luck was always with the German Navy. A method to penetrate deep into the fiords, to the very heart of their lairs had to be found.

A new secret weapon

For many months secret trials and practices

The Tirpitz *at anchor in Norway's Altenfiord surrounded by just two of the obstacles the X craft had to overcome – anti-submarine and torpedo nets.*

were carried out on the coast of Scotland, in Loch Scriven, as this was the nearest natural configuration to the fiords of Norway. Here the Royal Navy secretly tested and modified a new weapon, the 'X' craft.

X craft were midget submarines designed to hold four men, and small enough to pick their way stealthily through the many navigational hazards, to negotiate the tortuous and twisting route necessary to avoid minefields and patrol vessels and slip unseen into the battleship's lair. The small submarines were designed to carry a payload of high explosives, two-ton charges which were deployed either side of the craft and could be released by one of the submariners.

A plan of action was devised. The submarines were to enter the guarded anchorage at Altenfiord and worm their way through the heavy defences to place their lethal explosive underneath the *Tirpitz*. With the explosive in place the submarines would return by the route by which they came. The plan was ingenious and top secret and in early September 1943, with the trials in Lock Scriven complete, it was designated by an official code-name, 'Operation Source'.

Six Royal Navy midget submarines, HMS X5 to HMS X10 were to enter Altenfiord during the period September 20 to 25. This timing would give them the favourable weather conditions needed. The six X craft, after navigating the fiords, would place their charges under the battleship and leave the fiord.

All was set for Operation Source. Six conventional submarines towed the X craft to their target across the North Sea. But then misfortune struck – two of the midget submarines broke adrift while on passage and were lost. Another developed serious mechanical defects and was forced to abandon the operation. Only three craft were left to enter the predator's lair – the X5, X6, and X7.

First strike

The three midget submarines dived off the entrance to Altenfiord to carry out their task and travelled singly up the tortuous passage. One craft the X6, commanded by Lieutenant Donald Cameron, RNR, suffered mechanical defects; his periscope, the 'eye' of the submarine, was only partly effective. Nevertheless, the X6 was first to strike.

The *Tirpitz* was protected by a very heavy and intricate anti-torpedo net. This encircled her anchorage so that no submerged craft could get within striking distance. It was inpenetrable – or almost. One space had been left open for small

supply boats to ferry men and stores to the great ship. The X6, completely submerged, followed one heavily guarded supply boat through the encircling defensive net and entered the battleship's sanctuary. Before her, immense and threatening, lay the *Tirpitz*. But then disaster struck the brave little predator. While trying to manoeuvre into a position to drop the deadly explosive charges, the X6 smashed into a submerged rock.

Charges in position

The midget submarine was driven almost clear of the water. In the grey half light of morning, the guards on board *Tirpitz* sighted the submarine breaking surface. Though Lt. Cameron managed to regain control it was too late – the alarm had been given. With great courage and fortitude, Cameron brought his damaged submarine close in to the *Tirpitz*, but again disaster struck. Wires hanging over the side of the battleship became entangled with the X6, and for a few moments the midget submarine was trapped. Cameron skilfully managed to extricate his tiny ship and, diving deeper, right under the hull of the *Tirpitz*, he planted his charges.

By now alarm and confusion had spread throughout the Tirpitz at the sighting of the enemy submarine. Lt. Cameron knew the game was up – he could not escape with his damaged submarine. He surfaced close by and abandoned ship. The four submariners were hauled aboard the great warship and the X6 was sent to the bottom of the fiord.

One of the other craft, the X7, commanded by Lieutenant Godfrey Place, RN, had tried to go under the maze of anti-submarine nets. Then at a depth of 75 feet, the craft became entangled in the encircling web. With great skill the commander extricated his vessel and moved silently in on the target. Diving deeper underneath the belly of the mighty battleship Lieutenant Place, too, laid his charges in strategic positions. He turned and began to make his escape but once again the nets snared his ship. The explosive charges had a time fuse – and time was running out fast.

Explosion!

At 0812 hours, some 30 minutes after the charges had been laid, explosions rocked the 42,000 ton *Tirpitz*. Water and steam flew high in the air. Two simultaneous explosions thundered down the fiord, echoing to and fro in a deafening

Opposite The Germans lay smoke screens to hide Tirpitz *from aerial reconnaisance.*

Below The 42,000 ton Tirpitz *carried a crew of 2,400 and included eight 15-inch and 12 5.9 inch guns in her hardware. With a maximum range of 9,000 miles at 19 knots, she posed a fearful threat to the vital convoys.*

crescendo of noise. The *Tirpitz* lurched to one side, a great hole torn below the waterline in her keel. Oil poured from her fuel tanks and spread its slimy fingers over the surface of the water. On board the battleship there was chaos.

The explosions were so violent that the ensnared X7 was blasted clear of the entangling nets and thrust to the surface by the underwater shock waves. German gunners opened fire on the wallowing submarine with small arms, and threw hand grenades to try and sink the fleeing craft. Damage to the X7 was severe and Lt. Place decided to abandon ship. The crew scuttled

Ships in the *Tirpitz* action

Tirpitz (Battleship)	*Launched:*	February 14, 1939
	Tonnage:	42,900 displacement
	Dimensions:	length 823ft. beam 118ft. draught 35ft.
	Speed:	29 knots
	Armament:	8 15in., 12 5.9in., 16 4.1in., 16 37mm A.A., 70 20mm A.A., 8 21in. torpedo tubes, six aircraft launched from one catapault.
	Complement:	2,530
X craft (Submarines)	*Built:*	1942-43
	Tonnage:	27-30
	Speed:	6.5 knots (surface) 5.5 knots (submerged)
	Dimensions:	length 51ft. beam 6ft. draught 6ft.
	Complement:	4

the brave ship. Tragically only two of the four man crew escaped alive from this daring and courageous exploit.

The third X craft to enter the fiord, the X5, arrived on the scene after the explosion. The Germans, now alert and watchful, spotted her and fired. The X5 was apparently hit and went with her crew to the bottom of the icy waters without delivering a blow to *Tirpitz*.

A most courageous act

In the aftermath of the brave sortie came disappointment. Air-reconnaissance photographs showed the *Tirpitz* still at anchor – it seemed that little damage had been done. What was not known, and would not become apparent for a few months, was that *Tirpitz* had suffered a grievous injury. The hole in her hull had seriously weakened her main structure and her generators and dynamos had been virtually destroyed.

The mighty *Tirpitz* never again ventured out into the Atlantic and never again fired a shot in anger. The small defiant attack by the extremely gallant and courageous crews of the midget submarines had cleared the way for the convoys. The tenuous supply lines could be maintained. Russia received her precious armaments and the war continued against Germany on two major fronts.

It was not until two years after peace that the British public became fully aware of the gallantry of the men in the three tiny submarines. As a reward for the tremendous contribution they had made to the war effort the survivors of Operation Source were proudly presented to, and decorated by, King George VI at Buckingham Palace. An official report by the Admiralty predicted that this 'daring attack will surely go down in history as one of the most courageous acts of all time'.

Above left The X craft carried a crew of five and had a range of 1,200 miles at 4 knots and at 2 knots could travel submerged for 23 hours. 53 feet long and weighing 30 tons, the X craft carried a warhead of two external charges as well as limpet mines.

Right Route of the X craft to the Tirpitz. *Inset The convoy route threatened by the German battleship.*

Submarines against Tirpitz

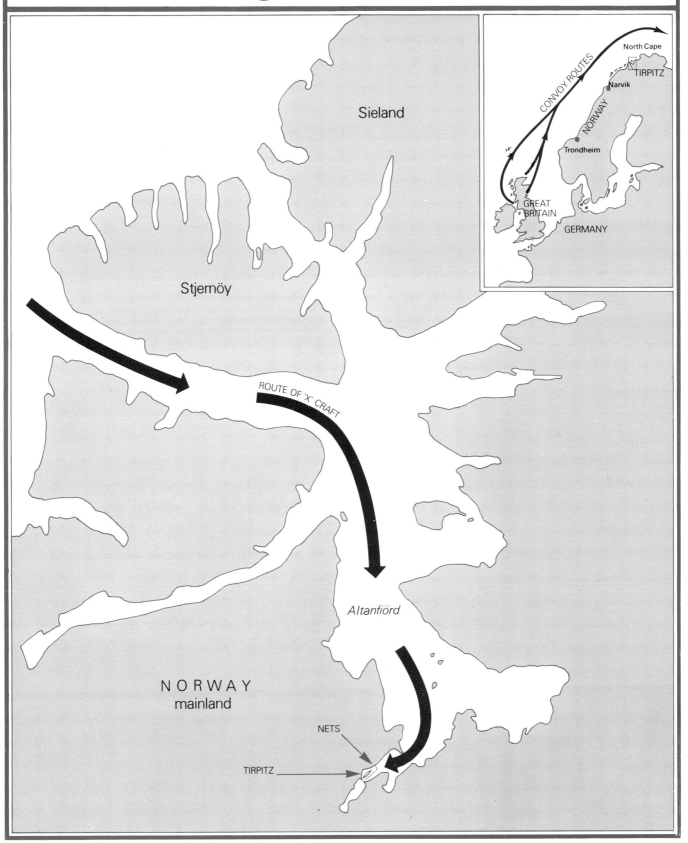

Sieland

Stjernöy

ROUTE OF 'X' CRAFT

Altanfiörd

N O R W A Y
mainland

NETS

TIRPITZ

CONVOY ROUTES

North Cape

TIRPITZ

Narvik

NORWAY

Trondheim

GREAT
BRITAIN

GERMANY

LEYTE GULF

In the greatest sea battle of all time, near the Philippine island of Leyte in 1944, over-matched American ships fought desperately against three Japanese fleets to keep the hard-won beach-heads open. And through bluff and bravery they succeeded.

'The President of the United States ordered me to break through the Japanese lines and proceed from Corregidor to Australia for the purpose, as I understand it, of organizing the American offensive against Japan, a primary object of which is the relief of the Philippines. I came through and I shall return.' Thus spoke General Douglas Mac-Arthur on his arrival in Australia in 1942, after the Allied forces had been virtually run out of the South Pacific by the southward advance of the armed might of Imperial Japan. Little else but Australia was left to the Allies in that theatre of war at that time. It took a bold man indeed to promise to halt the Japanese advance, let alone turn it.

But MacArthur did return, although it was not until October 20, 1944, that he was able to start the northward drive that was to carry him to victory. The build-up to the landings on the

Leyte Gulf, the largest sea battle of modern times was a vital step in America's fight to drive the Japanese from the Philippine Sea and thus sever her oil supply lines from Malaya and Indo-China. By doing this Japan's ability to wage war would be drastically impaired. Here the 33,100 ton Pennsylvania, *which fought at Leyte Gulf, leads an American battle line.*

island of Leyte, in the Philippines, that took place on that day was desperately fought. It was a matter of survival, pure and simple, for the Americans and their numerically weak Australasian allies; for the Japanese it was the final step in their dreams of a Pacific empire.

The last of the preliminary engagements, on June 19 and 20, had been especially costly for the Japanese. In this battle, known officially as the Battle of the Philippines Sea but sometimes irreverently, if accurately, referred to as 'The Great Marianas Turkey Shoot', the Japanese Navy suffered heavy losses. As well as the damage to their ships, they saw the American carrier-borne aircraft put over 500 of their planes out of action.

The largest sea battle

Both this action and the landings themselves, however, were destined to be no more than a prelude to the battle that followed. It took place in an area of the Philippines known as the Leyte Gulf, and remains the largest sea battle of modern times. Between October 22 and 27, 1944, over 230 warships and 1,996 aircraft took part in this terrible encounter between the forces of the

LEYTE GULF

Far left Admiral Soemu Toyoda,
Commander-in-Chief of the Japanese
Combined Fleet.

Left 'I shall return.' General MacArthur's
promise, made in 1942 came true in 1944
when American forces landed in the
Philippines.

Below American aircraft carriers under
attack off Leyte Gulf as seen from the
carrier White Plains.

United States and Imperial Japan. The battle was fought as an adjunct to the invasion of the island of Leyte, the vital stepping-stone in MacArthur's drive to rid the Philippines Sea of Japanese domination. The mighty sea-borne invasion force that he had mustered included no less than 17 aircraft carriers.

The landing on the beaches of Leyte itself, on October 20, met with little opposition, and by the midnight of the following day MacArthur had put ashore 132,000 men. Despite their recent heavy defeats, especially those they suffered during the latter half of June, the Commander of the Japanese Navy, Admiral Suemo Toyoda, was still far from cowed. He was seeking the sea-battle to end all sea-battles, the battle in which he hoped to blunt the American thrust towards Japan.

The Allied plan to land on Leyte was based on the theory that the Philippine archipelago lay directly along the main sea routes from Japan to her sources of oil in Malaya and Indo-China. The operation, to which MacArthur had given the name 'Operation Reno', was designed to cut these sea routes, and thus strangle Japan into surrender, and called on vast concentrations of air, land and sea forces. If these drives into the main life-blood of Japan, her oil routes, could be completed successfully, her ability to wage war would be severely impaired.

MacArthur lands

As soon as the USS *Nashville* had landed General MacArthur and his entourage on Leyte, the General, in his usual dramatic tones, spoke to his troops. Although fighting was still going on with

the Japanese not many yards away, a mobile broadcasting unit was set up and General Mac-Arthur spoke these, now famous, words: 'People of the Philippines; I have returned. By the grace of Almighty God, our forces stand again on Philippine soil, soil consecrated in the blood of our two peoples. We have come, dedicated and committed to the task of destroying every vestige of enemy control over your daily lives, and of restoring upon a foundation of indestructible strength the liberties of your people. . . .

'Rally to me. Let the indomitable spirit of Bataan and Corregidor lead on. As the lines of battle roll forward to bring you within the zone of operations, rise and strike. Strike at every favourable opportunity. For your homes and hearths, strike! For future generations of your sons and daughters, strike! In the name of your sacred dead, strike! Let no heart be faint.

Let every arm be steeled. The guidance of divine God points the way. Follow His name to the Holy Grail of righteous victory.' These words were indeed to bring the fighting spirit of the Philippine people to the surface.

Toyoda's last gamble

The time had come for Admiral Toyoda to make his last decisive gamble. Having heard of the American invasion, he set out from his base in Singapore with every ship he could muster. He

The American aircraft carrier Hornet, *27,000 tons. MacArthur's huge invasion force included no less than 17 carriers, but found itself stretched by the massive Japanese onslaught.*

divided the combined fleet of the Imperial Japanese Navy into three distinct groups: central force under Admiral Kurita, southern force rear group, under Vice Admiral Kiyohide Shima with southern force forward group, under Vice Admiral Nishimura, and northern force, under Vice Admiral Ozawa.

Toyoda's plan was for central force to pass through the San Bernardino Strait, north of Leyte, and then set course southwards for Leyte Gulf. Southern force would approach through the Mindanao Sea and Surigao Strait so that both fleets would converge simultaneously on the flanks of the attacking American naval fleet in a coordinated pincer-attack. Northern force, in the Philippines Sea, was to decoy the powerful United States Third Fleet from its job of protecting the entrance to Leyte Gulf.

The American naval forces involved in the Leyte invasion were disposed in two main bodies. The Seventh Fleet, under Vice Admiral Thomas C. Kinkaid, protected the southern and western entrances to Leyte Gulf, while the stronger Third Fleet, under Admiral Halsey, operated off Samar. It was his task to cover the San Bernardino Strait and the approaches from the north west.

Central force mauled

On October 24 General MacArthur moved his headquarters ashore. The *Nashville*, which had been his headquarters during the landing, moved into its position for the coming battle. During the day, Admiral Kurita's central force was put under constant attack by aircraft from the Third Fleet and could therefore only cautiously edge its way towards the entrance to the San Bernardino Strait. The first blows were falling to the American Navy: the *Musashi*, a new addition to the Imperial Navy, with nine 18.1-inch guns, was sunk. Her sister ship, the *Yamato*, was severely hit. Some Japanese cruisers were also damaged or put out of action, as were some of their smaller destroyers.

At 1553 hours the Japanese staged a temporary withdrawal of their central force, to enable them to regroup their now badly mauled formations. This was completed in less than two hours, and at 1714 hours the central force again advanced. Admiral Toyoda issued the following communique to his forces: 'All forces will dash to the attack, trusting in divine assistance.' He was determined to crush the American fleet with everything at his disposal.

Southern force ambushed

Meanwhile, the Japanese southern force, the other arm of the proposed pincer movement, was sailing at speed into the Mindanao Sea. The American forces had not been idle either: armed with excellent intelligence reports on the movements of the Japanese ships, they had prepared an ambush in a narrow passage at the entrance to the Surigao Strait with torpedo-boats, destroyers, cruisers and battleships.

The torpedo-boats and destroyers attacked the Japanese ships from both sides as they sailed in line astern formation into the entrance to the narrow strait. The cruisers and battleships, stationed ahead of the Japanese, then joined the action, using their big guns as soon as the Japanese came within range. The ambush was a complete success, and the whole southern force of the Japanese fleet was virtually annihilated. Indeed, this attack was almost perfect for only one Japanese destroyer escaped. The southern entrance to Leyte Gulf was completely cleared of Japanese naval forces in one swift defiant action.

Northern force's bad luck

At this stage only the northern force had made no contact and luck was to play a most important part for the Americans. The Japanese force was continually sending radio messages in order to advertise their position and lure the Americans into an unfavourable battle position. But a fault in their transmission systems prevented the Third Fleet from intercepting and acting on these signals. The American forces never knew of the enticement to fight that was being dangled in front of them! Vice Admiral Ozawa could not wage battle as he wished.

Due to the complete disaster that had befallen the southern force, and the lack of success of the northern force's tactics, the task of destroying a large proportion of the United States Navy now rested solely with Admiral Kurita and the regrouped central force of the Japanese fleet. At dawn on October 25 yet another battle took place.

Battle commences

A group of 16 escort carriers, nine cruisers and 12 destroyers of the Seventh Fleet were disposed east of Samar and the Leyte Gulf, directly in the path of the oncoming Japanese force. The light carriers of the American Navy were no real match for the massive battleships and aircraft carriers of the heavily armed Japanese central force. A battle between completely unequal adversaries commenced but the Americans realized the danger they faced should the Japanese break through and gain entrance to the Leyte Gulf. The powerful battleships, with their huge guns, could lay waste the beach-heads that MacArthur had just recently taken. The Americans planned their tactics accordingly.

At 0658 hours, the battleship *Yamato* fired her huge 18.1-inch guns, and the battle was on. Never before had the American fleet been subjected to such concentrated heavy firepower. In addition to the surface units, Kamikaze or suicide attacks were made on the American carriers by Japanese air units based in the Philippines. The central force continued to press home their attack, at

The American battleship Texas, *27,000-tons. Her main armament consisted of ten 14-inch guns. Two Japanese battleships carried 18.1-inch guns.*

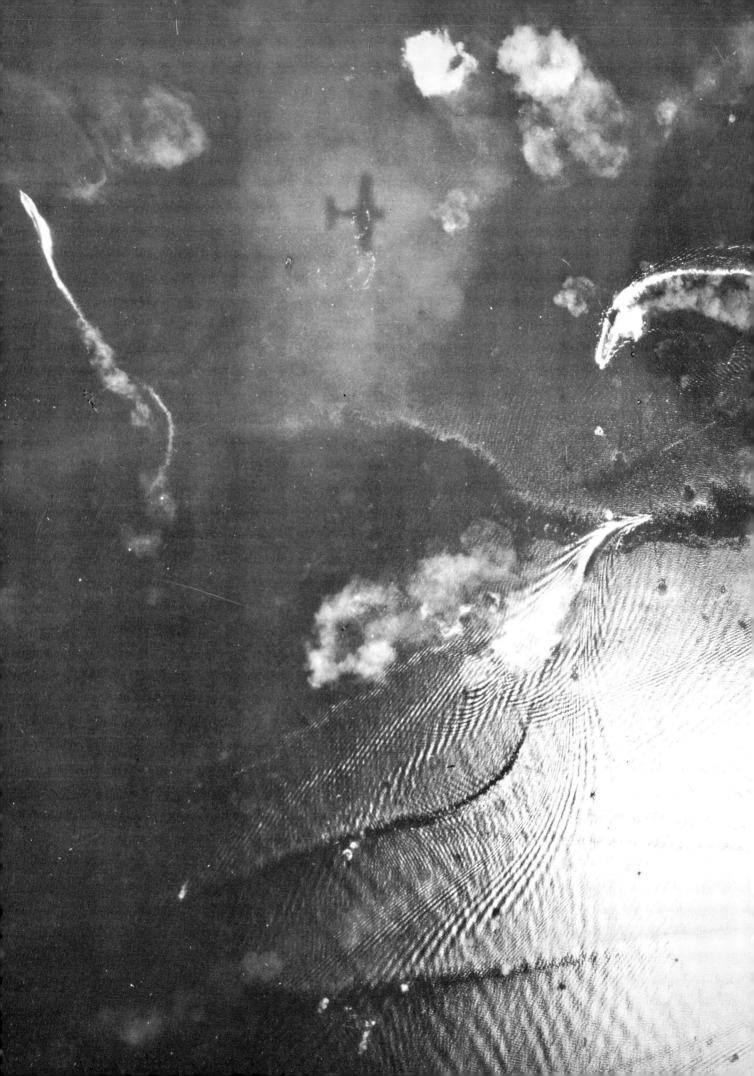

full speed. But the American fleet was not to be battered into submission quite so easily.

Battleships versus carriers

A brilliant display of co-ordinated counter-thrusts then took place. No sooner had Yamato's shells been fired than aircraft were launched from the American escort carriers, and the orders were to destroy or cripple the big guns as quickly as possible. The situation was rapidly reaching a critical point for both sides. The American fleet laid smoke screens – and used every tactical trick in the book: central force had to be stopped in its tracks by the weaker American fleet. The beach-heads must be protected at all cost.

The destroyer escorts were sent in to harry the enormous, and therefore slightly cumbersome Japanese battleships. Although they took heavy punishment, they pressed home their attack like dogs barking at the heels of a great dragon and started to inflict small but telling wounds on the mighty warships. Aircraft buzzed like hornets around the dragon's head, continually attacking and thrusting. But American ships were being put out of action and sunk and the battleships of the Imperial Japanese Navy thundered on. They were creating havoc amongst the American forces by now, their heavy firepower damaging the cruisers and destroyers severely. Kamikaze aircraft had smashed open the flight decks of the aircraft carriers, so that the returning planes had nowhere to land. Some were able to make for the sanctuary of the airstrip at Tacloban, but others, who had carried the battle to the limits of their range, and had expected to be able to return to their mother carriers, were compelled to ditch in Leyte Gulf.

Disaster now stared the Americans in the face. At 0900 hours the American forces issued this signal: 'Our escort carriers being attacked by four battleships, eight cruisers plus others. Request fast carriers make immediate strike.' Help was wanted quickly or they would perish, and already the American losses had started to mount alarmingly. After two and a half hours of continuous battle their ammunition was running

Left Japanese ships in the Tablas Strait take evasive action during an attack by American aircraft during the battle of Leyte Gulf.

low, their destroyers had expanded all their torpedoes and their planes had to be refuelled and rearmed many miles away.

Victory for Japan?

Victory lay within the Imperial Japanese Navy's grasp – but could they close their fingers and grip it? This was the desperate question passing through the minds of the men of the United States Navy. Then suddenly, the impossible happened. Inexplicably the Imperial Japanese Navy turned away: their units had sustained more damage than had been, at first glance, apparent and believing that the American forces were falling back in order to muster another attack, they retreated.

To the US carriers, this was a blessing for they had been receiving a terrible pounding, now instead of the Japanese advantage being forced home, they were being let off the hook. The American carrier forces and their destroyer escorts set up a huge smoke-screen behind which they, too, retreated to regroup.

The Japanese withdrawal lasted until 1120 hours when, after regrouping and making some quick repairs, the remains of the central force mounted one last attempt on Leyte Gulf. But fate again stepped in: unsure of their own strength, the Japanese commanders hesitated. Their central force was less than one hour from its objective, but their uncertainty made them

Above American patrol boats were used for spotting and attacking Japanese forces and for rescuing survivors. A cameraman on board the USS Hancock *pictures crewmen of PT 321 fishing a Japanese sailor out of the water.*

Right the scene of the Battle of Leyte Gulf and the positions of the contending fleets. Inset shows the position of the Philippines in the China Sea.

give up this last attempt. They turned round at 1236 hours, one hour and sixteen minutes after attempting their final assault in a mood of indecision that finally culminated in a complete withdrawal. The central force passed back out through the San Bernardino Strait, and by 2130 hours on October 25 the remains of the Japanese navy were scurrying home.

American bluff – and courage

The Seventh Fleet had held out despite a tremendous hammering and against almost overwhelming odds. In the end, by a good deal of bluff, they had persuaded the enemy that they were stronger than they really were. Thus the battle of Leyte Gulf drew to a close, with the Japanese navy completely routed.

When the engagement finished with small skirmishes on October 27, the toll against the Imperial Japanese Navy had been heavy. Of the 65 ships that started, 26 had been sunk, including

Leyte Gulf

Major ships in the Battle of Leyte Gulf

JAPANESE FLEET:

Central Force

	Name	Tonnage	Main Armament
Battleships	Musashi*	42,500	9 16in.
	Yamato	42,500	9 16in.
	Nagato	32,720	8 16in.
	Haruna	29,330	8 14in.
	Kongo	29,330	8 14in.
Cruisers	Chikuma*	14,000	8 8in.
	Suzuya*	14,000	8 8in.
	Atago*	9,850	10 8in.
	Chokai*	9,850	10 8in.
	Maya*	9,850	10 8in.
	Noshiro	6,000	6 6.1in.
	Kinu	5,170	7 5.5in.

Southern Force

	Name	Tonnage	Main Armament
Battleships	Fuso*	29,330	12 14in.
	Yamashiro*	29,330	12 14in.
Cruisers	Mogami*	14,000	8 8in.

'Northern Force'

	Name	Tonnage	Main Armament
Battleships	Ise	29,990	12 14in.
	Hyuga	29,990	12 14in.
Aircraft carriers	Zuikaku*	29,800	
	Zuiho*	12,000	
	Chitose*	9,000	
	Chiyoda*	9,000	
Cruisers	Tama*	5,100	7 5.5in.

AMERICAN FLEET:

	Name	Tonnage	Main Armament
Battleships	Arkansas	26,100	12 12in.
	California	35,190	12 14in.
	Idaho	33,400	12 14in.
	Maryland	33,590	8 16in.
	Nevada	29,000	10 14in.
	New York	27,000	10 14in.
	North Carolina	35,000	9 16in.
	Pennsylvania	33,100	12 14in.
	South Dakota	35,000	9 16in.
	Tennessee	35,190	12 14in.
	Texas	27,000	10 14in.
	Washington	35,000	9 16in.
	West Virginia	33,590	8 16in.
Aircraft carriers	Gambier Bay*	6,730	
	Hornet	27,000	
	Kitkum Bay	6,730	
	Lexington	27,000	
	Princeton*	11,000	
	Santee	12,000	
	St Lo*	6,730	
	Suwanee	12,000	
	Wasp	27,000	
	White Plains	6,730	

Vessels known to have been sunk

the entire force of Japanese carriers, three battleships, and ten cruisers. Even the flagship *Musashi* had gone down. For the sinking of these 26 ships the United States Navy had lost six capital ships out of a total of 166. The six ships sunk included a light aircraft carrier and some small carriers and destroyers. Four days of hard battle had ended in a Japanese defeat of great magnitude.

General MacArthur was naturally delighted that the American navy had managed to protect his landing. He sent this signal: 'At this time I wish to express to you and to all elements of your fine command my deep appreciation of the splendid service they have rendered in the recent Leyte operations. ... We could not have gone along without them.'

Right *The 11,000 ton aircraft carrier* Princeton *explodes. Fire caused by a bomb had reached the magazine. The* Princeton *sank.*

THE
PICTORIAL
HISTORY OF

BURTON GRAHAM

From the frail biplanes which whirled and fought over the trenches of France, aircraft have been transformed into sophisticated, supersonic jets, capable of delivering a nuclear strike to any part of the world.

This is the history of that development – a lavishly illustrated account of the men, the aircraft and the actions which have revolutionized the concept of warfare. Each chapter is devoted to an actual air battle, chosen to illustrate the many military roles which aircraft have played.

Among the operations described are those which have decisively altered the course of the war – the Stuka terror-bombing of Warsaw; the Battle of Britain. Others, less well known, are recounted in exciting detail – the destruction of Gestapo headquarters by Mosquito squadrons; the dreadful sacrifice of the Japanese Kamikaze pilots. In these actions the names of famous planes stand out – Hurricane; Messerschmitt; Zero; Flying Fortress; MiG and Sabre – names that live on in legend.

This is a book which conveys the special nature of air battles. Battles no less horrible than others, but fought at lightning pace above the clouds, where death strikes in the blinking of an eye. Vividly, in words and pictures, this book captures the 'feel' of those conflicts – the courage and the horrors, the men and the machines, the planning and the actions, which make up the history of war in the air.

CONTENTS

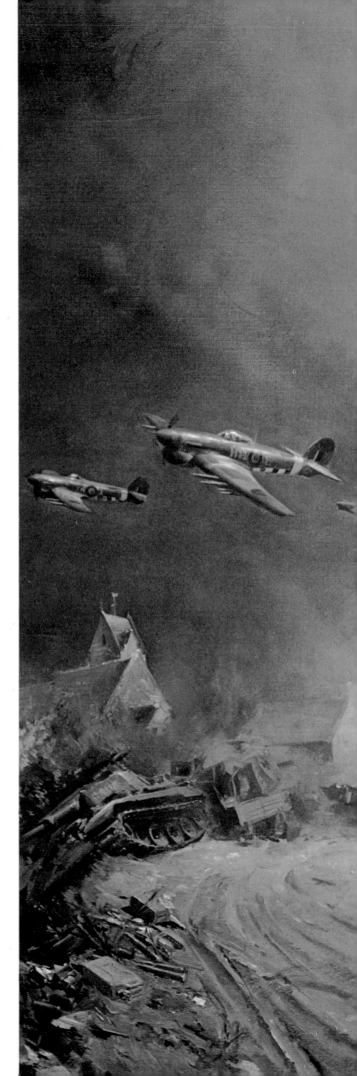

ZEPPELIN RAID

Zeppelin raids on Britain provoked a horrified outcry which was out of all proportion to the damage they caused. Relatively immune from ground-fire and able to out-climb aeroplanes, they bombed London with impunity. The outraged population demanded that the RFC strike back.

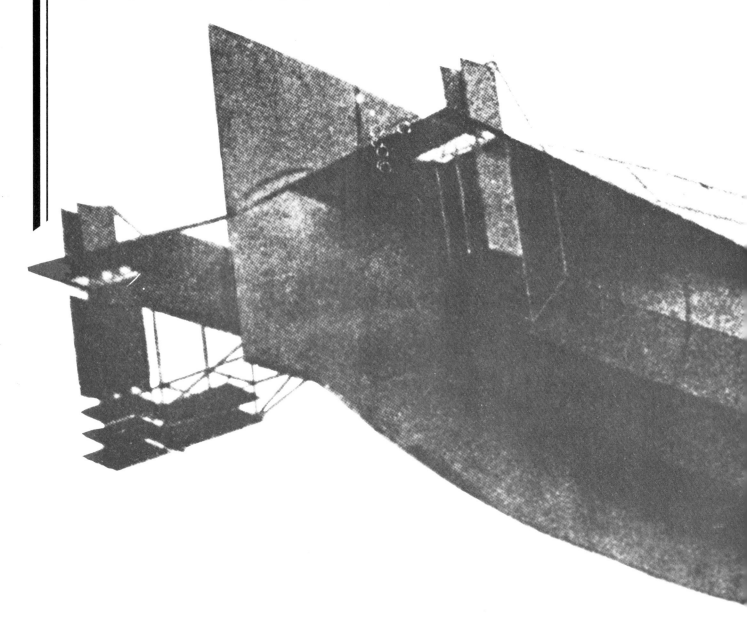

Like a gigantic prehistoric monster, a German Zeppelin lifts slowly from its mooring and gains height for its mission across the Channel. When Zeppelins first appeared over London they caused an uproar in a civilian population whose morale was already dented by the massive casualties sustained in France.

The weekend had been unbearably hot, but towards evening on Sunday, 6 June 1916, a brisk cold front advanced from the Atlantic and caused a rapid condensation in the heavy, humid atmosphere. By evening the whole of southern England shivered in a sudden cold snap and, as night fell, mist shrouded the Channel and brought shipping to a halt.

No light shone along the east coast of England for fear of aiding the German Zeppelins. A black-out had been in force since the first raid over Norfolk in January. Gun crews shivered in the isolated emplacements that were dotted about eastern England, and since the raid on London, only a week before, the ground defences around the capital had been increased. A few second-grade corvettes and light cruisers, armed with anti-aircraft guns, stood in the Thames to guard the eastern approaches.

At 10pm in a small upstairs room of a house on the Norfolk coast, an amateur radio enthusiast named Russel Clarke picked up some halting Morse signals on his home-made short-wave receiver.

Clarke, a barrister, adjusted his earphones and fine-tuned the frequency. The dots and dashes went on for a time, then stopped. Then, after a time, there came more – from somewhere closer. He took off his earphones and hurried downstairs to the telephone. He rang the Admiralty and gave them the frequency.

Clarke's message was received almost thirty minutes before one from the Navy's own listening station at Hunstanton, by which time the controller at Whitehall was already plotting the movement of an enemy Zeppelin force, assisted by stations and ships on the other side of the Channel.

Shortly after 11pm, Whitehall signalled the information to Commander Arthur Longmore, the officer commanding the RNAS at Dunkirk, and instructed him to alert his crews for possible action.

The course taken by the Zeppelins was carefully plotted, and at 12.45am on Monday, 7 April, Longmore took action both to intercept the Zeppelins and to shadow them back over the enemy lines and destroy their bases.

The hunters . . .

A few minutes later, Lieutenants Alexander Warneford and John Rose hurried across the mist-shrouded field to two Morane-Saulnier Parasols. As soon as they were in the cockpits, the ground crewmen swung the propellers and the engines spluttered into life, then settled down to a blasting roar. Presently, the two sturdy little monoplanes were jolting across the field. They turned into wind, throttled up to full boost, and sped through the grey-black darkness, climbing towards Ghent.

Two minutes later, Lieutenants John Wilson and John Mills climbed into their larger Farman bombers and took off in the wake of the fighters.

...and the hunted

The three Zeppelins moved slowly across the Straits of Dover at 12,000 feet – three huge, grey pencil-like forms nosing above the swirling mist which shrouded the whole of the coastline west of Flanders.

Each of the monsters was an army airship 536 feet in length; its cotton fabric envelope was painted a metallic grey and marked with a large black cross beneath its sharply pointed nose. Powered by four heavy-duty Maybach engines, it was slow in level flight, but, by discharging its water-ballast, it could out-climb any aeroplane, nosing upwards vertically at over 1,200 feet a minute to a height of 23,000 feet. It was armed with five machine-guns – two in each gondola and one in the turret on top of the hull – and it had a bomb-load capacity of almost 1,000lb.

Tonight, each of the three Zeppelins was carrying five 110lb bombs and fifty 7lb incendiaries originally intended for London.

The flight was commanded by Germany's newest hero, Captain Erich Linnartz, the veteran Zeppelin commander who, only a week ago, had bombed the British capital, inspiring German newspapers to declaim:

'England is no longer an island! At last, the long-yearned-for punishment has befallen England, this people of liars, cynics and hypocrites, a punishment for its countless sins of the past. It is neither blind hatred nor raging anger that inspires our airship heroes, but a religious humility at being chosen the instrument of God's wrath. . . .'

Captain Linnartz's Zeppelin LZ-38, with a crew of three officers and sixteen men, had lifted off from the new Zeppelin base near Brussels late that afternoon. Shortly before dusk, over Bruges, it had rendezvoused with the two sister Zeppelins LZ-37 and LZ-39. After dark they had crossed the Belgian coast between the lighthouses of Ostend and Zeebrugge. Linnartz knew

from experience that a westerly course from here would take them to the outer mouth of the Thames.

The full moon was due to reach its zenith at midnight, when he had planned to arrive over London. But tonight, as they flew seaward, the mist thickened over the Channel and closed right in, bringing visibility to zero. They cut engines and drifted for a time, hoping to find the bottom lip of the Thames estuary, from whence they would turn due west past Herne Bay.

As they drifted over the Straits of Dover, anxiously working out their position, a Morse message came from base:

Terminal weather unsuitable. Cancel mission.

They turned east towards France, and a further message came through:

At your discretion, strike alternative target.

The Zeppelin strike force altered course slightly towards Calais, while Linnartz studied his

Right Zeppelin crews were exposed to the elements during bombing raids and suffered more from exposure than from enemy air attack or ground-fire.

Below Ground-crew manhandle a Zeppelin to its launch position in preparation for take-off. Other flight-crew occupy machine gun positions on top of the gondola.

maps to locate the position of the secondary target – an important rail junction behind the British front.

The prey is sighted

Warneford and Rose kept in visual contact for a time, their two little monoplanes flying wing to wing south-west towards Calais. Warneford's sleek red and grey Morane-Saulnier was brand new, straight from the French factory a week ago. He'd fitted a rack beneath the fuselage to hold his bombs, and an improvised bomb-release, worked by pulling a cable that had been threaded through a hole in the cockpit floor. While he was waiting for take-off, his mechanic had loaded six 20lb bombs into the rack.

Suddenly, Rose was wobbling his wings to draw his colleague's attention. Warneford saw him give the distress signal and immediately tilt over and disappear into darkness.

The lamp on Rose's instrument panel had gone out, and he found himself flying blind by sense of touch. He knew that as soon as he lost visual contact with Warneford he would be in trouble, so he tried to make it back to base alone.

There was thick fog covering the flax fields near Cassel, and Rose's plane hit the earth hard and turned over on its back. The pilot climbed out unhurt.

Alone now, Warneford flew on, peering through the foggy darkness for a sight of the grey wraith-like shape of a Zeppelin. The Moraine-Saulnier's engine was so noisy that there was no hope of hearing the airship's Maybachs. He circled, throttling back . . .

Suddenly, guns opened up below him, a little to the right. He guessed that they were two

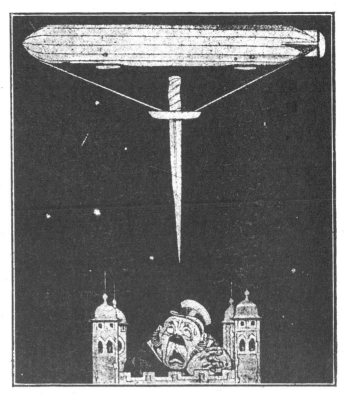

Left *A Naval Zeppelin bombs a fort on the southern English coast, while its crew look on. Such attacks were not pressed home with real zeal: usually, at the first sign of enemy ground-fire, the airship would drop its bombs at random and beat a speedy retreat.*

Right *The Zeppelin was a favourite subject of cartoonists during World War I. A German artist sees the giant airship as the ultimate weapon, suspended like the Sword of Damocles over a cowering John Bull. The British took a more jaundiced view of it.*

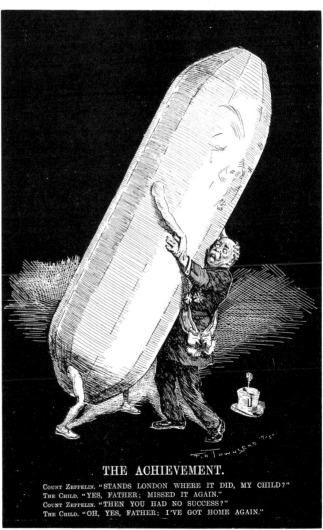

THE ACHIEVEMENT.

Count Zeppelin. "STANDS LONDON WHERE IT DID, MY CHILD?"
The Child. "YES, FATHER; MISSED IT AGAIN."
Count Zeppelin. "THEN YOU HAD NO SUCCESS?"
The Child. "OH, YES, FATHER; I'VE GOT HOME AGAIN."

particular German anti-aircraft guns his mates had warned him about. They were called Archibald and Cuthbert – high-velocity cannons which could hurl their shells to a height of 22,000 feet. They were firing at the sound of his engine. He cut the power and glided away and the noise of the gun-blasts faded behind him.

He flew on, hopefully anticipating the sight of the enemy, though he knew that his chances of seeing anything in this grey-black wall of mist were practically nil. He was now a few miles west of Ostend . . .

There it was! He couldn't believe his eyes. A great grey ghostly shape slid past his windshield and was nosing downwards ahead of him to port. He throttled back, keeping the long, glistening envelope in view, just following, not noting where he was being led.

It seemed to go on interminably. He stalked the eerie shape for almost an hour, staying as far behind as possible without losing him. A gusty head-wind had sprung up and he had trouble keeping up with the Zeppelin's four engines. The eastern sky was lit with an early pre-dawn glow and lightening with every minute. He had to stay out of gun-range as the LZ-37 began to lose height and nosed towards the distant Zeppelin base of Gontrode.

Suddenly a machine-gun chattered, and shells and tracer ripped past the Morane-Saulnier's wings. The gunner in the turret on the topside of the Zeppelin was blasting away at him to frighten him off. Lieutenant Rudolf von de Haegen, the LZ-37's master officer, grabbed up the intercom phone.

'What are you shooting at?' he demanded.

'An aeroplane,' the gunner said, 'Three hundred meters astern.'

Haegen alerted the four gondola gun-crews, and two of them opened up on the monoplane.

Warneford banked and climbed, keeping his distance, getting out of sight of the gondola gun-crews. He made a wide climbing circuit, content to bide his time, to watch for any sudden move, very aware of the Zeppelin's capacity to out-climb him.

Inferno in the sky

He let the minutes go by, content to stalk the monster, exhilarated at the chance of bagging such a prize with his pathetic bomb-load.

His chance came when Haegen suddenly put down the LZ-37's bow and headed for Gontrode, his four Maybach engines at full-throttle.

Warneford watched, bringing the Morane-Saulnier into position where he could turn and fly straight and level above the path of the diving airship. He throttled to bring his plane almost directly above – 900 feet above – then cut his power and dived in a tight spin, volplaning to within 150 feet, releasing his bombs and flattening away.

As he fled, frantically turning on full throttle to escape the blast, an enormous, jarring explosion rent the air and Warneford's midget monoplane was thrown up two hundred feet, whipping violently over on its back – the great Zeppelin had become a blinding ball of flame.

Private Roemer, the LZ-37's coxswain, felt the giant ship lurch, and the helm was ripped from his hands. He was skidding, almost flying across the sharply tilted deck, four other crew members with him. His head struck a metal upright and stunned him. He grasped it and held on. There was no-one else on the deck. They had all gone overboard.

Above him, the whole ship was a hissing, twisting, roaring inferno. He lay flat on the deck, the flames licking down on him, roasting him alive, as the deck fell and kept on falling. . . .

Warneford recovered, then circled, dazed, elated, trembling with shock and relief, as he watched the giant airship's dying minutes. There was a hissing roar as it threw off great ragged pieces of flaming debris. The huge envelope fell slowly to earth, twisting, contracting, writhing, shooting out bursts of coloured flame – red, blue, orange – lighting as bright as day the countryside around Mont-Saint-Amand.

The flaming forward section fell onto a dormitory of the Convent of St Elizabeth, the gondola crashing through the roof, setting fire to the building and killing two nuns and two orphan children and injuring many others.

Roemer, still alive, though terribly burned,

Right Zeppelin LZ 37 plunges earthwards engulfed in flames. To a war-weary Britain, Warneford's feat was a much-needed boost to a flagging morale. To the Germans, the disaster dealt a death-blow to their programme of Zeppelin raids on Britain. Increasingly, Gothas were used for long-range, heavy bombing.

felt himself somersaulting through the air, then blacked out. . . .

A black night for Zeppelins

Warneford was in trouble. The violent blast had knocked his fuel-line loose, and he knew he would have to make a forced landing behind enemy lines.

Thirty miles away, Lieutenants Wilson and Mills saw the glow as they were arriving over the big Zeppelin shed at Évère, where they had followed the LZ-38.

As their labouring Farmans roared across the target, the Zeppelin was already on the ground and being handled into its hangar.

Wilson banked in a wide turn to position his plane for a bombing run. Searchlights picked him up as he began his approach. On a sudden

inspiration he seized his flashlight and blinked it on and off through the wind-shield. The Germans held their fire.

In the confusion, Wilson and Mills made perfect runs over the hangar and dropped their bombs, which exploded through the iron roof with a clatter of sound and set the Zeppelin on fire. Linnartz and his crew escaped unhurt.

Meanwhile, Warneford had set his monoplane down safely in a clear patch of field. He quickly fixed his fuel-line with a piece of wire and took off again. But his engine was spluttering now and missing badly. In trying to urge some power out of it, he strayed off course in the deceptive half-light and lost his bearings.

After flying on for a time, trying to find his way, he turned north and headed for the coast, meeting the sea at Cap Griz Nez.

Realizing that he was thirty-five miles too far west, he banked and set course for Dunkirk. Then the engine cut out and he began to lose height quickly. He came down on a wide, flat stretch of wet sand left visible by the ebbing tide.

As daylight came he started to hitch-hike his way back to the squadron. He arrived back at noon and was welcomed by the cheers of his fellow pilots. Thirty six hours later he was awarded the Victoria Cross.

For Warneford, the next few days were a whirl as a grateful Parisian society lionised this daring young aviator. Mobbed by actresses, congratulated by George V, it is understandable if the hero of the hour did not think of the horrible fate of the crew of LZ-37. Only Roemer, thrown clear as the Zeppelin crashed, survived, and he would bear the hideous scars of his ordeal for the rest of his life.

In Germany, a shattered High Command analysed the disaster. So shocked were they by the loss of the two Zeppelins that they temporarily halted the army's airship raids. It was left to Captain Strasser's naval Zeppelins to make Germany's yearned-for, but abortive attempt to destroy London the following September.

Left Caught in the glare of searchlights, a Zeppelin seeks to escape the fire of anti-aircraft guns by jettisoning ballast – thus increasing its rate of climb.

Right Warneford's exploit was celebrated throughout Allied Europe. 'War Budget', a British propaganda magazine, bears a graphic illustration of the explosion which rent Zeppelin LZ 37.

THE
WAR
BUDGET
ILLUSTRATED

3D NET WEEKLY

FILMORE

FLYING CIRCUS

During the early years of World War I, superiority in the air see-sawed between the Allies and the Germans. By April 1917, the German Air-force, led by pilots such as Baron von Richthofen, seemed to have won complete dominance. It was a critical time for the Allied pilots.

There they came, gaining height over No Man's Land in a wide climbing sweep, the throaty roar of their primitive Mercedes-160 engines ripping the morning air. They were sleek-lined, V-strutted Albatros D IIIs – 20 of them – drawn from Germany's four crack hunting squadrons, led by Manfred von Richthofen.

There was something menacing in the sight of them. The Red Baron's machine was scarlet. The others in his legendary *Jasta* 11 were also red, but with individual markings: Allmenroder, a white tail; Schaefer, black tail and black elevators; Richthofen's brother Lothar, yellow strips. The rest of the planes in the awesome flying wedge had been painted in the whole spectrum of vivid colours, in every garish combination the Teutonic brain could conjure up.

Far beneath Richthofen's flight lay a section of the Western Front. They could see the lines of the great battle that had been raging since Easter Monday. Ragged puffs of white smoke told them where the enemy's barrage shells were

Aerial combat during World War I tended to be rather undisciplined. Each pilot fought for himself, seeking to build up a higher 'score' than his comrades.

bursting. The ground on both sides of the zig-zag lines of trenches was dark brown where it had been churned up by the heavy shelling of the past few weeks.

There was plenty of activity this morning. The British artillery was blasting a barrage all along the front, the greatest fire being concentrated near Arras and Vimy Ridge. Allied planes were operating with the guns, ranging them on the German lines. There were Martinsydes, Spads, Bristols, Sopwiths, Nieuports, RE8s, FE2s. . . .

Schaefer saw them first. He pointed below. The leader looked down and saw a flight of British planes. They were FE2s of 57 Squadron and Sopwith Pups of 3 (Naval) Squadron. Richthofen gave the signal to attack and the formation dived to intercept.

As they dived their minds were blank of everything but the action to come. Certainly they did not think that this attack was to herald a new concept in aerial warfare. For this was the first encounter by history's first *Jagdgruppe* – a fearsome flying Armada with enormous fire-power, against which no enemy machine operating singly could hope to survive. It was the last day of Bloody April 1917.

The bloodiest month

During the month, 316 British aviators had been killed or posted missing – one third of the flying strength of the Royal Flying Corps' 50 squadrons facing the Germans on the mainland of Europe.

Up till now, British machines had proved scandalously inadequate, and no match for Richthofen's Albatroses, with their raked wings, oval tail-plane and shark-like bodies. In fact, at least 50 of the Red Baron's personal 'kill' of 80 had been two-seater 'crocks', most of which were obsolescent and suicidal to fly. Had there been more twin-gun SE5s or French Nieuport 17s in service, the alarming ratio of German victories – over four to one – would have been considerably less.

As it was, by April 1917 the RFC's turnover of pilots and planes had reached the point where 18-year-old pilots, with only 10 hours solo experience, were sent into battle against German flying machines which could out-fly them and out-gun them.

Yet there seemed no end to the reservoir of British pilots, nor to the RFC's BE2s, FE2s

and RE8s. With the Allies and Huns locked in the bloody Battle of Arras, with appalling casualties in the trenches, Field Marshal Haig was calling on the Royal Flying Corps for a still greater effort. For its planes were needed now more than ever – for artillery spotting, bombing, photography and reconnaissance. The obsolete BE2s and RE8s were crossing the lines in increasing numbers, despite the appalling losses.

Yet despite their superiority in the air, the German high command wanted complete domination of the skies and to this end had conceived a new strategy. Now the time had come to put it into effect. They planned to introduce a new offensive element into aerial warfare – the *Jagdgruppe*.

This was a powerful formation of bombers and fighters which, because of its assembled fire-power, would be able to destroy any opposition the Allies could offer. Thus, with complete control of the skies, it would be able to sweep unhindered behind the enemy lines and bomb airfields, installations and grounded planes.

Such a strategy, they reasoned, would result in crippling the Allied air strength once and for all.

Thus it was on April 30, with the RFC reeling from the month's calamitous losses, the *Luftstreitkrafte* assembled 20 Albatros D IIIs of *Jastas* 11, 10, 6 and 4 – later to become known as *Jagdgeschwader* I (Richthofen's Circus) – and sent them up from Douai aerodrome to clear the skies over Arras.

Dog-fight

The seven British machines should have been cut down in the opening seconds by the formation's 40 Spandau machine-guns. But the technique of holding tight formation while bringing to bear a withering cross-fire had not yet been developed. The German formation wavered awkwardly, some planes crowding their neighbours.

The British pilots saw them coming and split up to make individual attacks. But not before three FE2s had taken hits, one by Lothar von

Left The Circus comes to town. German squadrons were highly mobile units which were transferred from place to place as they were needed. They came to be called Circuses because of the temporary camps which sprang up wherever they were based.

Richthofen. The Sopwiths came in, their Lewis guns spitting fire. The German flight floundered. Some of the planes stalled. Others dived out of danger.

Two of the FE2s were spiralling down out of control. The other was limping back across the lines with a wounded pilot and a dying navigator.

It took the Germans several minutes to regroup and form up again. East of Douai nine Halberstadts joined them, and with this greatly increased fire-power the formation continued its patrol.

Richthofen saw a ragged group of five British triplanes and six Bristol fighters reconnoitring the new trench positions. He signalled the attack.

This time the British pilots had time to manoeuvre. As the *Jagdgruppe* bore down on them, the Bristols scattered and came at the flight from all directions, their frontal guns chattering.

Once again the Germans broke and scattered, and it was every man for himself, with machines whirling, spinning, rolling all over the sky. It went on for minutes. Then three SE5s of 56 Squadron joined the battle. A few seconds later one of the Halberstadts fell out of the *mêlée*, turning over and over like a dead leaf. Then another stood on its tail, stalled and fell away. One of the SE5s dived out of control, pouring black smoke.

In those two short encounters the whole theory of the *Jagdgruppe* was cast into doubt. Perhaps it was because the German pilots had learned too well that the name of the game was 'kill or be killed'. In those early days of aerial warfare, every man was a lone wolf, with ambitions to become another Richthofen. The personal tally was the thing.

At any rate, from this point on, the battle reverted to the old-style dog-fight, with individual duels happening all over the sky.

The lone wolf

The Canadian ace, Major W A ('Bill') Bishop, entered the battle at this point. In the 53 days

Right A German Albatros swoops down on a flight of fighter bombers high over the Western Front. It was the Albatros which dominated the aerial war in 1916.

since his return from flying school in England, he had shot down 22 HAs (hostile aircraft), and he and his sleek silver Nieuport 17 were fast becoming a legend over the Western Front.

Just before 1000 hours, Bishop had taken off, leading C Flight of 60 Squadron. Wedged into the cockpits of their tiny French-built Nieuports, they had climbed at full bore in a wide arc over Lens, to level out at 10,000 feet and get their bearings.

Now, far below, they saw two British DH4s patrolling the German trench system. One of Bishop's men waved frantically, pointing downwards. Bishop looked quickly in that direction and saw four red Albatroses of Richthofen's squadron bearing down on the DH4s. Bishop signalled the attack.

Each man picked his target and dived. Bishop pushed down the stick and gave his Le Rhone engine full throttle. The little plane reacted so sharply that the fuselage went beyond the vertical point. He felt himself falling inside the cockpit and the next moment struck his head against the windscreen. There was a blur, and panic swept him as he fired his gun then pulled back the stick. The Nieuport gradually righted itself and levelled out.

The Hun had vanished and so had the rest of his patrol. He looked quickly about the sky, banked to cover his tracks and make sure there wasn't a Hun on his tail. Then he swung west and climbed. Altitude, get altitude, was the first rule.

He got up to 8,000 feet and almost immediately saw two enemy bombers making a run over the Allied artillery positions. They were mammoths— the huge three-seater Gothas which soon would be launched against London. He'd never seen them on the Western Front before. He closed in on them from behind, now a little below their flight line. As he drew closer they seemed to grow to monstrous proportions, and he felt, as he wrote later, 'like a mosquito chasing a wasp'.

They had seen him.

One of the Gothas banked around in a slow spiral to get at him. Bishop turned with him, under him, as he came around, trying to stay in the German pilot's 'blind spot'.

Suddenly there were bullets coming at him. The second Gotha was diving at him from a slight angle, its three machine-guns rattling.

Below Von Richthofen, the most famous of all combat pilots, lands his Fokker DR1 Triplane after a raid on Allied territory. His room was decorated with the remains of aircraft he had shot down.

Richthofen's score

Through the chances of war, all but one of the aircraft Richthofen was officially credited with shooting down were British (the exception was a Belgian Spad). As with all aces, most of his victims were reconnaissance, not fighter aircraft. The drawings below illustrate the full tally of 20 types of Allied aircraft that fell to Richthofen.

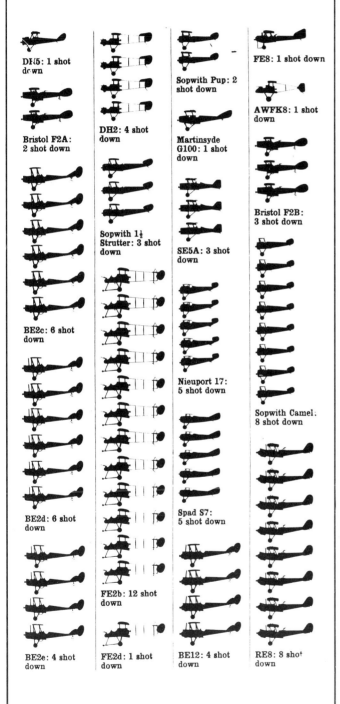

DH5: 1 shot down

Bristol F2A: 2 shot down

BE2c: 6 shot down

BE2d: 6 shot down

BE2e: 4 shot down

Sopwith Pup: 2 shot down

DH2: 4 shot down

Sopwith 1½ Strutter: 3 shot down

FE2b: 12 shot down

FE2d: 1 shot down

Martinsyde G100: 1 shot down

Nieuport 17: 5 shot down

Spad S7: 5 shot down

BE12: 4 shot down

FE8: 1 shot down

AWFK8: 1 shot down

Bristol F2B: 3 shot down

SE5A: 3 shot down

Sopwith Camel: 8 shot down

RE8: 8 shot down

Bishop dived, let the giant plane pass overhead, then pulled his nose up under the belly of the first Gotha and opened fire.

His gun had jammed! There was no time to do anything about it. He looped out of trouble, rolled and flattened out. He banged at the gun with the heel of his hand, then tugged at the cocking device. It wouldn't budge.

There was no option. He swung west and made for base. He was out of the fight. He flew back, cursing all the way at having to let the two giant Gothas get away.

First kill

It took only a few minutes for the mechanics to fix the wire cocking device known as 'Nicod's gadget', and Bishop was back in the air south of Lens by 1100 hours.

Eight minutes later, he spotted three two-seater German planes about two miles away and a

Above A group of German 'Aces'. From left to right they are Testner, Schafer, Baron von Richthofen, Lothar von Richthofen and Kurt Wolf. To qualify for the title of 'Ace', a pilot had to shoot down five enemy planes.

Left Von Richthofen's 'score'. The 'Red Baron' celebrated his victories by ordering an engraved silver cup to mark each kill: eventually he stopped the practice as it was proving too expensive.

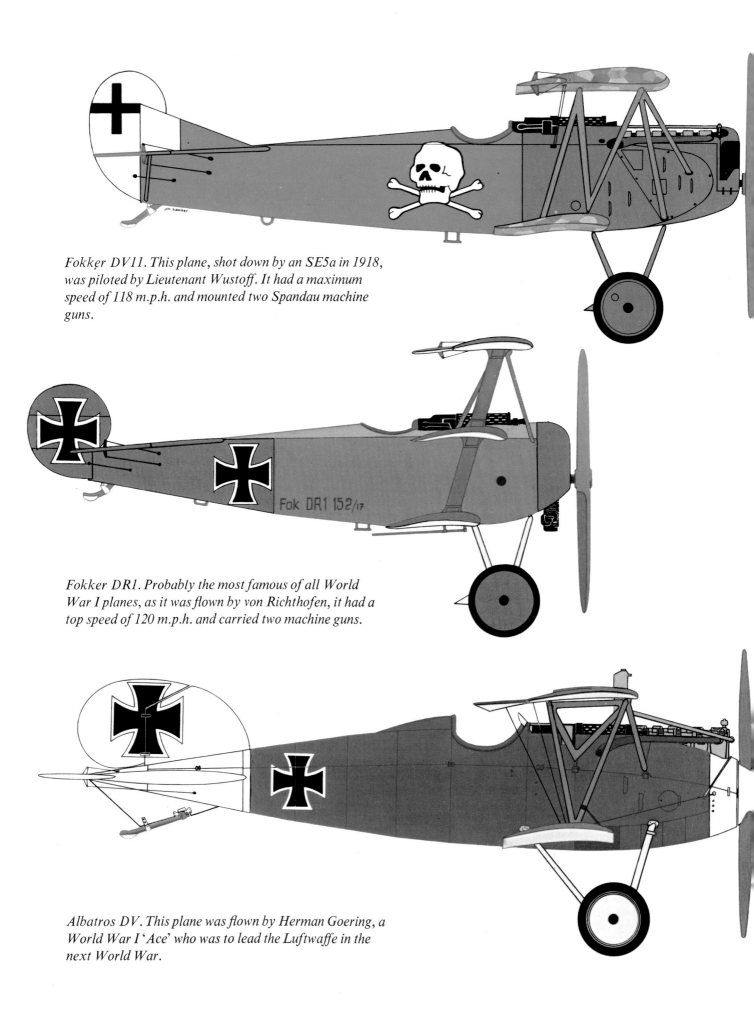

Fokker DV11. This plane, shot down by an SE5a in 1918, was piloted by Lieutenant Wustoff. It had a maximum speed of 118 m.p.h. and mounted two Spandau machine guns.

Fokker DR1. Probably the most famous of all World War I planes, as it was flown by von Richthofen, it had a top speed of 120 m.p.h. and carried two machine guns.

Albatros DV. This plane was flown by Herman Goering, a World War I 'Ace' who was to lead the Luftwaffe in the next World War.

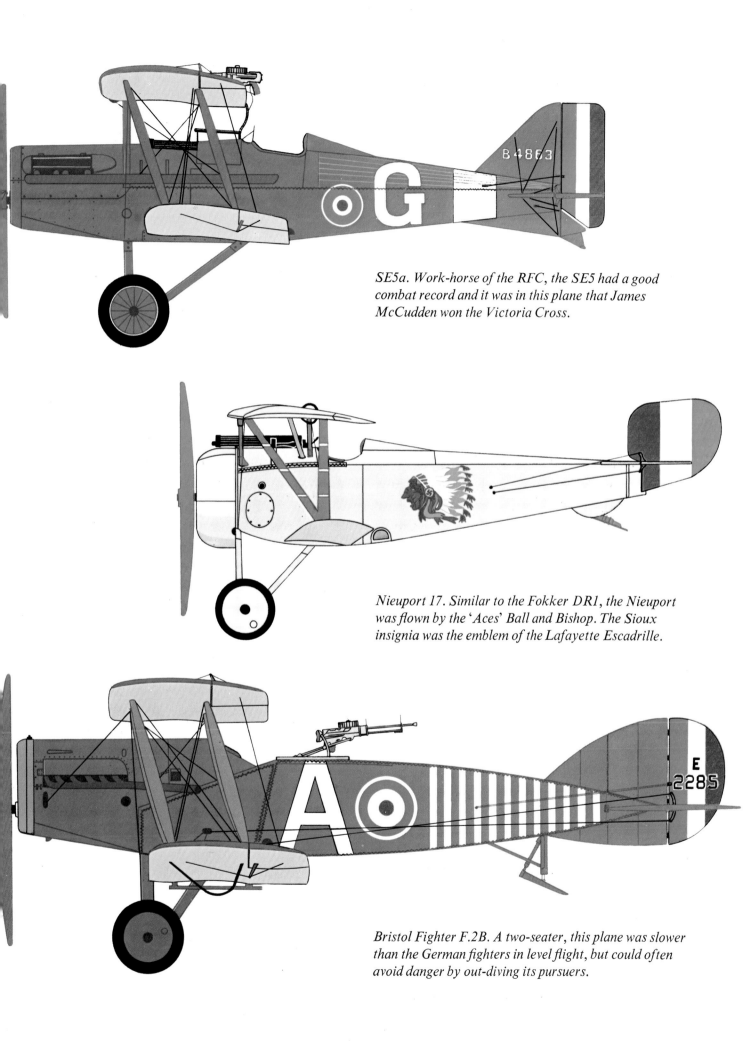

SE5a. Work-horse of the RFC, the SE5 had a good combat record and it was in this plane that James McCudden won the Victoria Cross.

Nieuport 17. Similar to the Fokker DR1, the Nieuport was flown by the 'Aces' Ball and Bishop. The Sioux insignia was the emblem of the Lafayette Escadrille.

Bristol Fighter F.2B. A two-seater, this plane was slower than the German fighters in level flight, but could often avoid danger by out-diving its pursuers.

little below him. They appeared to be spotting for the German artillery. He got the nearest one in his sights and opened fire.

But suddenly he was in trouble. He'd begun firing too early, warning the enemy, and the three planes banked to face him, all guns rattling. He found himself in a cross-fire from three Spandaus.

Miraculously he flew through the hail of bullets in his first pass. He banked around to find that the three two-seaters had turned away and flew after them.

Just in time he saw the trap they had led him into. Five scarlet Albatros D IIIs led by Richthofen, were waiting to pounce and they swarmed down on him. He banked violently, rolled and levelled out, split-arsing away and pouring on the power to get height.

That had been close, and Bishop cursed himself for almost falling for the trap laid by the two-seaters. He continued climbing until he was well above the red Scouts, gradually getting himself into position for an attack. He dived to intercept them, firing at the last second.

The Albatros pilots waited for him to pass through their formation so that they could get him in their sights. But just before he reached their level he pulled the Nieuport's nose up and zoomed out of range. He repeated this manoeuvre three times, giving the Germans no chance of returning his fire. They scattered and left him alone.

Bishop gained more height in the hope of spotting the two Gothas again, but they were nowhere to be seen. At 1115 hours, south of Lens, at 8,000 feet, he saw two Halberstadts on artillery observation and banked round in a gentle arc to intercept them.

Waiting till the last second, he dived on the nearest Hun, giving a burst of 20 rounds. The plane's observer opened fire almost simultaneously and his bullets ripped through the Nieuport's strutting. Bishop pressed home the attack as the second Halberstadt banked round to meet him almost head-on. Bishop passed over him and banked sharply, to see the first machine slip violently to one side, then stand on its nose and go into a spin.

Bishop turned to attack the second machine. The German dived away. Bishop followed, finishing his drum into him. The HA continued diving eastwards and got away.

Bishop levelled out and watched the other Halberstadt spiral down to earth and explode in a ragged stab of flame. He flew south, calmly re-arming his frontal guns ready for the next encounter.

It came at 1125 hours, east of Monchy, at 6,000 feet. He saw five of Richthofen's fighters chasing two BE2s and made one long pass at them, firing 20 rounds without result.

Then at 1130, east of Wancourt, at 5,000 feet, he saw two more Halberstadts doing artillery observation and attacked the leading plane head-on.

As they closed on each other – at an aggregate speed of something over 200 miles an hour – they each opened fire.

The German's bullets ripped through the Nieuport's struts not three feet from Bishop, and Bishop's tracers streaked into the HA's engine. At the last instant they pulled away, the Halberstadt diving sharply, Bishop's plane flashing above it.

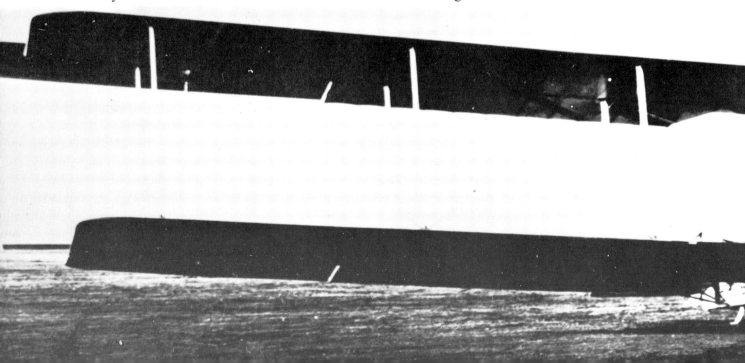

After banking round and levelling out, Bishop saw the German plane some distance away, still going down in a long glide, apparently under control. There was no sign of any smoke. Bishop followed, watching him. It had been the Canadian's closest shave in almost a hundred encounters. He wondered how the German was feeling. He turned west. He had very little ammunition left by now. And he was hungry.

He took part in two more skirmishes before landing safely back at base in time for lunch.

A dubious strategy

During the afternoon, Allied bombers pockmarked Epinoy aerodrome, unchallenged except by German anti-aircraft batteries. At Lozingham, enemy bombers which blasted the aerodrome were chased by Naval fighters which later shot down five of 12 Albatroses which they jumped during an attack on two RE8s.

On the day's air-fighting, the odds were about even. But strategically the RFC had won through – by containing the enemy and proving his *Jagdgruppe* theory to be unworkable.

Bloody April proved to be the turning point. In May and June, 757 British machines reached France and the picture changed. British losses

Right Major W. Bishop, *VC, DSO, MC, signs an autograph before returning home in 1918.*

Below A Gotha G5 heavy bomber. After the failure of the Zeppelins to carry the War to England, the huge Gothas were the mainstay of the German bombing offensive.

dropped by 61 and the Germans' rose by 73 for the month of June. By the end of the half-year, the Allies were able to claim 1401 hostile aircraft and 52 kite balloons destroyed, compared with the enemy's claim of 955 aircraft and 45 kite balloons destroyed.

Yet, despite the lessons of April 30, the German high command persisted with its *Jagdgruppe* obsession, using larger formations led by Manfred von Richthofen. But the Circus's inexperience in mass manoeuvre continued to invite disaster, and the concept of fighter support for bombers found no unanimity. Certainly, an escort was vital. But how close to the bombers should it fly? The experience over Arras in 1917 should have influenced the *Luftwaffe's* strategic thinking 22 years later, when it sent its mass-formations of Heinkels and Dorniers over Britain, surrounded by a 'beehive' of Messerschmitts.

STUKA!

Stuka dive-bombers, born in the hell of the Spanish Civil War, were an essential weapon of the blitzkrieg. *In August 1939, as German forces prepared to unleash the attack on Poland, Stuka units were entrusted with the first vital missions of World War II.*

On the night of 31 August 1939, the long flat airfield was covered with patches of fog. The ghostly skeletal shapes of aircraft stood like dozing dinosaurs around the low, squat line of hangars and administration buildings.

The airbase was the scene of quiet unhurried activity, of black figures moving in and out of the beams of truck lights, as maintenance crews serviced the aircraft, armed them up with fragmentation bombs fitted to racks on the sloping struts, and fueled them from the tankers. Each plane had a black cross on its fuselage and wings, and a rakish, fixed trouser-type undercarriage. They were the ugly gull-winged Junkers Ju 87Bs of *Luftflotte 1*, under the command of General Kesselring.

Since sundown, all along the border, the night had been filled with rumblings of tanks and armoured trucks coming into position, odd clangings of steel on steel, and distant sounds of shunting trains.

Despite rumours and intelligence reports of German troop concentrations, few in Poland believed that war would break out. Nobody doubted for a moment that Great Britain and France would keep their pledge to help Poland if Germany attacked, and they thought that Hitler was mounting his greatest bluff, that he would not risk a European war. However, during 31 August, Poland belatedly began to mobilize her troops to prepare for the threat.

Preparations for war

At 0330 hours on 1 September, a long row of dimmed headlights came through the fog and exhaust fumes along the winding road from the barracks. Before long, *Luftwaffe* command cars and crew trucks were pulling in before a low flat building near the tarmac.

Among the first groups to enter the briefing room for last minute orders and weather reports and a cup of hot coffee, were six men who comprised the crews of three dive-bombers of *3rd Gruppe* of *Stukegeschwader 1*. The leader of this *kette* was Hauptmann Bruno Dilley.

More and more Stuka crews filed in as vehicles

Left Stuka dive-bombers first saw action in the Spanish Civil War, when they demonstrated their power to strike at mobile targets and terrorize the ground troops.

continued to arrive. They grouped themselves in tight little knots around their leaders. The atmosphere in the long narrow room was buoyant. All depth-briefings had taken place a few hours before. Now, pilots and navigator-gunners were concerning themselves with changed flight-plans because of the closed-in weather all along the Eastern Front.

At 0410, Dilley's group fastened on their helmets, checked their parachute harnesses and filed out of the building. On the tarmac they split into pairs and walked to their aircraft, where ground-crew men were standing by to give them a hand aboard.

One by one the Jumo 211D engines burst into life, and the tarmac area was shattered by a deafening roar. The three Ju 87Bs stood motionless for a time except for the bucking of the wings and tailplane as the bombers, locked by their airbrakes, resisted the pull of the whirling propellers.

Dilley's plane moved forward with a jerk and began to jolt across the field in the direction of the airstrip. Fifty yards behind him came the second plane, then further back still came the third member of the flight.

They reached the end of the field and swung round to face upwind, up the runway, positioned in line astern. Their engines roared to a crescendo. Dilley released his brakes and the Stuka began its rush down the runway, quickly gathering speed. The second plane began to move, following him, then the third. One by one they swept up in a surge of power and cleared the trees and the low ridge of hills into the darkness. The take-off was at 0426.

Once above the clouds the sky was clear. There was no moon and the whole of the eastern horizon was lit by the dull pink glow of dawn. Dilley's navigator slid open the Stuka's side-screen. A cold blast of air whipped into the cabin, carrying with it the suddenly deepening roar of the engine. He looked down to get his bearings, but most of the countryside was covered in cloud. He looked at the stars and checked his compass, then slid the screen shut. After a few seconds he made a slight adjustment to his course. He opened his microphone and spoke a few words into the intercom. The pilot acknowledged, then switched over to radio telephone and spoke to the two other pilots in the flight. They checked in and altered course with him. Dilley pressed the stick forward and

throttled back. The three Stukas sank slowly through the clouds. Dilley turned his instrument lighting down low to minimise distraction. Down, down they swept, crossing the border at 0431.

Attack at dawn

The altimeter subsided slowly around its little glass dial as Dilley's plane came down in a smooth sweep of controlled power and the land came up at him. The other two Stukas hung close behind. He raised his plane a fraction to skim over a low wooded hill. They followed like a double shadow. Now they were hedge-hopping toward the low-lying valley of the Vistula. The navigator was 'right on'. There was the river lying diagonally across their path like a gleaming riband of pink glass. They banked sharply to get in line with it, turning north.

The target was the twin bridges at Dirschau. Their mission was not to destroy them, but to *save* them. The German High Command knew that once the Panzers crossed the border, the Poles would demolish the Dirschau and other bridges in an effort to buy time. An armoured train, carrying units of the German shock troops, was due to cross the border at 0450, the moment

Right *In 1939, the Polish military machine was no match for the mechanised might of the Wehrmacht. It possessed few armoured or motorized divisions.*

when armoured groups from west Germany, Czechoslovakia and East Prussia would roll into Poland.

The daring Stuka mission was aimed at preventing the Poles from destroying the bridges across the Vistula before the armoured train could arrive.

To do this, it was necessary to knock out the detonator charges the Poles would have placed along the banks, and which would be wired to explosives fixed to the bridge supports. It had been reasoned that the Stuka, armed with fragmentation bombs, was the ideal weapon.

It was a hazardous mission for which hand-picked crews had been training for several weeks at Insterburg airfield. Dilley and three other pilots had even visited Dirschau by train to make a first-hand inspection of the bridges and the surrounding terrain, and particularly of the approach from the south.

The *kette* leader had realized at once that it was not a dive-bombing mission, for which the Stukas had been built and for which the pilots had been trained. No, this had to be low-level bombing while flying straight and level. Great precision was required if the strike was to be effective; therefore the Stukas would have to fly at the lowest possible level and drop their bombs at the very last instant.

At 0435, the three Stuka pilots saw the twin bridges rushing towards them. At full throttle the Jumo engines wound up to a wailing scream as the planes flattened out to thirty feet and swept towards the target.

They released their bombs to straddle the shelving river banks and the row of shacks that lay at the foot of the bridges, then zoomed up over the bridges and away.

The bombs exploded in a flat crackle of blasts. Ragged splashes of flame stabbed the darkness and threw the gaunt understructures of the bridges into spectral relief against the sky, and lit the base of the low-hung clouds.

It was all over – so quickly – leaving the surrounding countryside in a quaking silence. Then men began to cry out in alarm. Somewhere a dog barked. A whistle sounded. Some buildings on the shore had caught fire.

The three Stukas, now above the clouds, headed for home, Dilley and his crews feeling justifiably proud at having been entrusted with the first bombing mission of World War II.

They had every confidence that their mission had been carried out successfully, and indeed it had. The Stukas had succeeded in severing the leads to the detonators. What they didn't know was that the Poles, even now, were putting in place fresh leads with which they would destroy one of the bridges before the German armoured train arrived.

Blitzkrieg weapon

In the first strike of the war, the Stuka had demonstrated its accuracy in low-level attacks.

But its greatest asset was to be seen a little later on that same day, as it had been demonstrated in Spain – its power to terrorize a civilian population and to destroy the morale of enemy troops.

During the Spanish Civil War, in which Germany supported the Nationalists, enemy soldiers subjected to Stuka dive-bombing were found to be paralysed with terror and put into a state of stupor. General Ernst Udet, the founder of the Stuka, conceived the idea of multiplying the effect – increasing the natural howl of the power dive – by building a siren into the leg of the landing gear. This simple device had a devastating effect on anyone being attacked – especially in combination with the roar of the engines and the blast of exploding bombs.

Even the appearance of the Stuka was frightening as its ungainly black shape hurtled out of the sky with its banshee wail – which *Luftwaffe* pilots had gleefully christened 'The Trombones of Jericho'. The lines of its gull-shaped wings had been coarsened for mass-production, and for the same reason it had fixed landing gear, to which ugly cantilever fairings were fixed over the main legs. With its high vertical tail-fin it was indeed a nightmare of a machine.

But its uses went far beyond the psychological. The Stuka was a vital element in the German army's new *blitzkrieg* technique. Its deadly accuracy in attacking bridges, grounded aircraft, shipping, gun batteries and troop trains gave the Poles no chance of mounting a counter-offensive against the German's 15 Panzer divisions. With control of the air almost after the first day, the Stukas were a major instrument for destroying vital objectives in the heart of the enemy's industrial centres.

There were 219 Ju 87B dive-bombers on the Eastern Front, and during the days that followed they pulverized the Polish defenders in surprise attacks far ahead of the lines. Swiftly following the ebb and flow of the land battle, they were brought in at the crucial moment in their screaming dives and pin-point bombing.

On the first day of the war, 120 Stukas attacked Poland's tiny naval units and harbour installations. They sank the destroyer *Mazur* at

Left *Like avenging angels of death, Stukas peel off to attack a ground target. In battle, their main role was to soften up enemy armour and disrupt communications.*

Below *Los (Elk) bombers were the only modern bombers which Poland possessed in 1939, and these were destroyed within the first few days of the invasion.*

Gdynia and damaged submarines *Rys* and *Sep*. They also sank the gunboats *General Haller* and *Kommandant Pilsudski*, and minesweepers *Czajka, Czapla, Jasolka, Mewa, Rybitwa, Zuraw* and several auxiliaries. After the attack the Polish Navy ceased to exist.

But the real horror of the war for Poland was still to come. If the Dirschau strike had been the Curtain-Raiser, the mass bombing of Warsaw was to become Act One of a horrendous tragedy and a heroic struggle.

The horror of Warsaw

Almost before the sun rose that morning, the people of Warsaw awoke to the sound of aircraft over the city. They were German reconnaissance planes, and Polish fighters took off to engage them. The German planes fled. At 0900 a second wave came over. They were Dorniers and Heinkels, and they dropped bombs on the centre of the city – both incendiary and high explosive. Once again the Polish fighters went up to intercept them and a brief dogfight ensued before the bombers left. The raids continued throughout the day.

Dilley was back in the air during the afternoon when his Stuka squadron attacked Warsaw's radio stations at Babice and Lacy, but their bombs failed to destroy the huge concrete-embedded masts.

The attacks on the city continued day after day. On Monday, 4 September, the muttering of distant guns could be heard, and by the end of the week the German Army had fought its way to within five miles of the city, which by now had been turned into a well-defended fortress by the determined Polish Army.

Above Nobody could call the Stuka – properly named the Junkers Ju 87 – an elegant plane. Its coarse lines were deliberately designed for mass production.

Right A Stuka releases its bombs after a near vertical dive. Throughout the early years of the War this was a terrifying sight on every battle-front; then Allied fighters demonstrated how vulnerable the Stuka was.

The Germans pushed on east, surrounding the city, but they dared not leave such a strong-point in their rear. They dropped leaflets appealing to the people to abandon the capital and threatened to lay waste the city, regardless of the fate of civilians, unless it surrendered by the night of 17 September.

In answer, General Czuma and the Mayor refused the demand and ordered 100,000 men to entrench themselves and to be prepared to defend the city street by street and building by building. The Mayor broadcast a moving appeal for help to the peoples of the civilized world.

Goering ordered Richthofen (a relative of the World War 1 fighter ace, and now commanding a Stuka group) to smash the city's morale, and from this moment the German raids became more frequent and more violently destructive. Over 1,000 civilians were killed each day in the almost continuous bombardment. Churches, hospitals, power stations, and finally the water-works were destroyed. Hospitals, schools and churches were full of maimed humanity – of shattered skulls, broken limbs, torn chests and gaping stomachs. Hundreds of corpses lay on the streets and pavements and wreckage was everywhere. Warsaw was burning. And the procession of walking wounded was an agonized and unending march of death.

STUKA!

Below German stormtroopers mount an attack on Polish troops who have entrenched themselves in Gdansk's central Post Office. Resistance was severe and the German troops were forced to call up an air-strike of Stukas before the position was taken. There was little defence against the dive-bombers. Polish fighter squadrons had been annihilated during the first days of the War, and the burden of defence fell to badly-equipped anti-aircraft units which had received little training.

By now, Russia had entered the war – on the German side – and her armies were pouring across her eastern frontiers onto Polish soil. But Warsaw remained defiant.

Furious, Hitler sent over 400 planes, including 240 Stukas from eight *Gruppen*, which dive-bombed the beleaguered city hour by hour, using high-explosives and incendiaries.

It was the nightmare of the Stukas, with their evil presence and their hideous howl, as much as the death they dealt, that caused the city to finally break. The end came on 27 September when, after almost three weeks of heroic defence, the Germans captured the forts defending the city.

Hitler's use of the Stuka as a 'weapon of terror' had justified itself on military grounds as, during the whole campaign thus far, only 31 Stukas had been lost. The relatively quick result at Warsaw saved the very much worse destruction that street fighting would have caused, as Stalingrad was to prove later.

The most important factor was the reputation the Junkers Ju 87B had earned for itself – a reputation which would over-awe opposition and break the morale of enemy troops, to whom the word 'Stuka' would mean death, defeat and despair. It would be almost a year later, over the green fields of southern England, that the weaknesses of the Stuka would be exposed and the legend of the 'terror bomber' shattered.

BATTLE
FOR BRITAIN

After Dunkirk, Britain stood alone against the Nazi menace. During the long, hot summer of 1940, Goering, on Hitler's orders, launched a massive air-assault on southern England in preparation for Operation Sealion — the threatened invasion of Britain.

501 (Volunteer Reserve) Squadron were relaxing when the telephone rang. One of the pilots near the table pounced on the receiver and brought it quickly to his ear. All eyes were on his face. Almost at once he turned, urgently motioning to the other pilots – *scramble!*

Everyone in the crew-hut sprang to his feet and started for the door.

The first man out yelled: 'Start up!'

The pilots were racing across the bomb-pocked field to the Hurricanes dispersed among the trees. As each man reached his machine, he grabbed his 'chute, swung it on, clipped on the catches and scrambled onto the port wing and into the cockpit.

A Rolls-Merlin engine coughed, belching black smoke, propeller spinning. Another came to life, then another. In seconds they were all roaring. The Squadron Leader was moving, then his wing man, Lacey. Throttle knobs forward, brakes released, the Hurricanes jolted away, taxiing into position amid the roar of engines and the lash of prop-wash.

The Squadron Leader gave full throttle, gathered speed, bumped, then touched, skimmed and lifted away from the field, leaning into a slight turn. His wing-man lifted off only thirty yards behind him, then Red Three. Behind them came the other three Vs, undercarts retracting, sticks back, banking, cutting off the leading echelon in tight turns, closing the gap and forming up, climbing south-east into the patchy sky.

There was a rush of static in the pilots' earphones. The Squadron Leader's voice came through:

'Check in, Red Section.'

Lacey said: 'Red Two.'

'Red Three,' came a voice.

'Check in, Yellow.'

One by one the pilots checked in – Yellow, Blue, Green. All twelve pilots were in the flight.

Now the Controller's voice was heard:

'Pinetree Leader. Victor one-three-zero. Angels fifteen. Fifty-plus raid approaching over Folkestone.' He repeated the message.

The Squadron Leader acknowledged and Control said: 'Good luck.'

The formation altered course slightly, gaining height at full bore.

It was 15 September 1940, a beautiful autumn morning with clouds beginning to drift in from the west . . .

High above the clouds, a Hurricane squadron seeks out its prey. In the Battle this versatile fighter equipped over 60 per cent of Fighter Command squadrons, but was overshadowed by the faster and more famous Spitfire.

A nation alone

The scene had been set some twelve weeks before when, with Dunkirk over, the flower of France's fighting strength defeated in Flanders, and all but one division of the British Army gone, only a few RAF squadrons and the Navy stood between the *Wehrmacht* and final victory in Western Europe.

With the conquest of France and the Low Countries complete, Germany had 2,000 miles of coastline from which to mount air attacks on Britain. At the nearest points, the *Luftwaffe* could reach the English coastline in 15 minutes flying time, and the most distant point was only 400 miles away.

The Germans began their feverish preparations for what was intended to be a history-making conquest – the invasion of Britain – the first since 1066. Hitler was confident that Britain, worn down by the U-boat blockade and reeling from round-the-clock air attacks on her ports, cities and industries, could be over-run. Ports along the French, Belgian and Dutch coasts became crammed with vessels of every description, while German assault troops practised landing exercises in preparation for Operation Sea Lion.

However, before a successful landing operation could be effected, the German High Command knew that the first objective must be to wipe out the RAF fighters. Nothing less than their total elimination was demanded, after which Goering's bombers, unescorted, would be able to range free and annihilate the aircraft factories and arms plants.

Against Goering's air armada of nearly 3,000 aircraft, Britain had 45 RAF squadrons – a force the German Marshal believed could be brushed aside by his fighters. What he did not anticipate was the skill and resolution of the RAF fighter

Below Scramble! Fighter crew, who were not available in sufficient numbers during 1940, were on constant alert throughout the Battle of Britain.

pilots or the fighting qualities of their planes. Nor could he guess the major role which Fighter Command Control would play in dictating the course of the battle to come.

Unknown to Goering, the RAF had evolved an elaborate control system which could plot the movements of enemy aircraft from their appearance over the Channel to their intended targets. All fighter squadrons were linked to this central control, and could be alerted and directed to the enemy force as a single, co-ordinated unit. The key to the entire system was the use of radar.

Radar – the use of radio beams for aircraft detection and direction finding – had been developed by the National Physics Laboratory's Radio Research Centre, and a network of RAF radar stations had been set up to send information by landline and radio to Fighter Command Control. In addition, intelligence came from Naval patrols, patrolling RAF aircraft, and from

Above *The Operations Room at Headquarters Fighter Command during the hectic summer of 1940.*

Below *Squadron Leader Douglas Bader (front centre) with Canadian pilots of 242 (Canadian) Squadron RAF.*

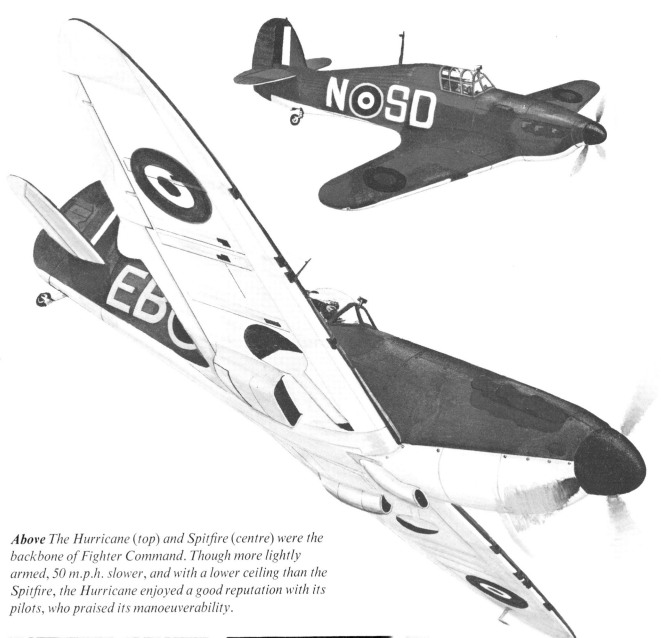

Above The Hurricane (top) and Spitfire (centre) were the backbone of Fighter Command. Though more lightly armed, 50 m.p.h. slower, and with a lower ceiling than the Spitfire, the Hurricane enjoyed a good reputation with its pilots, who praised its manoeuverability.

Far left Air Marshal Goering, the corpulent supreme commander of the Luftwaffe, was, despite his exalted career in World War I, something of a playboy, who had the habit of promising more than he could reasonably achieve.

Left Air Marshal Dowding, called 'Stuffy' by friends and enemies alike. His quiet manner and gloomy expression concealed a stubborn belief in the fighting qualities of his Command.

over 1,000 Royal Observer Corps posts serviced by 30,000 volunteer observers in 32 centres throughout the British Isles.

The eagle flies

The destruction of Britain's fighters in the air and on the ground was to be carried out in three phases: during the first five days, within a radius of 60 to 100 miles south and south-east of London; in the next three days, within 30 to 70 miles; and finally, for five more days, within a 30 mile radius of London. The plan entailed deep penetration by the *Luftwaffe* bombers to seek out and bomb the airfields where the fighter squadrons were based. This would irrevocably win absolute air superiority over England and fulfil the Fuhrer's mission. Goering, supremely confident, christened this first phase: Operation Eagle, and promised Hitler action within three days of

getting fine weather. It came on 12 August.

Known British radar stations were attacked with the first wave: Dunkirk (near Faversham, Kent), Pevensey (near Eastbourne), Rye (near Hastings) and Ventnor (near Dover). Ventnor was hit and knocked off the air, a serious blow to Fighter Command's warning system. Rye suffered slight damage and a few casualties, including one AA trooper killed and six others wounded. Attacks were also made on RAF stations and fighter airfields, including Biggin Hill, Northolt, Martlesham, Croydon, Kenley, Middle Wallop, Manston, Hawkinge and Lympe, causing damage to airfields and installations. And bombers and dive-bombers, escorted by

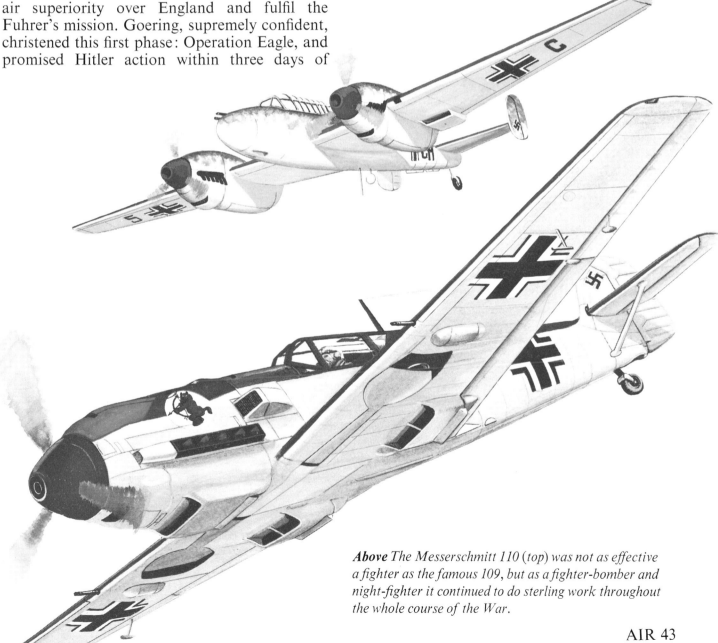

Above *The Messerschmitt 110 (top) was not as effective a fighter as the famous 109, but as a fighter-bomber and night-fighter it continued to do sterling work throughout the whole course of the War.*

Surrounded by his staff officers, Goering (fifth from right) discusses the air battle raging only a few miles away across the English Channel.

fighters, made mass attacks on Dover, Portland, Weymouth and other coastal towns, damaging port installations and shipping. The ferocity of the offensive grew alarmingly as the area of the battle widened.

In the first ten days 697 German aircraft were shot down for the loss of 153 British fighters.

Daily, almost continually now, bombers converged on London in formations of 40 or more, escorted by Messerschmitts, at heights of 15,000 feet and upwards.

The struggle went on without respite, increasing in intensity. The brilliance and courage of the British pilots, flying the Spitfire and Hurricane eight-gun fighters in tremendous and spectacular battles, brought Churchill's never-to-be-forgotten tribute:

'The gratitude of every home in our Island, in our Empire, and indeed throughout the World, except in the abodes of the guilty, goes out to the British airmen who, undaunted by odds, unwearied in their constant challenge and mortal danger, are turning the tide of the World War by their prowess and by their devotion. Never in the field of human conflict was so much owed by so many to so few.'

But the situation was serious. The *Luftwaffe's* offensive on airfields had cost Fighter Command 295 fighters and 103 pilots killed, with a further 170 planes badly damaged and 128 pilots wounded.

At the end of those two desperate and bloody weeks, Goering came near to defeating the RAF, for, compounding Britain's aircraft losses, all but crippling damage had been inflicted on communications, including the Operations Room itself.

Yet – at the very moment of victory, with the RAF reeling and diminished under the *Luftwaffe's* blows, with her fighter control system all but paralyzed – Hitler unaccountably stopped the decisive battle against the British fighters in favour of an all-out assault on London.

A costly blunder

It was Hitler's most colossal blunder of the War. First, he had ceased bombing the radar stations – a costly error. Now – believing that he could crush the spirit of London – he ignored the advice of his advisers and let the fighter airfields off the hook.

The onslaught came on 7 September. Hundreds of bombers came over London with the aim of destroying the docks. They came with fighter escort in massive daylight raids, and by night as well, inflicting enormous damage with high explosive and incendiary bombs.

It was the gravest blow that had been struck so far by the enemy in the great battle of the air, and it brought this scathing judgment from Churchill of his mortal enemy:

'This wicked man . . . this monstrous product of former wrongs and shame . . . has now resolved to try to break our famous island race by a process of indiscriminate slaughter and destruction . . .'

On 11 September, 60 German aircraft were shot down for the loss of 26 British fighters; the following day, 61 German machines for the loss of 13; next day, 78 Germans for the loss of 13; 14 September, 31 German aircraft for the loss of 11 British, while Goering's newspaper, *National Zeitung*, proclaimed: 'At an extraordinary rate London drifts towards its fate . . .'

Then came 15 September . . .

On the other side of the Channel, Goering felt victory almost within his grasp. Perhaps this sunny autumn day was to be his crowning glory. Perhaps, with London crumbling in ruins and with only a handful of British fighters left, today's assault might be the last in Operation Eagle . . .

Air Marshal Sir Hugh Dowding, Commander-in-Chief of Fighter Command, and Air Vice Marshal Keith Park, AOC II Fighter Group (Southern England), who was largely directing the Battle of Britain, knew better than anyone in England, including Churchill, what England's chances were of survival. All they could do today, with greatly diminished forces, was to send up the fighters, squadron by squadron, in the hope of breaking up *Luftwaffe* bomber formations before they reached their target, and go on inflicting heavier losses on the enemy than the RAF was sustaining. These men knew that Britain's fate depended on what was left of 'the few' . . .

Battle of eagles

The throbbing roar of the German Armada filled the whole sky. The massed *Kampfgeschwader*, flanked by Messerschmitt 109s and 110s, swarmed across the Channel towards London.

In II Group Ops Room, Churchill watched in silence as the Controller, Wing Commander Eric Douglas-Jones, sent up twelve squadrons. While these intercepted the enemy formations and fought them all the way to London, he kept another twelve squadrons in reserve. Now he called on 12 Group for reinforcements.

Squadron Leader Douglas Bader, the legless commander of the Duxford wing of five squadrons, met the bombers on the city's southern fringe and found them already in disarray from

Below A Spitfire Mark 1A of 19 Squadron RAF is re-armed after a sortie over southern England. An acute shortage of fighters throughout the Battle of Britain meant that ground-crew had to work round the clock.

Right Hawker Hurricanes of 501 Squadron RAF take off to intercept a heavy force of German bombers.

fighter attacks. Their bombs fell over a wide area, doing little strategic damage. One heavy bomb hit Buckingham Palace. Another fell on the lawn. A Dornier crashed through the roof of Victoria Station. The sky was alive with snarling aircraft, chattering guns, the crash of bombs and the whining roar of Dorniers and Heinkels falling out of control and plummeting to earth.

The twelve Hurricanes of 501 squadron had reached 10,000 feet over Ashford when the Controller gave his warning. They flew on, gaining height, each pilot tensely searching the sky, and checking his sights and guns. They reached 12,000 feet . . . 13,000 . . . 14,000 . . .

'Bogies twelve o'clock high!' someone shouted on the RT.

There they were at 20,000 feet, a big formation of Dornier 17s – twin-engined 'flying pencils' – and tiny shining shapes dotted the sky around them – Me 109s.

'Tally-ho!' the Squadron Leader called, and led his Hurricanes into a steep climbing turn.

Red Two – Sergeant Pilot James Lacey – pulled back on the stick to bring one of the Dorniers into his sights. But it was too soon, and as the enemy formation came into range his Hurricane was standing on its tail, airspeed slipping. He pressed the silver gun-button and his eight Brownings rattled. He felt the violent shudder of the aircraft as it absorbed the recall.

The Hurricane stalled, air-speed all gone. It fell away, dipping to the right, and began to spin, nose down, out of control, the engine racing. Forget the enemy, his mind said. He let her dive, applied opposite rudder. She stopped spinning and straightened, going straight down, nearly pulling the wings off. Gradually, he pulled her out, throttling back, easing back the stick. The blood drained from his head in the pull, as the green blur moved backwards and the nose came up to meet the horizon.

The Hurricane levelled out at 5,000 feet, and Lacey looked about him. There was no sign of the flight. He pressed the microphone switch.

'Red Two to Red Leader. Where are you?'

A rush of static filled his earphones. The Squadron Leader's voice came through:

'Red Leader to Red Two. Just north of Maidstone.'

Lacey banked sharply, at full throttle, gaining height, straining his eyes ahead and upwards, searching the sky for the rest of the squadron . . .

He was suddenly on a collision course with a bunch of Me 110s. He pushed the stick forward and dived below their flight path, waited until they were overhead, then pulled hard on the

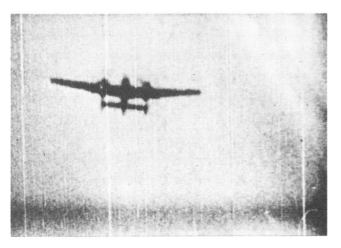

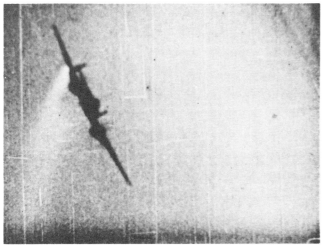

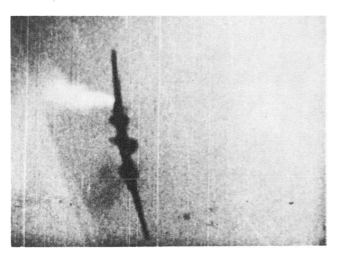

Left A Heinkel III passes across the Thames just below Tower Bridge. Hitler's decision to turn his Luftwaffe on London, just when the RAF was at breaking point, was one of the major blunders of the War.

Above A gun-camera mounted in the nose of a British fighter records the last moments of an Me 110 – an aircraft which was not well-suited to a fighter role.

stick. The Hurricane zoomed up and the last of the Me 110s came into his sights only 150 yards ahead of him. His thumb found the firing button, pressed it, and the eight Brownings roared.

The 110 seemed to stagger. He saw his tracers streak into the engine and fuel tank. The next instant black smoke poured out, and the Me dipped to one side, sliding away from the formation. A second later it burst into flames and plunged earthwards.

Lacey rolled, then came in behind the Mes again. They hadn't seen him. He lined up the trailing German, pressed the firing button. His shells ripped into the Me's fuselage and wings. Pieces flew off and flashed past his windscreen. The Me's coolant had been hit, white smoke began to stream from him. He'd never get home. Without coolant his Daimler-Benz engine would over-heat...

The other Mes had spotted him. They had split up into two groups and were coming round to attack on both sides, one of them trailing. Lacey banked hard left to stand on the port wing. The Me was suddenly in his sight. He pressed the button and the Hurricane's guns chattered, then cut out, the whole eight, one by one. And tracers were flashing past him from six different directions. He plunged the stick forward and dived out of the trap.

A little later he levelled out over the familiar patchwork of greens and browns. He was not far from Kenley, alone, and out of ammunition. He went down to land, touching down at 1235...

The eagle is plucked

In his luxury train at Boulogne, Field Marshal Goering paced anxiously. His personal assistant Christa Gormans brought him a glass of water and two pills. As he swallowed them, his aide said encouragingly:

'They must be at their limit now. Today's assault must surely complete the operation.'

Goering said nothing.

In British Fighter Control, the Command was equally anxious. They knew that the outcome of the battle was precariously balanced. The coloured lights on the large Ops Room table told the story. The tiny red bulbs showed that all 11 Group squadrons had been committed. And 12 Group reserves.

Air Vice-Marshal Park stood by the British

Prime Minister. They stared at the large map of England and at the confusion of tokens and markers that told how the battle was going. There was a silence.

Churchill cleared his throat.

'What other reserves do we have?' he asked.

'There are none,' Park replied.

All through the day the battle raged. The *Luftwaffe* made 1,300 sorties. Their Mes fought until the last moment before making for home, and more than 60 of them had to ditch in the Channel or on French beaches and fields.

Appalled by the reports coming in, General Kesselring telephoned Goering and told him:

'We can't keep this up! It is a disaster!'

Churchill had returned to Chequers, exhausted and dispirited. He lay down for his afternoon nap. At 8 pm his private secretary woke him. Churchill shook his head, muttering: 'Catastrophic . . . errors . . . delays! What a repellent day for England!'

'But we shot down 186 Germans for the loss of 40 of ours, sir,' his secretary told him quietly.

In fact, as post-war figures revealed, the 'bag' for the day was 56 shot down – in addition to those which crash-landed on the way back to base – for the loss of 26 British fighters.

The *Luftwaffe* had to face the bitter truth. It had been routed by an air force it had written off as defeated. 'Eagle' had lost his tail feathers.

But Goering, purple with rage and frustration, refused to believe it. He pounded the table in his railway carriage.

BATTLE FOR BRITAIN

'We can destroy him! We must keep at him with all our means! In four or five days with such heavy losses, he will be finished!'

He persisted with the raids, but with changed tactics, sending over formations of thirty bombers escorted by 200 to 300 fighters. On 30 September, the *Luftwaffe* made a last attempt to annihilate London – and lost 47 more planes.

RAF Fighter Command had won the Battle of Britain. Britain was safe – for the time being.

By the end of 1940, Hitler's dream of an invasion of Britain was shattered. Many of his bombers – like this Dornier – were burnt-out wrecks, and increasingly, as the Nazi leader turned his attention towards Russia, the Luftwaffe was transferred to the Eastern Front.

CORAL SEA

Japanese confidence after Pearl Harbour ran high, but they needed to extend and strengthen their defensive perimeter. In May 1942, an invasion force set sail for Port Moresby, in New Guinea. Barring its way was an American carrier fleet — a great battle was inevitable.

The lone Avenger flew on in dense dark cloud. At 0811 it banked around to commence the last leg of its search for the elusive Japanese flat-tops. The USN reconnaissance plane was over a 100 miles from its own carrier *Yorktown*, and well east of the furthermost island of the Louisiade Archipelago, east of New Guinea.

For 48 hours the two opposing carrier forces had been blindly searching for each other across vast stretches of ocean in murky tropical weather. It was a war of phantoms, in which the prize targets were the flat-tops themselves, which alone carried the means to strike from afar.

Cloudy weather and continuing rain squalls had hampered air reconnaissance over the Coral Sea for the past two days, and the crews searching in dense cloud only caught sight of the sea occasionally, through ragged gaps in the clouds.

But at first light this morning, the Americans had found themselves without protective cloud-cover. Their carriers *Yorktown* and *Lexington*, steaming in a glistening sea under a clear, orange-tinted sky as the sun came up, presented a target which could be seen for miles.

In a desperate bid to find the enemy flat-tops before the Japanese planes located the US carriers, Rear-Admiral Fletcher sent off 18 reconnaissance planes.

About 100 miles to the north of the American formation, the Avenger pilots ran into a cold front, where warm air had condensed to form thick cloud, and rain squalls reduced visibility to near zero. They continued their search with grave misgivings, for the Japs held all the cards this

morning. To find their carriers in this weather would be a thousand-to-one fluke.

The fleet is sighted

The time passed without a sighting. The Avengers were almost out of fuel. One more leg and they would have to turn back. A relief group would have already taken off from *Lexington*.

At 0815, an Avenger nosed down through the sleet, groping for the base of the cloud-bank.

'Ships at two o'clock!'

The radio-navigator yelled through the inter-com, and the pilot saw them – a large flat-top and two cruisers, some destroyers. There might have been more, but they were smudged out by the cloud.

The pilot nosed down, and ragged tufts of cloud streaked past the windscreen. Presently he saw a patch of sea again, and the flat-top, a single-engine fighter taking off from it. At that instant an explosion rocked the plane as a shell burst near the port wing-tip, and a moment later he saw the flash of a gun from one of the larger vessels. He gunned the Avenger up to full boost and climbed back into the clouds.

He headed back toward the US carriers while the radio-navigator pinpointed the Japanese position, encoded a message and began to tap out slow stuttering Morse with his key . . .

For three days and nights, the opposing carrier forces had played hide-and-seek under a blanket of low-hung tropical clouds and in almost un-ceasing rain squalls. But today – 8 May 1942 – a confrontation was almost inevitable. A decisive battle would be fought – a battle which would decide the fate of Port Moresby – and of Australia – once and for all.

The stage is set

At the end of April 1942, the Japanese High Command made the decision to seize Tulagi, in the Solomons, and Port Moresby, in New Guinea, with the object of cutting the America-Australia supply route and at the same time establishing a springboard from which to invade Australia.

On 30 April, the main Japanese attack force, which had assembled at Truk, in the Carolines, sailed southwards towards Rabaul, the assembly point for the invasion force.

Vice-Admiral Shigeyoshi Inouye, the overall commander of the operation, had five separate naval forces at his disposal, plus land-based support to the tune of 86 bombers and 63 fighters, in addition to 12 seaplanes.

Although the carrier Shoho was the smallest in the Japanese invasion fleet, she provided valuable air-cover and was a constant menace to the Allied fleet assembled in the Coral Sea.

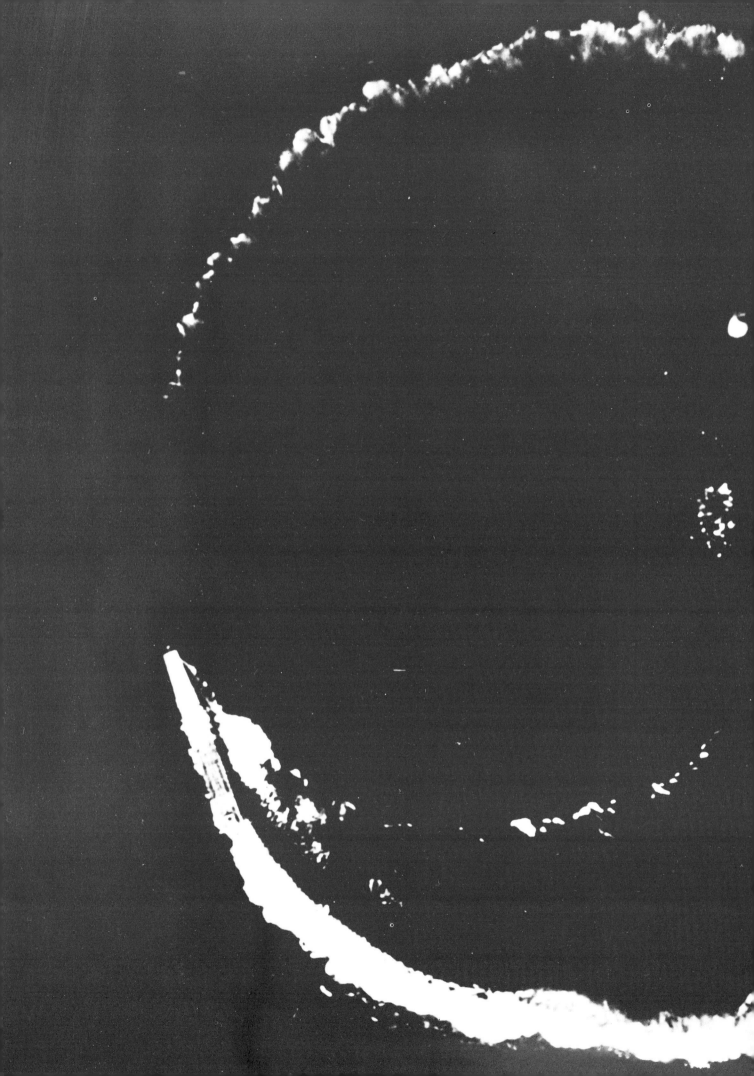

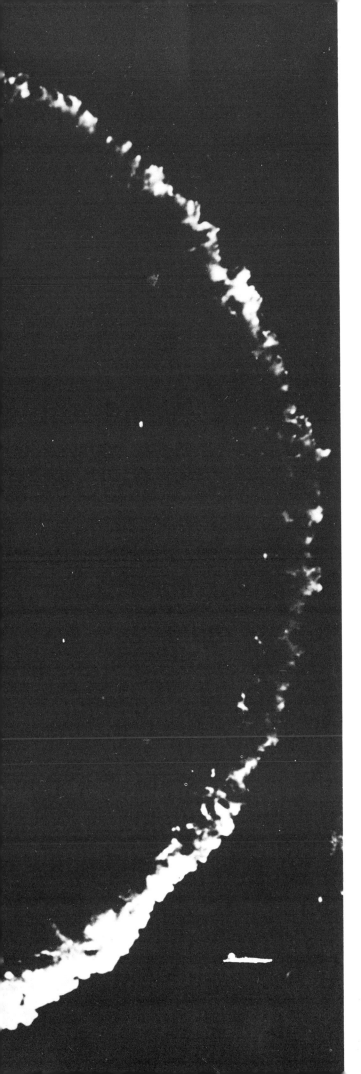

The main strike force, from Truk, comprised the aircraft-carriers *Zuikaku* and *Shokaku*, two cruisers and a screen of destroyers, under Rear-Admiral Tagaki. The Port Moresby invasion force comprised five Navy and six Army transports, plus a number of auxiliary vessels and a destroyer escort. In addition, Inouye had a main covering force, under Rear-Admiral Goto; a small strategic strike force under Rear-Admiral Shima; and a separate support group for the invasion fleet, under Rear-Admiral Marushige.

To prevent the invasion and destroy the Japanese naval forces, Admiral Nimitz sent Task Force 17 to the Coral Sea, under the command of Rear-Admiral Frank J. Fletcher. The task force comprised carriers *Yorktown* (Fletcher's flagship) and *Lexington*, four cruisers and a screen of destroyers. To this was added an Allied force under Rear-Admiral Crace, RN, comprising the Australian cruisers *Australia* and *Hobart*, USN cruiser *Chicago*, and a destroyer escort.

In his opening moves, Inouye brought his carrier force down from Truk via a course well eastward of the Solomons, where they could stay beyond the reach of Allied air-reconnaissance for as long as possible. Then, on 3 May, he sent Shima's force to occupy Tulagi.

Fletcher replied by attacking Tulagi with planes from *Yorktown* on 4 May. They hit the base and destroyed five seaplanes, four landing barges, three mine-sweepers, heavily damaged the destroyer *Kikuzuki*, causing it to beach, and strafed destroyer *Yuzuki*, killing her captain and several crew members. The Americans lost three planes.

On 5 May, Admiral Takagi's force cleared Cristobal, turned west and passed north of Rennell Island, the bad weather still hiding it from Allied reconnaissance planes. At 0930 on 6 May, he turned south.

Meanwhile, the Port Moresby invasion force of five Navy and six Army transports, with a number of smaller craft and a destroyer escort, had sailed from Rabaul under the command of Rear Admiral Kajioka, flying his flag in the light cruiser *Yubari*. They rendezvoused with Marushige's support group off Buin, Bougainville, then set course for the Jomard Passage, en route to Port Moresby and the invasion.

Left *First victim of the Battle of the Coral Sea. Shoho desperately manoeuvers in an attempt to avoid the attack by planes of Lexington and Yorktown.*

Opening moves

By 6 May, in squally weather under the unbroken cloud-cover, the two forces were closing fast. At one time during the evening they were only seventy miles apart, but neither side was aware of the presence of the other. During the night they both changed course and the distance between them widened again.

Before dawn on 7 May, Fletcher detached Crace's force of three cruisers and two destroyers and sent them at full speed ahead to close the southern exit of Jomard Passage. His Task Force 17, comprising carriers *Yorktown* and *Lexington*, four cruisers and a screen of destroyers, held a steady westward course 225 miles south of Rennell Island. At first light, he sent off two spotting planes to try to find the enemy carriers.

At this time, the Marushige-Kajioka invasion force was nearing the Louisiade Archipelago, with Goto's covering force close at hand, including the light carrier *Shoho*.

At 0736, one of Fletcher's reconnaissance planes spotted six elements of Goto's force, including the carrier, and signalled their position back to the *Yorktown*.

Fletcher, believing it to be the main force, struck with all his strength and, three hours later, the *Shoho* was found and sunk. This loss deprived the invasion force of its air cover, and Inouye was forced to hold it north of the Louisiades until the Jomard Passage had been cleared.

However, the Japanese forces were prepared to hit back. The three-cruiser force heading for the Passage under the command of Rear-Admiral Crace, RN, had been spotted. Early in the afternoon the Allied ships were heavily attacked by successive waves of shore-based torpedo bombers using the same tactics and in the same strength as

the force which sank the *Prince of Wales* and *Repulse* in the opening phase of the Pacific War. By skilful handling and good fortune not a ship was hit.

A running battle

But Fletcher's position had now been disclosed to the enemy and, with his planes away on the strike, he was in a serious plight. Luckily the weather worsened during the afternoon, and the enemy had no radar. The Japanese knew an encounter was inevitable, and they launched an attack from *Shokaku* and *Zuikaku*, using 25 bombers and torpedo bombers.

But in the squally, murky weather the planes missed their target. They searched the area where they had estimated the American carriers would be until almost nightfall, when they had to drop their bombs and torpedoes into the sea and return to their carriers.

As they flew back in the thickening gloom, they passed close to Fletcher's force and were detected on the radar screen. A patrol of Wildcats from *Lexington* intercepted them and shot down nine Japanese planes for the loss of two. A further 11 enemy planes did not reach their carriers and had to ditch in the sea.

With *Shoho* gone and Crace's force blocking the Jomard Passage, Inouye ordered the transports back. Thus the invasion force intended for Port Moresby never passed through the Passage into the Coral Sea. It remained north of the Louisiades until finally ordered to withdraw.

Now, with only the carrier forces of Fletcher and Takagi on the scene, the tactical situation remained a stalemate until one of the forces was destroyed. The coming encounter was inevitable.

During the night the two forces drew further apart, neither risking a night attack.

As 8 May dawned, it was the Japanese who held the advantage, sitting under the shelter of low-hung cloud, while the American ships steamed ahead in brilliant sunshine.

At 0600 the Japanese sent out a search mission, and at 0625 Fletcher ordered 18 reconnaissance planes from the *Lexington*.

At 0815, one of Fletcher's search planes located the Japanese carriers and signalled their position.

And at exactly the same time, *Yorktown*'s radio-operators intercepted a signal from a plane close by which made it plain that the Japanese had located them.

To the south-west, hundreds of miles away, were the towns and cities of Australia, oblivious

Revenge for Pearl Harbour. Shoho, overwhelmed by the sheer number of bombers and torpedo bombers which attacked her, was hit many times and sank with heavy loss of life.

that they were the prize in the great battle about to be fought.

Carrier versus carrier

There was a heavy sea running and the massive decks of the two flat-tops rose and fell with the swell. A huddle of fighters stood at the elevator end, lashed down by steel cables. Three machines were lined up behind the catapult launcher. Each carrier swung into wind as a bull-horn from the bridge boomed out:

'Prepare to launch aircraft!'

Overalled groundcrew came from everywhere and threaded their way among the aircraft, secured the chocks and released the cables. Almost at once the fighter pilots came quickly from the briefing room and boarded their aircraft.

A starter-cartridge exploded with a flat *crack*, and the first engine came to life with a roar, its propeller a gleaming, shimmering circle. Another cartridge exploded, another engine started; then another, and another. The whole scene was a dazzle of spinning propellers and the flightdeck thundered with the roar of engines.

'Prepare for first catapult launch!' rasped the controller.

The pilot in the leading Wildcat gunned up his engine to a throaty roar and the machine bucked,

held to the runners. The catapult officer whirled one finger above his head while the blast of the motor increased. Then he whipped his right arm down and the catapult fired.

The Wildcat was hurled down the deck and off the forward edge of the carrier at 120 miles an hour. It dipped over the choppy waves for an instant, then climbed away in a tight circuit.

Twice more the catapult fired, to thrust two more fighters into the clear blue sky. They clawed for height, chasing the leader, closing on him to form a patrol to guard the carriers while the rest of the planes got airborne.

Now it was 'chocks away', as one by one the fighters came into position, roared to full boost and hurtled off the flight-deck.

While the last of the fighters was getting off, the bombers and fighter-bombers, their wings folded above them, were coming up in the elevators.

By 0925 the Americans got off a striking force of 122 aircraft.

Below *At the time of Coral Sea, the Mitsubishi Zero was the best fighter operating in the Pacific theatre. It was fast, well-armed and highly adaptable.*

Above right *At the time of Pearl Harbour, the Grumman Wildcat was the standard American single-seat fighter. Its tubby appearance belied its fine fighting qualities.*

The Japs had launched 121 during the same time.

And both forces were heading towards each other's surface vessels in the strangest hide-and-seek air battle in history.

They passed each other on their way to their targets.

Attack and counter-attack

The *Shokaku* and the *Zuikaku* were eight miles apart, steaming at thirty knots toward the enemy position. Each carrier was protected by two cruisers and several destroyers. Since dawn they had been in a cold front; hidden in thick low cloud and rain squalls.

The *Shokaku* came into the light as the first wave of American torpedo planes arrived. They let go their torpedoes from too far back. The carrier twisted to avoid them, and Japanese patrols swooped on the attackers. Now bombers came in and hit the *Shokaku*. One bomb fell forward and hit the capstan compartment. It exploded. The second bomb hit the engine repair shop, aft, and set it on fire.

The carrier zigzagged to avoid more torpedoes as the damage-control squads fought the flames with extinguishers.

Now *Zuikaku* emerged from the weather-screen, saw the *Shokaku* blazing and dodged back under the front. The American planes circled in vain, searching for her, while Jap patrols circling the carriers dived on the bombers and torpedo-bombers and shot down three.

The American carriers had no such natural protection. They steamed into the north-north-east wind in bright sunshine. The Japs found them at 1055, their decks empty and a dozen Wildcats circling far below the attackers.

The Japanese came in with the sun at their backs. The American ack-ack gunners pumped shells at them, their aim wild. But for a time they kept them off. Wave after wave came in and several were sent crashing into the sea, while the *Lexington* and the *Yorktown* twisted and turned.

After 23 minutes, the attackers spread out and came in from both sides of the *Lexington* at zero feet. They launched their torpedoes from a thousand yards. The *Lexington* had no time to evade them, and she took a hit on the port side, then another, and water flooded into three boiler rooms. A fountain of water rose to port. A near miss. Another to starboard. Then a bomb hit her and ruptured some of her plates. Now there was black smoke, streaked with flame, coiling in heavy rolls from the burning carrier. But she was still operational, though with a heavy list.

At 1120 the *Yorktown* was attacked with torpedoes. She leaned at crazy angles, curving to

avoid them. One after another passed her bows or stern. The gunners were blasting away. They shot down several of the attackers.

But then came the dive-bombers, and a 750lb bomb went right through the flight-deck and three decks below it before it exploded. The vessel shuddered violently with the impact, and now a fire had broken out below and black smoke was pouring through the hole in her deck.

66 men had been killed in the blast.

The brief, furious battle was over, and both air attack forces were straggling back to their carriers.

The jubilant Japanese pilots reported both American carriers hit and sinking. But the combat effectiveness of the *Lexington* and the *Yorktown* remained unimpaired, and Fletcher still had 37 attack aircraft and twelve fighters fit enough to take to the air.

The Japanese planes had returned to the crippled *Shokaku* and most of them were forced to ditch. They had only nine planes left operational.

The odds could be said to have been even.

But at 1247 came a bitter and tragic anticlimax. An explosion occurred deep inside *Lexington*, and she caught fire. She was abandoned shortly after 1700.

In the running fight both sides had inflicted severe damage on the enemy. The Japanese had lost the small carrier *Shoho*, sunk; destroyer *Kikuzuki*; *Shokaku* heavily damaged; *Okinoshima* and *Yuzuki* damaged; four landing barges sunk. The Americans had lost *Lexington*, with heavy loss of life; destroyer *Sims* and tanker *Neosho* sunk; and carrier *Yorktown* damaged. In addition, 66 American aircraft and 543 men were lost; while Japanese losses were 80 planes and about 900 men.

In the material debit and credit of the clash, the battle was perhaps largely indecisive. In its strategic implications, its results were of immeasurable importance to the Allies and the future of the Pacific War. Japan had gambled her biggest stake on the conquest of Australia – a potential Allied offensive base – and the gamble had failed.

Left USS Lexington is torn apart by a gigantic internal explosion. She was bombed by Japanese planes attacking from both sides simultaneously and was hit by two torpedos and two bombs. Escaping gas built up inside the ship and her crew and planes were taken aboard the Yorktown. Shortly after, the 'Lady Lex' blew up and sank.

DAMBUSTER RAID

In 1943, despite RAF Bomber Command's intensive programme of raids on the Ruhr, Germany's industrial output had not decreased significantly. The need to destroy strategically important targets — such as the Ruhr dams — became increasingly urgent.

The Lancaster came swooping out of the dusk and levelled out over the still dark waters of Uppingham Lake. An Aldis lamp had been fitted under the bomber's nose and another under the tail, and their two thin beams made pale round discs of light that rushed along the surface, gradually converging as the plane came lower.

'Down, down, down,' the bomb-aimer's voice droned through the inter-com. 'That's it, hold it, steady . . .'

The two small patches of light had converged. The bomber flew straight and level at exactly 150 feet. Wing Commander Guy Gibson, DSO, DFC, held it steady for half a mile, then swept up over the hills and made for base.

As soon as he returned to his office, the commanding officer of Squadron X – a new squadron which had been created for one top-secret mission – rang Dr Barnes Wallis, the scientist, and reported the results of the flight.

'The lights work. We were spot on one-fifty. No trouble.'

'Good!' Wallis sounded vastly relieved.

'Tomorrow I'll have the lights fitted to all aircraft and we'll start training in earnest.'

'That's good news. By the way, tomorrow I want you to make some more drops at a hundred and fifty feet to see what happens at various speeds.'

They did just that, Gibson dropping Wallis's incredible two-and-a-half ton aerial mine to test its practicability. On the first run the balloon-like projectile burst on impact with the water, as it had several times before. On another run it bounced along the surface like a stone across a pond. The results were inconclusive. Time was running out and there was still a lot of work to be done.

When the two men met at Brooklands on the following afternoon, the inventor looked tired and depressed. He took Gibson into a small theatre and showed him some films of the tests. When the films finished, Wallis switched off the projector.

Like dozing monsters, Lancasters line up on the runway in readiness for a raid. More than any other plane, the Lancaster carried the War to the heartland of Germany, at a time when the Allies were on the defensive.

Gibson said: 'I don't understand why it works sometimes and not at others.'

'The speed-to-height ratio,' the inventor explained, and showed him a graph on the blackboard. 'As you see, it works at a hundred and fifty feet, but at an excessive speed. At lower speeds the mine breaks up, as we saw today.'

'Then what's the answer?'

Wallis pointed to the bottom of the graph. 'It wouldn't break up at forty feet.'

'Forty!'

'Well, sixty would be ideal. Sixty feet at two hundred and thirty-two miles an hour. It's either that or call the whole thing off.'

Testing time

Gibson rose and picked up the phone. He got through to his squadron and spoke to someone named 'Hutch'. He gave orders to alter the angle of the Aldis lamps on G George to make their beams cross at sixty feet below the aircraft. He hung up and said to Wallis:

'We'll have a crack tonight.'

Shortly after nine that night he took his Lancaster over Uppingham Lake once more. As he came down, his bomb-aimer watched the twin discs of light converge on the ink-black surface.

'Down, down, down, still further . . .'

Gibson found it uncomfortably low. They seemed no more than tree-top height.

'That's it, stay on that, up a bit, steady . . .'

Yes, it was possible, and the lights were a god-send.

As soon as he returned to base he rang Barnes Wallis and told him.

The inventor muttered his grateful thanks.

Next day, all the twenty-five Lancasters of Squadron X – now officially named 617 Squadron – were fitted with lights angled to converge at sixty feet. Night after night, dawn after dawn, the bombers flew across the Wash to get used to flying in complete darkness across

water at precisely the required height.

As the days passed, the crews made guesses about the target. Somebody said he had it on good authority it was the *Tirpitz*. But during those early weeks of training, Gibson was the only member of the squadron who knew their destination.

One afternoon early in May 1943, the skippers and their navigators were assembled in the briefing room at RAF Station, Scampton. Gibson, sitting relaxed on the window sill, told them why they and their long-suffering crews had been training at such a relentless pace for the past five weeks.

Below left Wing Commander Guy Gibson, DSO and Bar, DFC and Bar (on ladder), about to lead his crew into a Lancaster of 617 Squadron.

Below The Avro Lancaster, along with the American Flying Fortress, was the most effective heavy bomber of World War II.

The targets

The most highly industralized area of Germany was the Ruhr, he told them, and nearly eighty per cent of the total water available to the Ruhr Valley was contained in a complex of dams. Breach these, and the resulting shortage of water for industrial and domestic purposes would be a disastrous blow to the enemy, quite apart from immediate damage by flooding.

Number One Target was the Moehne dam across the Ruhr Valley, a tremendous Gothic structure built in 1911, and the pride of the German nation. It was half a mile long, 140 feet thick at its base, and as high as a fifteen-storey building – a mighty barrage dam which held back 140 million tons of water contained in a valley twelve miles long.

Number Two Target was the dam across the Sorpe, which consisted of a sloping bank of earth extending 600 feet on either side of a water-tight concrete core.

A secondary target was the Eder dam, a little larger than the Moehne. It held 202 million tons of water, and was built to prevent winter flooding of agricultural land and to improve the navigability of the lower Weser River. The Eder was also important for providing water for the Mittelland Canal, one of the main transport arteries of Germany.

As far as was known at present, Gibson told the crews, the dams were only lightly defended.

A ripple of excitement – and scepticism – ran through the room.

One of the pilots said: 'But, Christ! A bomb shelter is only three or four feet thick. What kind of a bomb can penetrate a hundred and fifty feet of concrete?'

Gibson told them about Dr Barnes Wallis's experiments, aided by photographs. He described how Wallis had blown up a dam in Wales, using a charge most experts would have considered totally inadequate.

He explained: 'Wallis worked out a charge on the scale of one which a Lanc could carry, placed it at the base of the structure and detonated it. A fountain of water spurted a hundred feet in the air and, when the spray cleared, Wallis saw that a gaping hole had been torn in the dam.'

The trick was, Gibson told them, that the bomb had to be placed against the base of the structure on the bed of the lake. The other important requirement, if Wallis's theories were correct, was that the dam had to be full – up to four or five feet from the top – to ensure that it held the maximum amount of water, and that there was still a protruding lip against which the aerial mines could be thrown.

The projectiles had to fall so that they would sink into the water actually touching the dam

Below With engines roaring, a Lancaster stands on a darkened runway waiting for the signal which will send it on its dangerous mission. The odds against it returning were appallingly high.

wall, about forty feet down. If they were not touching, they would be useless. When the mine was exploded by a hydrostatic fuse, a crack would appear at the base of the dam. With succeeding explosions, the wall would shift backwards before the pressure of the water, until it rolled over.

The training of the squadron proceeded at a relentless pace. Two dummy towers had been put up on the water at Reculver – the same distance apart as the towers of the Moehne. It was found in low-level runs at them that an ordinary bomb-sight wouldn't work. The mines had to be dropped well before the target. If the plane over-shot, the mine would go over the top. If it undershot, nothing would happen. If too close, the mine might hit the parapet and explode under the aircraft's tail. The mine should explode when the aircraft was a hundred yards across the wall and thus protected from the underwater blast.

A special bombsight was invented, using age-old range-finding principles. A corporal knocked up a prototype out of plywood, and Gibson tested it out over a dam in Sheffield. He found he could achieve extraordinary accuracy with it.

For several weeks, RAF reconnaissance aircraft had been keeping a close watch on the Ruhr dams. So as not to alert the Germans, they passed near the dams as if by accident. On 17 April the water was some fifteen feet from the top of the dam wall. By the beginning of May it was only ten feet. On 16 May the water level was only four feet from the top – just right for the attack.

The Lancasters taking part in the raid had been modified to take Wallis's queer-looking aerial mine. The bomb doors had been removed, as had the mid-upper turret and some of the armour, and there was an ugly protrusion below the belly. They looked ungainly and dangerous to fly.

Take-off

The moonlight was so bright on the night of 16 May that all other missions over Europe had been cancelled. Nineteen Lancasters of 617 Squadron took to the air at 2128 hours. The crews included thirteen Australians, two New Zealanders and two Americans (members of the RAF). Flying in two main groups, they flew a course designed to take them through the Dutch flak belts, to the north of the Zuider Zee.

The first formation of nine Lancasters, led by Wing Commander Gibson, was to attack the Moehne Dam, then, if successful, carry on to the secondary target, the Eder.

The second formation of five Lancs was to act as a diversionary force and to attack the Sorpe. The other five aircraft would be useful to fill in gaps, as required, during the operation.

The flat, dark land-mass of Holland slid under the low-flying aircraft as the two flights threaded their way through the defences and wireless masts, lifting to clear windmills and bridges.

Gibson's navigator, Pilot Officer Taerum, warned: 'Small town coming up.'

'O.K., Terry.'

Gibson banked gently to the north-east, cleared the huddle of dark buildings, and swung back on course, easing up to clear some high-tension wires.

Now they hugged a long straight canal until it

reached the German border west of Duisburg.

Before they skirted Eindhoven, ack-ack guns opened up and one of the Lancasters of Number Two Flight was hit. Severely damaged, it turned and limped toward the Channel.

The canal led them to the Rhine and the entrance to the Ruhr Valley. The river glistened in the moonlight, and presently guns opened up from emplacements along its banks. The Lancasters' gunners replied with rattling bursts of fire.

They were suddenly over an airfield, and the three front planes in Gibson's flight were caught in the searchlights. They flattened low over the tree-tops and soon lost them. One of the Lancasters following, dazzled by the searchlights, nosed up sharply and went out of control. It stalled and crashed in a field and burst into flames. Five seconds later its mine exploded.

The intention was to converge south-west of Munster, but the Sorpe force had lost four of its five aircraft, leaving Flight Lieutenant McCarthy to attack and return alone.

The reserve force, too, had been shot up during the hazardous journey, and only two of its aircraft remained.

Gibson's flight, now numbering eight, swarmed part Dortmund, then swung between Hamm and Soest.

'We're there,' Spafford reported on the intercom.

There, suddenly, it was, already lit up by concentrated flak. The Moehne dam. It looked huge and squat and impregnable. Barnes Wallis must be mad, was Gibson's first impression. Their aircraft felt so small and frail, and the dam looked as solid as the countryside. Its defending guns showered out flak all along its length. But there were no search lights.

Presently Gibson called over the RT:

'Hello, all Cooler aircraft. I am going to attack. Stand by to come into attack in your order.'

A few seconds later, he said:

'Hello, M Mother. Stand by to take over if anything happens.'

Flight Lieutenant Hopgood answered him:

'Okay, leader. Good luck.'

Gibson banked, circling wide to come round down-moon over the steep hills at the eastern end of the lake. Still two miles away, he straightened up, skimming the tops of the fir trees to begin his long gradual dive across the water.

The Moehne is breached

There was the dam, straight ahead, a solid wall, now huge in spectral relief against the haze of the valley beyond, its towers and sluices clearly seen. From end to end came the flak, in red, green, yellow and tracer bursts, all doubled by the reflection from the still black waters of the reservoir.

Gibson's steady voice came through:

'Terry, check height . . . Speed control, Flight-engineer . . . All guns ready, gunners . . . Coming up . . .'

Taerum had the Aldis lamps on, and their two ghostly spots were streaking along the surface of the water below the aircraft. The navigator's voice was steady as he brought the skipper down.

'Down . . . down . . . down . . . steady . . . that's it . . . hold it . . .'

Pulford was controlling the airspeed; Spafford was lining up the towers with the gunsight; the fusing switches were on; Gibson was looking through the make-shift sight across the windscreen, aiming the aircraft at the midpoint between the towers; Spafford had his thumb on the button.

The dam came up large. The flak came at the Lancaster and the Lancaster's guns spat back at them. Tracers and shells whipped past the bomber as it held course sixty feet above the water, flying straight and steady.

'Mine gone!' Spafford yelled, and Gibson pulled back the stick, eased the bomber over the parapet and the dam sank away behind them.

A few seconds later there was a tremendous explosion. A great cauldron of water rose up and spilled over the dam.

Someone on the RT said: 'Good show, leader! Nice work!'

The dam held. There was no way of knowing whether any damage had been done. But if Barnes Wallis's theory was correct, there was already a crack in the base of the concrete wall.

Gibson waited before ordering in the next attack. The reservoir was awash with ripples from the explosion, and he waited for the surface to become smooth again.

Right *Capable of carrying up to ten tons of bombs, the Lancaster carried a crew of seven and was armed with ten Browning .303 machine guns.*

'Hello M Mother,' he called. 'You may attack now. Good luck.'

'Okay. Attacking,' came Hopgood's terse reply.

Gibson came down with him to draw off some of the flak. But the German gunners had him in their sights early and he flew into a wall of fire –

'He's been hit!' someone yelled.

The Lancaster was on fire. Hopgood dropped his mine. It fell onto the power house and exploded. The bomber lurched across the top of the dam and exploded with a vivid flash as one of its wings fell off.

Heavy, cumbersome and relatively slow, the Lancaster was particularly vulnerable to attack by fighters. Its main defence lay in maintaining close formation, so that each aircraft was protected by the machine guns of its neighbours. Even so, casualties were high.

Flight Lieutenant Micky Martin came next, and Gibson made the run in with him. It was a perfect drop and his mine hit the wall and slid down into the water at the base of the wall. Again the water billowed up and surged over the dam. Martin was safe and away.

The dam still held.

Gibson called: 'Okay D Dog. Watch the flak.'

Gibson came in as a decoy, his gunners firing with all guns and flicking on the identification lights to confuse the defences. Squadron Leader Young's run-in was perfect and his bomb accurate. He cleared the dam.

This time a colossal wall of water swept right over the dam, and Gibson could have sworn it moved. But it still held. He called in Number Five: Maltby.

It was a perfect drop, and again there was the white surge of water across the wall of the dam. But it was hard to see now. The whole valley was

full of smoke and spray. Gibson called up Shannon to attack.

But as he came back he saw what had happened.

A great section of the wall had rolled over. He couldn't believe his eyes. The breach in the dam was a hundred yards wide, and millions of gallons of water were rushing through the gap and flooding into the great wide Ruhr Valley below.

He called Shannon and told him to wait. Then he told Hutchinson, his wireless-operator to report the result to base.

Back in the Operations Room at Bomber Command, Barnes Wallis had been waiting, and the only news that had come in so far had been bad – in fact, disastrous. He had a haunted look as he stood, shoulders hunched, his hands deep in the pockets of his overcoat.

Hutch's slow morse began to come through:

Dash-dot . . . dot-dot . . . dash-dash dot . . . 'Nigger!' someone gasped.

The scientist jumped, his face almost wild with relief. It was too much. He danced for joy.

The Eder crumbles

Gibson told Martin and Maltby to go home. Then he mustered the remaining five aircraft and told them to follow him, and headed for the Eder.

They found the dam in a deep valley with high hills around it, densely covered with fir trees. The approach was hazardous. An attacking aircraft had to dive steeply over a Gothic castle, dropping quickly from 1,000 to sixty feet, flatten out, let go the mine and zoom up in a climbing turn to miss a rocky mountain on the other side of the dam.

Shannon's first approach was too steep, and he had to pull out at full bore to avoid hitting the mountain.

He tried again. No good. He tried three more times, but wouldn't allow his bomb-aimer to let go the mine.

To give him a break, Gibson called in 'Z Zebra' – Maudsley.

Maudsley made two tries, then came round for his third. Gibson watched him. He came down, a good approach, flattened out. His spot-lights came together. He headed straight for the wall. His Verey light went off, showing that he'd dropped his mine – but too late. It hit the top of the dam and exploded on impact. The Lancaster disappeared, blown to smithereens.

There was a pause as the planes circled in the moonlight.

Gibson called up Shannon:

'Okay, Dave. Attack now. Good luck.'

Shannon came in. Another dummy run. He went round again. He came in, diving sharply over the castle. This time he was in position and made a perfect approach. He came down to the water, levelled out, held it, dropped his mine and banked away, clearing the mountain.

The mine exploded and the water surged up, spilling over the wall. But the dam held.

Knight came next. Two abortive runs. Gibson looked anxiously at the sky. The time was 0140, and the eastern horizon was beginning to lighten. They were far from home. He told Knight to call it off and turn for home.

The Australian said: 'One more crack, skipper.'

He dived in, carrying the last weapon left, made a perfect approach, levelled out, dropped his mine, and was away.

Gibson, from four hundred yards back, saw the explosion. The whole base of the dam seemed to shake. Then the whole great structure rolled over. Thousands of tons of water surged through the valley toward the doomed town of Kassel.

The survivors set course for home.

The terrible price of success

McCarthy, the lone survivor of Number Two Flight, had found the Sorpe in the hills south of the Moehne, its valleys full of mist. After three dummy runs he placed his mine accurately and saw it explode by the dam wall. And when he came back over it a minute later, he saw water tumbling across the crest and headed for home.

The controller at Bomber Command wanted to make doubly sure of the Sorpe and called up Gibson, asking if there was anyone left who could be diverted to the Sorpe. Hutchinson signalled back 'None'.

Brown, of the reserve force, was sent to the Sorpe. He found the valley hidden in swirling mists and made eight runs in an endeavour to get close enough, but without avail. Then he dropped incendiaries all around the banks and set fire to the trees on both sides of the dam. In his tenth run, he dropped his mine accurately. When he came round again all he could see was a huge ring of smoke around the base.

Anderson, also of reserve flight, was sent to the Sorpe, but by now the whole valley was filled with mist and the target completely hidden. He turned homewards with his bomb.

Ottley, in C Charlie, was ordered to attack the Lister Dam, another of the secondary targets. He acknowledged the message but was not heard of again. And Townsend, in O Orange, attacked the Ennerpe, hitting it after three runs. He joined up with Anderson to fly home.

Ten of the nineteen Lancasters were coming home, with the sky lightening with every minute, increasing the risk from German fighters. They flew low over the fields of Holland, dodging the flak. Squadron Leader Young's aircraft was hit and had to ditch in the Channel.

Photo reconnaissance in the next few days revealed two empty reservoirs and scenes of flooding and damage. An airfield was under water. And the town of Kassel was strangled.

The total cost to 617 Squadron was 54 members lost, nine Lancasters destroyed and four others damaged. Gibson was awarded the VC, and 32 other aircrew were also decorated.

Such was the strategic air offensive's most famous operation.

Right Before and after. The Moehne Dam was the pride of Germany – a mighty barrage dam almost half-a-mile long and containing 140 million tons of water. The Dambusters blew a breach 200 feet wide in it, releasing millions of tons of water which rushed down the valley and flooded villages, factories and roads. After the War, critics questioned the strategic importance of the raid, but it was undoubtedly a major blow to the Third Reich.

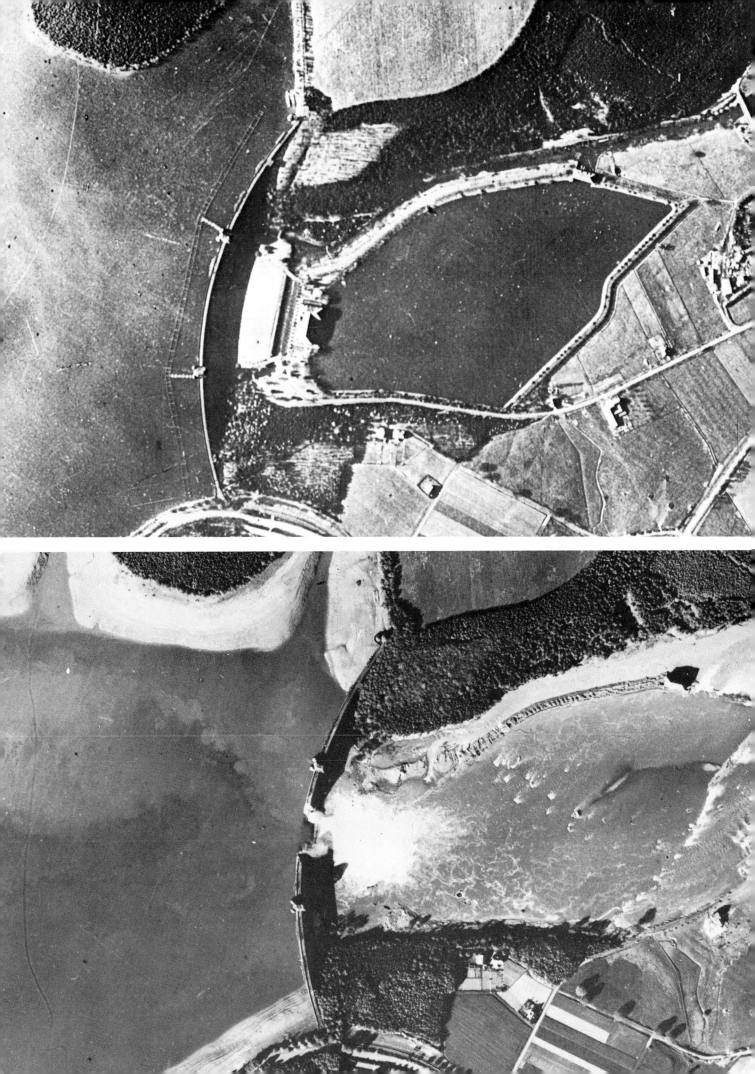

ATTACK ON SCHWEINFURT

While the RAF bombed Germany by night, the USAF had the unenviable task of carrying out daylight bombing raids on key targets, such as the ball-bearing plants at Schweinfurt. Flying unescorted over Germany, the American bombers were cut to pieces by the Luftwaffe.

The mission had begun and there was no turning back. The weather was overcast and the B-17 pilots had to use their Gee-equipment to find the leaders as they climbed over the Channel toward the Belgian coast.

It was 14 October 1943, and there were 291 Flying Fortresses in the air – 149 from the 1st Bombardment Division and 142 from the 3rd Bombardment Division – most of them oil-streaked, battle-scarred veterans of other daylight raids over Europe. Their guns bristled from every turret and window, and they were manned by men who knew that those who stayed alive this morning would have to burn their way through guts and blood.

All the groups were formed up now and heading for the enemy coast. One B-17 struck engine trouble and had to turn back. Each successive flight was a little higher than the one in front. And, flanked on either side and far above them were the tiny glistening P-47 fighters – Thunderbolts – which would protect them as far as Aachen.

The American fliers had a lot to think about this morning, for there had been hopes during the past few days that the mission would be called off – that the whole programme of bombing deep into Germany by daylight was about to be abandoned, following the disastrous losses of the past few weeks. The Eighth Air Force was operating in a state of despair, its remaining crews weary and demoralized. There was a

palpable feeling abroad that their beautiful, massively-armed bombers could not adequately defend themselves, unescorted, against heavy fighter resistance.

Into the jaws of death

The crews had plugged in their ear-phones, and the checking procedure was still going on –

'Pilot to navigator.'

'Navigator. Course checked, Oxygen okay.'

'Pilot to radioman.'

'Equipment okay. In contact. Oxygen checked.'

'Pilot to tail-gunner.'

'Okay, sir. Checking guns.'

A jarring rattle of sound as he fired a short burst into the Channel.

'Okay, sir.'

'Pilot to waist-gunner . . .'

The checking finished, there was a silence on the intercom, broken only by occasional, mono-syllabic orders. The R/T was on strict radio silence.

Pretty soon they were over Belgium. A navigator reported:

'Some flak coming up over there, Skip.'

The pilot said: 'Okay. Watch it. Some fighters at eleven o'clock high. Keep your eyes on them. The P-47s are splitting them up.'

They flew on through the broken clouds, the patchwork of greens and browns below them. Ack-ack came up at them. But the Me 109s were largely leaving them alone, the P-47s keeping them away from the bomber formations.

A B-17 was suddenly on fire. It fell away

Left A huge force of Boeing B-17 Flying Fortresses flies high over Germany, heading for the heavily guarded ball-bearing plants at Schweinfurt.

sideways and blew up. No word was spoken on the R/T.

The Fortresses flew on.

Eventually, Aachen came up – 240 miles from the English coast; the point where the P-47s had to turn back.

From here on to Schweinfurt the bombers would have to fly on without a fighter escort.

Some of the P-47s waited till the last moment before wheeling away with a final 'good luck' rock of their wings.

The Fortresses stayed on course.

Now they were on their own. From now on the Luftwaffe would give them their full attention.

A pilot said: 'Okay. Watch it now. Keep your eyes peeled. Don't fire till you get them in range. Short bursts. Hold them down now. Here they come, here they come! Let 'em have it, boys –'

The cost of daylight bombing

Once again the unbelievable US concept of high-level, unescorted, daylight bombing was being stubbornly put to the test, with almost three hundred bombers going back to Schweinfurt.

Only two months before, the deepest daylight penetrations of Hitler's Fortress-Europe had been attempted – by Flying Fortresses of the Eighth Air Force on their famous Regensburg-Schweinfurt raid. Of the 315 bombers which took part, 60 were shot down with their ten-man crews.

And this morning – 14 October 1943 – the Eighth was going deep into Germany to attack the Schweinfurt ball-bearing plants again.

Daylight bombing had been the subject of much high-level and press controversy. The British had produced bombers that could carry 8 ton block-busters, and they were concentrating on satura-tion-bombing at night. The Americans preferred daylight bombing of specific targets, using its Flying Fortresses with their strong defensive armour and precision Norden bomb sights to

Right P-51 Mustangs – which eventually were to replace the P-47 Thunderbolts as long-range escorts. They were to prove the deadliest fighters of the War.

Overleaf Flying Fortresses, so called because of their fire-power and armour, head into Germany, while above them the vapour trails of escorting Thunderbolts create stark patterns against the sky.

strike at ball-bearing and synthetic rubber plants, research stations, steel plants, electric-power installations, railroads, dams and dykes; and later the V-1 and V-2 launching sites. The RAF struck at all these targets, too; but at night.

Beginning in January 1943, as Operation Overlord was being planned, the combined Allied air forces began round-the-clock bombing of Germany, hitting such targets as the huge Ploesti oil refineries in Rumania, the submarine bases at St. Nazaire and Lorient, the Skoda arms plants in Czechoslovakia, the Diesel works at Nuremburg, and the vital ball-bearing plants at Schweinfurt.

The Luftwaffe attacks

'Here they come!' yelled a waist-gunner. 'Three o'clock high! A dozen or more.'

A rattle of cannon-fire blasted above the roar of the engines.

The Luftwaffe had been waiting for the P-47s to turn and go home. Now they unleashed an air-to-air attack on a scale never seen before, with the

Below A Messerschmitt 410, one of the least successful German fighters, peels off in a death-dealing dive to attack a Flying Fortress.

aim of destroying the morale and fighting efficiency of the Eighth Air Force once and for all.

A running air-battle began which ranged over hundreds of miles and developed into epic proportions. Masses of German fighters came swarming down like wasps, tearing at the formations. Some attacked singly. Others dived in groups, isolating a flight and completely destroying it. They used cannon, air-to-air rockets, and air-to-air bombing from above, to blast the bombers out of the sky. Groups circled the formations, picking off stragglers like sitting ducks.

Never before had the enemy made such full and such expertly co-ordinated attacks. It was obvious that they had waited for this moment to attack in strength, knowing that the Allied fighters had turned back.

The Fortresses flew on, closing their ranks as bombers blew up, or dived away out of control, or fell behind, crippled. Their gunners blasted streams of shells and tracer at their deadly attackers, as the formations pressed on towards the target.

Wave after wave of fighters attacked. A screen of Me 109s streaked in from the front, firing 20mm cannon and machine-guns until almost crashing into the bombers head-on.

Behind them came large formations of twin-

Above The horrors of daylight bombing. A Flying Fortress, hit by enemy cannon-fire, breaks up in mid-air. A ten per cent loss of aircraft was the cost of unescorted daylight raids over Germany.

engine fighters in waves, each plane unleashing rockets from projectors beneath both wings, lobbing them into the middle of the formations from a range of 1,000 yards.

Others attacked from the rear, firing at the leading V, knowing that the normal spread of their shell-bursts would be certain to give them hits.

The fighters made their diving passes through the formations. Some of them kept on going, trailing smoke. The rest swooped up to gain height and reform, then came swarming down again. The twin-engine rocket carriers, having expended their rockets, climbed and came down in the role of fighters, blasting into the bombers with large-bore cannon.

By now, more than half of the Fortresses had been hit. One flight of the 1st Bombardment Division, which had borne the brunt of the attack, had been completely wiped out by the air-to-air rockets. The 40th Combat Wing had lost seven of its 49 planes, and several more were so badly damaged that they dived away and turned for home. 28 B-17s were destroyed with their ten-man crews before the badly mauled force reached the target.

Bombing run

A sudden change of course south of Schweinfurt confused the enemy fighters, whose attacks diminished as the Fortresses banked, then levelled to make their bombing run.

The leading bombardier said:

'Switches one, two, three, four, okay. Open bomb-bay doors.'

The turret gunner said: 'Bomb-bay doors open.'

'Okay. Everything's all set.'

'Clutch in.'

The bombardier threw the switch onto the automatic pilot, which gave control of the aircraft to the bomb-sight. Then he lined up the course.

'Clutch in. Estimate target in thirty seconds.'

Visibility was good over the target, and the flak was thick. Their bursts became closer. 20 seconds . . . 15 seconds . . . 14 . . . 13 . . . 12 . . . the fighters were coming in again.

'Christ, how long is this going to last? Can't you get rid of those bombs?'

'Shut up. A few more seconds . . .'

The needles in the sight came together. They felt the great plane buck as the bombs left her.

'Bombs away. Let's get the hell out of here!'

Considering the mauling the 1st Bombardment Division had received, their bombing was unusually effective. The first force straddled the target with hundreds of bombs. By the time the second force came in, its bombardiers were handicapped by clouds of smoke from the burning plant. Even the crippled 40th Combat Wing dropped more than half of its bombs within 1,000 feet of the aiming point.

Of the 291 Fortresses that had left England, 228 succeeded in dropping their bombs – 1,122 of them – on or about all three of the huge Schweinfurt ball-bearing plants. 88 direct hits were scored on the factory buildings and a further 55 bombs fell in the plant area.

Running for home

As the straggling force headed for home, the German fighters continued to tear at them. The

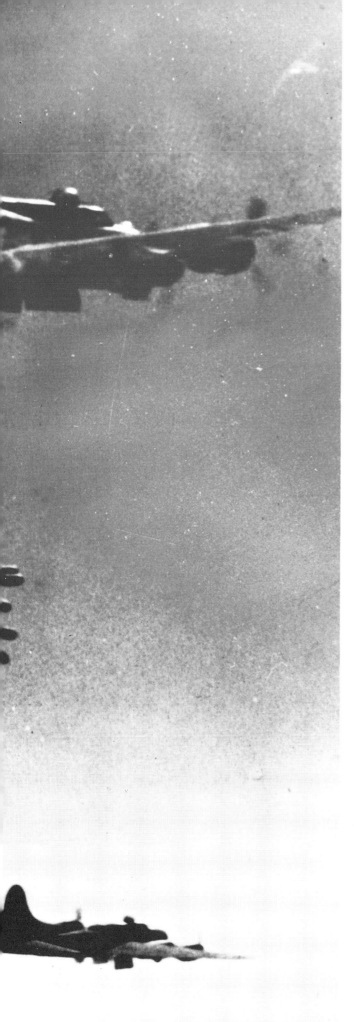

ground forces were waiting for them too, and a renewed hail of flak came up at them, knocking down a few more, and causing the pilots to make wasteful detours as they sought to husband their precious gallons of fuel.

Two squadrons of RAF Spitfire IXs arrived to take on the Me 109s, and a running, whirling dog-fight went on for over 200 miles along the withdrawal course which took them over northern France.

Further relief came to the labouring bombers as they passed Mèzières, when a large group of USAF Lightnings arrived to join the Spitfires in driving off the Messerschmitts.

At last the bombers were safe from air attack and ground fire as they headed across the Channel, a crippled and bleeding force, with many of the crews killed or wounded in 144 of the 237 planes still flying.

Six of the damaged Fortresses crashed in England trying to land. In all, the Eighth Air Force lost 60 B-17s and their ten-man crews. 17 more had suffered irreparable damage. And 121 others sustained hits and many crew members had been killed or wounded. The Luftwaffe lost over 120 fighters, and a further 100 were damaged.

General Arnold, then chief of the US Eighth Air Force, was later to write about the Schweinfurt raid: 'No such savage air battle had been seen since the war began.'

Strategically, the raid was the most important of 16 made by Allied bombers on the Schweinfurt ball-bearing plants. It caused the most damage and the greatest interference to production. But it demonstrated to the Americans that the cost of such deep penetrations by daylight, without fighter escort, was too high to be borne for long.

However, the Americans were still unconvinced, stating that losses of up to 25 per cent were acceptable when hitting heavily fortified strategic targets of great importance, the destruction of which could damage enemy war production.

To obscure the argument forever, in mid-October the weather shut down foggily on southeast Germany for most of the remainder of the year, after which Operation Overlord dictated different tactics.

Left Although one wing of this Flying Fortress is blazing fiercely, the pilot manages to hold his aircraft on course long enough to allow his bombardier to drop a full bomb-load on the target.

OPERATION CARTHAGE

As the liberating Allies pushed through Europe in the Spring of 1945, the Gestapo ruthlessly clamped down on the growing resistance movements. In answer, Mosquito squadrons of the RAF staged daring pinpoint attacks on the headquarters of the Nazi secret police.

The three Mosquito formations, with their Mustang escort, swept over the dark boisterous sea at a little above wave height. The navigator in the leading Mosquito, Squadron Leader E. B. Sismore, checked and rechecked his calculations. His job was to guide the formation across the North Sea and hit the Jutland coast exactly at the gap in the German anti-aircraft defences. A miscalculation would alert the enemy AA network and fighter squadrons and the surprise element would be lost.

It was a pretty high-powered 'show'. The first wave was led by Wing Commander Bob ('Pinpoint') Bateson (with Sismore as navigator) and included Air Vice-Marshal Basil Embry and four Mosquitos of 21 Squadron, among them Wing Commander Peter Kleboe. The second wave comprised six Mosquitos of 464 (RAAF) Squadron, led by Wing Commander Bob Iredale, and the third, six Mosquitos from 487 (RNZAF) Squadron, led by Wing Commander F. H. Denton. All the Mosquitos carried 'still' cameras, and unarmed Mosquitos Mark IV of Film Photographic Unit flew with the first and third waves.

Chosen for the job was the Mark VI Mosquito built by de Havilland largely of wood. Its crew of two was housed side by side in the compact, glass-canopied cockpit. Often used in high-level bombing, it was in low-level strafing or bombing attacks that the 'wooden wonder' was most deadly. Able to carry a bomb load of two 1000lb bombs to a range of 1,000 miles or more, it was ideal for this mission.

Through the enemy defences

Bateson fought to control his tossing, bucketing aircraft, and Sismore strained forward, straining his eyes for a sign of the enemy coast. Sea spray had dried on the windscreen; the washers had run out of glycol and the blades of the wipers were jerking across the screen, scratching marks in the dried salt, making vision almost impossible. Sismore checked his watch anxiously and strained forward.

The faint line on the horizon came up at last. Sismore breathed a sigh of relief. He recognised the familiar landmarks of Jutland.

As soon as they reached the coast, Bateson waggled his Mosquito's wings, then throttled up to 275 miles an hour. This was the signal for the planes to fan out into loose formation as they streaked across the north of Funen and the Great Belt at tree-top height. The wind was not so savage now, but visibility remained extremely limited as the wind-screens clouded over with dust and pulverized insects. They reached the coast of Zealand south of Kalundborg.

Lake Tisso slid under, a grey splash in the pleasant landscape. Bateson waggled his wings again. At this signal the second and third echelons banked round in a wide circle, leaving

Left The de Havilland Mosquito, called the 'Wooden Wonder' by its admirers, was probably the most adaptable aircraft of the War. It was used with success as a fighter, bomber and reconnaissance plane.

Bateson's flight to bore on to the target alone with some of the Mustangs.

The two waves made a wide circuit of the lake. Then the second echelon levelled out and headed for the target, leaving the third wave to do another circuit. This separated the three echelons by approximately a minute.

By now, Bateson was leading his flight toward the target. The six Mosquitos were strung out thirty feet apart. Fields and roads and high-tension cables flashed below, then houses on the outskirts of Copenhagen. A bridge appeared ahead of him, and he saw some tall light-standards sticking up and eased the Mosquito over them. Sismore had the bomb bay doors open now and was straining forward, his eyes squinting to pierce the murky windshield. He pointed suddenly to draw the pilot's attention to the small bunch of lakes and beyond them the camouflaged building on Kampmannsgade – the Danish headquarters of the Gestapo and the target of Operation Carthage . . .

Count-down to liberation

On June 6 – D-day for the invasion of Europe – fifty Danish saboteurs destroyed the Globus factory, which made aircraft parts and components for V-2 rockets. And during the next two months, many such raids were carried out, including the devastating action against the Rekylriffel Syndiket works and the German barracks at Jaegersborg.

The SS retaliated violently, executing eight saboteurs on 23 June, and proclaiming a state of emergency in the capital.

In answer, 10,000 workers from Denmark's largest shipyards went on strike, to be joined by tens of thousands of factory workers. On 30 June, Hitler's special plenipotentiary in Denmark, Dr Werner Best, cut off all supplies of electricity, gas and water and executed eight more saboteurs. Copenhagen declared a general strike and open rebellion broke out, during which 700 people were killed or injured.

The strikes and sabotage in Jutland had the effect of holding up several German divisions which were being moved from Norway and Denmark to the Western Front to help stem the invasion.

Werner's answer was an SS raid on every police station in Denmark, in which nearly 10,000 policemen were arrested, 2,000 being deported to concentration camps.

The Allied Command immediately acknowledged Denmark's contribution to the fight against Germany, and decided to help the Danish resistance. They knew that the Gestapo headquarters in Aarhus, Copenhagen and Odense were centres for interrogation, and that they stored a dangerous accumulation of information concerning the resistance movement.

On 31 October 1944, twenty-five Mosquitos of 21, 464 and 487 Squadrons hit Gestapo headquarters at Aarhus. In eleven minutes they destroyed the two Gestapo buildings of the university, killing Schwitzgiegel, the Gestapo chief in Jutland and more than 200 of his subordinates, and destroying the vital records of the Danish resistance.

In November, Air Vice-Marshal Embry suggested the raid on Shell House, Copenhagen. Svend Truelsen, head of Danish intelligence in London, supported it. At the briefing, he explained to crews the necessity for the raid despite the presence of prisoners in the building, who were expected to be executed and were undergoing torture before being finally shot by the SS.

Gestapo Headquarters was a shallow U-shaped building that faced south on Kampmannsgade, with two short wings running northwards along Nyropsgade and Veder Farimagsgade. Built in 1934 as the headquarters in Denmark of the Shell Oil Company, it had been commandeered by the Gestapo in May 1943, since when it had become the Baltic nerve centre of the various Nazi departments concerned with sabotage, resistance, espionage and counter-intelligence. Besides the prisoners who were brought daily from the *Vestre Faengsel* for interrogation and torture, the building housed a dangerous accumulation of information concerning the Danish resistance movement. The destruction of this information and the release of the prisoners was the purpose of Operation Carthage.

On the morning of the raid, selected prisoners who needed special 'treatment' had been brought to Shell House from the *Vestre Faengsel* (West-

Right Pilot and navigator climb aboard a Mosquito. The Mosquito was faster than most German fighters and, unloaded, had a ceiling of over 40,000 feet – qualities which stemmed from its light, all-wood construction.

ern Prison). Others, who had endured the night's interrogation, were being held in cells on the sixth floor of the building.

The cells in the west wing facing Nyropsgade were full. Poul Bruun, one of the last prisoners to arrive, was sitting at a table playing patience, waiting to be interrogated. In the last cell, Mogens Prior lay on his bed. On the fifth floor, Captain Peter Ahnfeldt-Mollerup and Poul Borking were being interrogated. Gesso Pedersen had been moved out of cell 14, leaving Brandt Rehberg alone to think about his dreaded meeting with the Gestapo chief.

When the prisoners heard the sound of aircraft coming in low across the city they concluded that they were the usual German fighters playing games – sweeping low over the building to

Left Operation Carthage was not the first operation mounted against Gestapo H.Q. In October 1944, Mosquitos bombed Gestapo H.Q. at Aarhus, killing many occupants – including Schwitzgiegel, the notorious Gestapo chief in Jutland.

Below The accuracy of low-level bombing by Mosquitos is demonstrated in this photograph of Gestapo H.Q. at Aarhus, taken by a photographic Mosquito. The centre of the building, which housed the Nazi staff, has been destroyed, while the rest of the building is untouched.

frighten the prisoners. Then they heard a rattle of machine gun fire – and a few seconds later a huge explosion rocked the building . . .

Triumph – and tragedy

Bateson, in the lead Mosquito, bore in on the target, keeping his nose pointed at the pavement of Kampmannsgade. As the building rushed towards him, filling his windscreen, machine gun bullets and tracers ripped at him from sandbag emplacements on surrounding roof tops. He released his bombs and pulled back the stick and the Mosquito swept up and cleared the long facade.

Embry came in next, pressed the bomb release and swept up over the building, flattening over the streets to avoid the heavy anti-aircraft fire. Carlisle was right on his tail. The first three loads of bombs had hit the target.

Then tragedy struck. Kleboe, trailing half a mile back, not in formation, flashed across Dybbolsbro station to find a light standard in his path, rising 130 feet above the shunting yards. He saw it too late, tried to lift over it, and just nicked it with his tail-plane, which tore apart. He instantly jettisoned his bombs onto Sonder Boulevard, killing eight people. Horrified Danes

on the streets and looking out of windows saw the Mosquito rise sharply, turn on its side and crash onto a garage in Frederiksberg Alle with a great burst of flame.

Henderson, close behind him, was just able to miss the light standard, banked sharply, then levelled to drop his bombs through the roof on the Nyropsgade side. Then, skimming over the roof tops behind Shell House, he looked for the leaders. He saw Bateson's Mosquito, but not Embry's, and presumed that the old man had 'bought it'. Embry was at that instant right under him, and Henderson, flattening lower to avoid the anti-aircraft fire, was forcing him down to the chimneys. It was a close thing for a few seconds, then they split, heading for the coast.

The second wave – the Australian squadron led by Wing Commander Bob Iredale – levelled out from Lake Tisso and roared toward the target. As they swept towards it they could see a pall of smoke over the city. A yellow stab of flame from the Alleenberg garages, where Kleboe's plane had crashed, added to the confusion, and neither Iredale nor his navigator could identify the target; so Iredale banked away from the line of attack and made a wide circuit to try to get his bearings. This time he was able to pick out St Jorgen's Lake, and he swept in on Shell House and dropped his bombs on the corner of the building.

The rest of 464 Squadron's effort was abortive, two Mosquitos dropping their bombs on the Frederiksberg fire by mistake.

The New Zealanders, led by Wing Commander F H Denton, flew into a barrage of fire and were misled by the Frederiksberg fire, dropping their bombs on the garage and nearby buildings. Another pilot saw the error but was too late to correct it and dropped his bombs in the sea as he turned for home.

Now the Mustangs came in over the city, machine-gunning the anti-aircraft positions. One of the fighters was hit and it crashed in flames in a public park.

In four minutes the raid was over.

In addition to Kleboe's Mosquito and the crashed Mustang, four other aircraft failed to return to base. One Mustang crash-landed on the west coast of Jutland and the pilot was taken prisoner; two 464 Squadron Mosquitos were shot down on the way home; and one of 487 Squadron's Mosquitos crashed on Hven and the crew were killed. Many of the planes were badly

damaged, one belly-landing at Fersfield. The raid had cost the RAF six planes and nine lives.

And there had been other, more tragic, losses. A red brick Catholic school – the Jeanne d'Arc School – adjacent to the garages in Frederiksberg, was destroyed by wrongly directed bombs, and, of 482 children, 86 were killed, as well as seventeen adults.

But the nerve centre of the Gestapo in Denmark had been destroyed, and a vast collec-

tion of files and indexes, containing dangerous information concerning the Danish resistance movement, incinerated. Many of the prisoners escaped and there were casualties among the Germans and their collaborators. And there was a bonus. From the ruins, resistance workers salvaged two filing cabinets containing a complete list of Danes in the pay of the Germans – a list which was held for use after the liberation.

With the complete destruction of records at Aarhus, Copenhagen and Odense – the latter destroyed by RAF Mosquitos on 17 April – the power of the Gestapo in Denmark was smashed. Liberation came only eighteen days later.

Below Shell House after the raid. The tactical success of the raid was completely overshadowed by the large number of aircraft lost and the tragic death of 86 children, killed when a bomb hit their school.

KAMIKAZE

After the costly battles of Leyte Gulf and Iwo Jima, the Japanese in 1945 were a beaten nation. But it was in defeat that they proved most deadly; for out of the desparate defence of their homeland were born the Kamikaze pilots — volunteers for certain death.

The Operation Kikusui pilots had risen early. After a light breakfast they assembled in the crew-hut and took part in a brief formalized ritual conducted by a veteran pilot of renown. In an atmosphere of spiritual zeal and extraordinary solemnity, each man was given the black ceremonial belt on which was inscribed the code of *Bushido*. He put it on, than drank a toast to Emperor Hirohito, to the everlasting survival of Nippon, and to a glorious death.

Then they joined lustily in singing *The Kamikaze Song of the Warrior:*

> *In serving on the seas, be a corpse saturated with water;*
> *In serving on land be a corpse covered with weeds,*
> *In serving in the sky, be a corpse that challenges the clouds.*
> *Let us all die close by the side of our Sovereign.*

After the ceremony they broke off and went back to their barracks, where they waited for their orders and wrote letters to their families.

One, Reserve Ensign Susumu Kaijitsu, wrote:

'My activities are quite ordinary. My greatest concern this morning is not about death, but rather of how I can be sure to sink an enemy carrier. . . . Please watch for the results of my meagre efforts. If they prove good, think kindly of me and consider my good fortune. Most of all, do not weep for me.'

Presently a whistle sounded – the signal for them to prepare for take-off. They left their sealed letters on their beds and hurried out to the parade ground.

Volunteers – for death

Several hundred clear-eyed young *Kamikaze* pilots assembled in their groups and flights under the fluttering *Kikusui* flag, on which was the emblem of a half-chrysanthemum floating on water. *Kikusui* stood for 'Floating Chrysanthemum', the symbol of spiritual purity, and represented the air-sea nature of Operation Kikusui as well as the moral grandeur of the suicide volunteers, who had deliberately accepted death in the

Left A group of young kamikaze pilots, carrying samurai swords, pose for a final photograph before flying their one-way mission against the American Pacific Fleet. The inset shows an officer presenting flowers to a pilot.

vitally important defence of Okinawa.

One by one, as they answered the roll call, they saluted their superiors and the comrades they had met during the few short weeks of training, then they made their way to the trucks which would take them across the field to their designated machines.

The sky over the Kyushu airbase had begun to clear and there was a slight breeze coming from the haze-shrouded sea as the trucks jolted across to the waiting aircraft.

They were a weird collection of machines: single-engined Zeke and Zero fighters with 600 lb bombs fixed beneath their bellies; Baku mass-produced planes of crude and minimal construction, entirely without armour, but with 550lb of TNT encased in the nose, set to explode on contact; giant conventional bombers which had been modified to carry the Ohka – a piloted version of the German V-1 glide-bomb, made of wood, with a 2,640lb bomb built into the fuselage.

Once inside their machines, the pilots locked

themselves in the cockpits and waited with oriental serenity for the signal to begin their last one-way journey on this earth.

Presently, engines began to burst into life, and soon there was a roar of a score of deafening motors, a hundred, two hundred . . . and the first planes began to move towards the take-off point.

Now they were thundering down the runway, singly at first, then in groups of twos and threes, lifting over the ocean towards Okinawa, where a huge Allied Armada of 1,500 vessels, mostly American, was strung out for miles around the beachheads.

Once airborne, each *Kamikaze* pilot awaited his bitter-sweet destiny and prayed for the sublime courage to die for the homeland and to conform to the code of his ancestors in his last noble act.

Left A comrade tightens the 'hachimaki' – a symbol of manly courage – round the head of a kamikaze pilot. The young suicide pilots seemed to draw moral courage from the ceremonial preceding their missions.

Below To the cheers of their comrades and ground staff, kamikaze pilots warm up the engines of their bomb-laden planes, in readiness for an attack on American ships assisting in the invasion of Leyte Gulf.

Divine wind

The *Kamikaze* legend had been born during the Battle for Leyte Gulf, when Vice-Admiral Takijiro Onishi, commander of the Japanese air forces in the Philippines, sent out his pilots in bomb-laden Zero fighters in an effort to damage the flight decks of the American carriers and thus prevent them from launching their planes. The volunteer pilots responded with zeal, crashing their planes on the flat-tops and inflicting hundreds of casualties. But the attacks failed, and the Americans dealt a decisive blow to the remnants of the Japanese Navy.

But after Leyte Gulf and the costly invasion of Iwo Jima, the greatest battle of the Pacific War was still to be fought – the Battle for Okinawa.

The largest of the Ryukyu Islands, Okinawa stood between the Allied forces and the Japanese mainland and was of the utmost importance strategically, being half as close again to Japan as Iwo Jima. The Japanese had to make a stand here or lose the war, and its garrison of 70,000 troops were prepared to fight to the death to defend it.

Onishi, without enough planes to prosecute conventional attacks, was faced with the task of depriving the Americans of Okinawa's airfields which had the potential to handle 5,000 planes.

Left A Zero, only a split second away from destruction, aims straight for an anti-aircraft position whose gunners have failed to hit the hurtling plane.

Above While crew members row for safety in a lifeboat, a Japanese fighter-bomber, which has shot down an American plane, circles above them.

He decided to stake all on suicide tactics.

He called together his remaining pilots and told them that the salvation of Japan was in their hands. He invited them to volunteer for the *Kamikaze Tokubetsu Kogekitai* (*Kamikaze* Special Attack Squad), and offered them a glorious death for the Emperor and the homeland.

The pilots volunteered to a man.

Onishi's strategy was a stream-lined version of the *Banzai* charge, and was based in the ritual Japanese veneration of the Emperor and on belief in the life of the spirit after death. In a favourite Nippon legend, a *Kamikaze* (Divine Wind), sent by the Sun Goddess, wrecked the huge fleet of the Mogul conqueror Kublai Khan in 1281. Now Onishi's glorious young men would become the Divine Wind which would destroy the hateful invaders and save the homeland. They were his secret weapon.

And so, late on the morning of 6 April 1945, 355 planes, divided into two waves, took off from Kanoya and Shikoku to break the spirit of those weak Americans who considered earthly life so precious.

Waves of death

There were 195 navy planes in the first wave, including eighty *Kamikazes* of various types,

Though badly damaged by anti-aircraft fire, a blazing Japanese dive-bomber presses home its attack on USS Kitkun Bay – part of the Leyte Gulf invasion force. The photo inset shows the destruction caused by a kamikaze when it crashed onto the flight deck of the USS Belleau Wood. American carriers, unlike their British equivalent, did not possess armoured flight decks and were particularly vulnerable to the plunging vertical dives of the suicide planes.

eight Type One bombers carrying Ohkas and 107 escort fighters. The army's *Tokubetsu* of 160 assorted *Kamikazes* took off a little later, forming the second wave.

Aboard the hundreds of ships that made up the Allied fleet – flat-tops, battleships, cruisers, destroyers, troopships, transports, landing craft, ancillary vessels – almost a quarter of a million Americans saw the first wave of *Kamikazes* come over the horizon.

First of all, as the alarms sounded, they were specks – a dozen or so – dimly seen in the morning haze; moving specks that surged into view, growing larger. Behind them came more, and more, a hundred . . . you lost count. And now you heard the sound of their engines. They came swarming across the ocean like angry wasps.

They were at varying heights, and in no particular formation. There were over 200 in the opening attack. Allied Navy fighters – mostly American, some British – swooped down on the leading wave and shot down over a score in the opening seconds.

And now the ships, some of them manoeuvring to present a difficult target, began to pump out a blistering fire of anti-aircraft shells. Some of the Jap machines exploded in the air. Others crashed and were swallowed up by the waves.

The *Kamikazes* came on, in straight and determined flight, not weaving or turning from the barrage of fire or from the attacks of fighters. The sky was dotted with bursts. And now even the big guns thundered, point blank, sights lowered, lifting enormous fountains of water below the attackers.

Like moths into flame, the suicide planes descended on the fleet in the most eerie and blood-chilling spectacle of the war. It was like watching a mysterious force at work, not human, but unbelievably gallant and stupid.

Escorting fighters – Mitsubishi Zeros, flown by veterans – engaged the American and British fighters which were still coming off the carriers to meet them. And all hell was let loose, plane after plane hitting the sea and exploding, destroyers and other small ships veering wildly to dodge the *Kamikazes*, listing to 45 degrees in abrupt turns,

while their gunners desperately tried to fight off the attackers.

Destroyer *Bush* was hit by a diving Baku, then by two more in quick succession. *Colhoun*, nearby, shot down five planes, then was hit by three Bakus. The attack transport *Logan Victory* was

Right Zeros, code-named Zekes by the Allies, were the mainstay of the Japanese fighter force and were highly effective throughout the War, both as conventional fighters and suicide weapons.

hit, and her cargo of ammunition exploded and split here in half. Minesweeper *Emmons* was sunk; transport *LST*-447 was struck by two Ohkas and sunk; fleet carrier *Hancock* was hit, as were light carrier *San Jacinto*, eleven destroyers, four escort vessels and five minelayers. More seriously damaged were destroyers *Haynsworth* and *Taussig*, each disabled by two hits.

One hundred and thirty-five *Kamikazes* sacrificed themselves or were shot down in that first attack. Of the eight Ohka-carrying bombers, five were shot down. By now the battle was

spread over a wide area and the sky was dotted with explosions and streaked with ragged patterns of smoke from exploded aircraft.

The ultimate sacrifice

Reserve Ensign Susumu Kaijitsu had been shot clear of the mother-plane by activating the first of his three rockets. Now he was diving into the holocaust at 600 miles an hour.

He saw a flat-top – the most glorious prize – and, guiding his flying-bomb towards it, hurtled out of the sky in an almost vertical dive.

He was chanting softly as the strain on his body began to build up:

'May my death be as sudden and as clean . . . as the shattering . . . of a crystal. . . .'

Down he dropped, following the movement of the carrier, exultantly conscious that it carried a supply of inflammable fuel. The littered ocean rushed towards him.

'Let me fall . . . clean and radiant. . . .'

Shells ripped up at him in those last glorious seconds, tearing off his port wing, and his plane began to twist away as the super-structure of the carrier filled his windshield. . . .

'Life is like a delicate flower. . . .'

A blinding flash filled his brain, then blackness. . . .

A terrible cost

The battle could not keep up its furious pace, and for long periods there was silence across the vast smoking scene. Then another wave would come and the fury would begin again. But by nightfall they had dwindled to a few individual attacks by small groups of Bakus. During its first day, Operation Kikusui had cost the Japanese 248 machines and pilots.

On the following morning, only 114 planes, sixty of them escort fighters, could be assembled. They came over the glistening sunlit sea, to be cut to pieces by large patrols of Thunderbolts

and Hellcats. But a few got through, one crashing on the already damaged deck of the fleet-carrier *Hancock*, killing forty-three men, another setting fire to the battleship *Maryland*. Among the other ships hit were destroyers *Gregory* and *Bennett*, both of which were heavily damaged. The Japanese sacrificed over 100 machines.

The incredible battle raged for eighty-two days and nights, on some days the Japanese mustering only a few planes, but on others mounting great and costly attacks.

On 12 April, over came 350-plus aircraft from Kyushu in two main assaults. They spent themselves in unprecedented fury, crashing their planes on fleet-carriers *Enterprise* and *Essex*, battleships *Missouri*, *New Mexico* and *Idaho*, light cruiser *Oakland* – also on ten destroyers, three destroyer escorts, three minesweepers, two gunboats and one landing ship. Though these ships were heavily damaged, some having to leave the battle zone, only one – the destroyer *Mannert L Abele*, hit amidships by an Okha piloted bomb – was sunk. The Japanese lost 330 aircraft.

Operation Kikusui went on, taking an alarming toll in lives and ships: 16 April, 155 planes attacked Task Force 58 and ships anchored off Okinawa, two *Kamikazes* hitting the deck of carrier *Intrepid*, setting fire to her, and damaging a score of other ships; 27 April, 115 planes; 28 April, 200-plus – hitting hospital-ship *Comfort;* 3 and 4 May, 305 planes; 11 May – *Bunker Hill* hit, 400 killed, *New Mexico* hit again.

On 15 May, the fleet carrier *Enterprise* left Okinawa on a mission to attack airfields on the Japanese mainland. During the morning twenty-five *Kamikazes* swept over the horizon from the south-west and were immediately intercepted by patrolling fighters. Most of the suicide planes were shot down by anti-aircraft fire and the Hellcats, but one got through, crashing onto the centre of the flightdeck, penetrating three decks and killing fourteen seamen. A 30-ton elevator was torn from its mountings and hurled into the air. Quick fire-control saved the carrier.

History's verdict

By 21 June, the Americans had lost 40 ships sunk and 368 ships damaged – and had lost 763 aircraft in battle against the *Kamikazes* and their escorts. Operation Kikusui had cost the Japanese approximately 7,800 aircraft and pilots before the last *Kamikaze* pilot had died in a crowning explosion of sublime courage and patriotism.

A Strategic Bombing Survey, originated later in the United States, concluded that the Japanese suicide pilots and planes had wrought such damage that if their attacks had been introduced earlier in the war, and if they had been sustained in greater power and concentration, they could well have caused the Allies to withdraw, or to revise their strategic plans.

But whatever the lessons learned – whatever the strategists or politicians of the future may postulate – one shining fact that emerged from those terrible weeks was the sublime spirit of the *Kamikaze* corps, whose pilots brought to the world a forgotten message of human courage.

Left Enough kamikazes got through to their targets to seriously worry the American High Command – who saw the morale of their men sink dangerously low. But few suicide planes survived the hazardous run-in.

KOREAN JET-WAR

In 1951, Korea, torn between Government and Communist forces, became the theatre for the first jet-war. High above the hostile terrain MiGs and Sabres met daily in supersonic combat. Death struck swiftly and it was not always the UN forces which triumphed.

The Red jets came out of the sun at 20,000 feet over 'MiG Alley' – that rugged, hostile area between the Yalu and the Chongchon rivers.

The flight leader of a patrol of twelve UN Sabres of 51 Fighter Wing saw the red-nosed, swept-wing fighters at twelve o'clock high, moving to nine o'clock in preparation for the attack, and yelled:

'Aircraft attacking nine o'clock high! Break starboard!'

Down the MiGs came, banking in behind the Sabres' tails, between thirty and forty of them, in groups of twos and threes, their guns chattering.

Flight Lieutenant Johnny Swifte saw tracer zip above him from behind, then felt his plane shudder. Then it flipped over on its back and spun down out of control, with clouds of smoke coming up through the floor of the cockpit.

'I've been hit!' he called, and in his panic thought of the sea. He must get to the sea and Dumbo.

At 10,000 feet he levelled out and wrenched the Sabre's nose violently towards the east, where the rugged mountains were silhouetted against the sea.

He reported on his radio:

'Still flying. On fire. Heading seawards.'

Fighting to survive the scorching heat, he urged his burning aircraft towards the coast, knowing that reaching the sea was his greatest hope. There was no chance of making it back to base, and the MiG pilots never followed UN planes out to sea for fear of being jumped by patrolling USN fighters. Also Dumbo would be there.

Dumbo was a specially equipped USN airsea-rescue flying-boat, the courage and vigilance of whose American crew had already saved the lives of hundreds of UN pilots during the two and a half years since the war began.

The leader had brought his flight of Sabres overhead now to keep the MiGs off Swifte's tail and cover him to the rescue point.

Operation Control at Seoul had heard the leader's call for another flight of fighters to take over and was already alerting two US helicopters to stand by.

Out to sea, beyond Chongju, flying-boat Dumbo was circling, with six USN fighters weaving above. The pilot and wireless-navigator were both listening on the fighter frequency and had heard the Australian pilot's message. The flying-boat was already heading toward the shore.

Swifte was in trouble. The Sabre was blazing fiercely, and he knew he'd never make it to the sea. He reached for the ejector button.

From above, the leader saw the smoking Sabre's canopy shoot backwards and the ejector seat flying out with the pilot in it, then the chute blossomed.

The Sabre kept on going, rolled gently on its back, and dived steeply, now enveloped in flames, until, with a vivid red flash, it exploded into a dozen flaming pieces which twisted and turned lazily as they fell to earth.

Swifte swung gently in the harness, looking below at the wooded hills and valleys, the rice fields, the curious U-shaped houses. He looked about him. Three Sabres were still overhead, and some MiGs were heading away to the northern mountains. To the west, he could see the sea about five miles away.

One hour away from the United Nations air bases and carrier forces were the cold blue hostile

Right Sabre F-86 jets, alerted by radar, take off to intercept hostile aircraft over 'MiG Alley'. The Sabres proved to be the most effective fighters of the Korean War – due largely to superior pilot training.

skies of North Korea, where the horizon lay miles inside China, and the meandering Yalu River marked the main line of resistance.

Behind the Yalu, he could see the region from which the Chinese and North Korean pilots, in their beautiful Russian-built MiGs, took off daily, swarming across the river in their hundreds to meet the sleek US Sabre Jets flown by American and Australian pilots...

The first jet-war

After the first year of the war had ended in defeat for the Communist forces in the field, there followed two years of dragging stalemate, with ninety Communist divisions facing General Ridgway's UN and South Korean forces along a ragged line that crossed the whole peninsular.

With the advent of the stalemate between ground forces, the need for close air support in the field was considerably reduced, so a new UN strategy was introduced. It was called 'Operation Strangle', and it was an all-out air offensive aimed at severing the Communist forward zone from the rest of North Korea. UN aircraft rained bombs on the roads in an effort to stop 3,000 tons of supplies reaching Communist troops daily. Then, when it was found that the roads could be repaired almost as quickly as they were damaged, the campaign was broadened to include the railway system as well, and in particular the bridges.

As the operation went on, the Communists became experts at dispersion and camouflage. Dummy airfields were built, with straw aircraft on them. Good airfields were camouflaged to look as though they were riddled with craters. Trains were kept in tunnels, and trucks in caves, to be taken out and moved during the night.

Generally, the US Air Force concentrated on the western side of Korea, and the USN carrier planes on the eastern part, both being co-ordinated from Seoul.

Left A Sabre peels off to attack a Communist supply and communications centre deep in the mountainous heart of North Korea. The rugged nature of the terrain made it difficult for the UN forces to engage the enemy.

Inset By the time of the Korean War, pilots were trained to a pitch never seen before. Their equipment reflects the sophisticated nature of jet warfare.

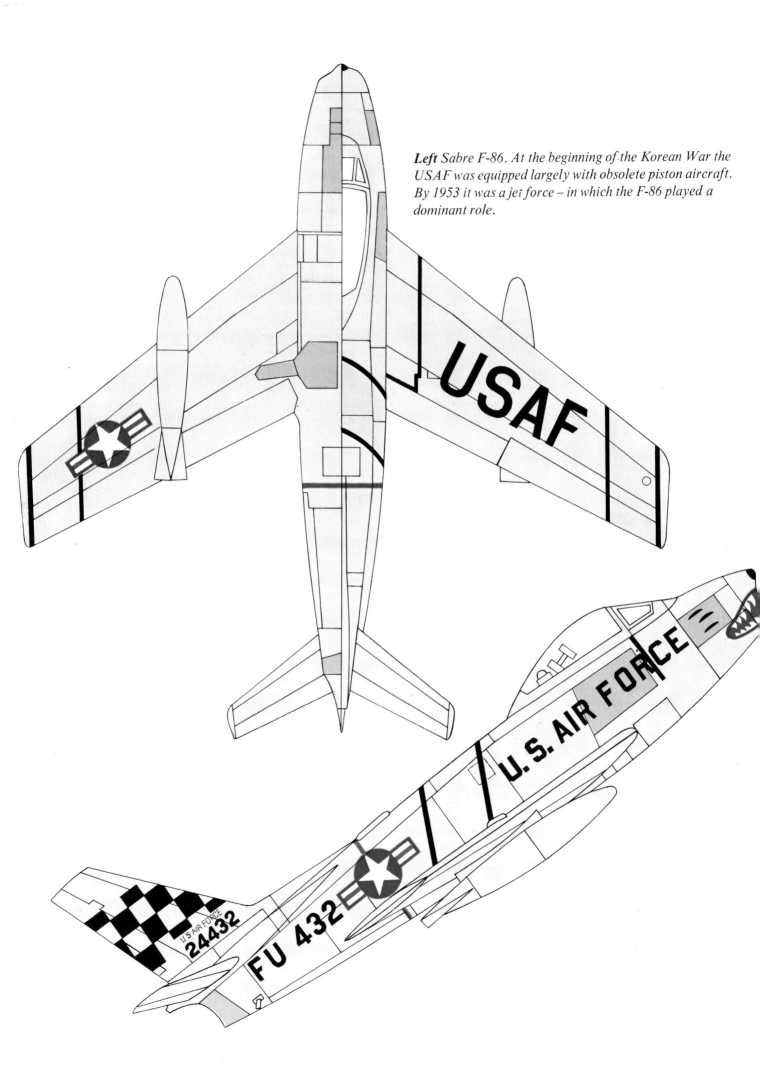

Left *Sabre F-86. At the beginning of the Korean War the USAF was equipped largely with obsolete piston aircraft. By 1953 it was a jet force – in which the F-86 played a dominant role.*

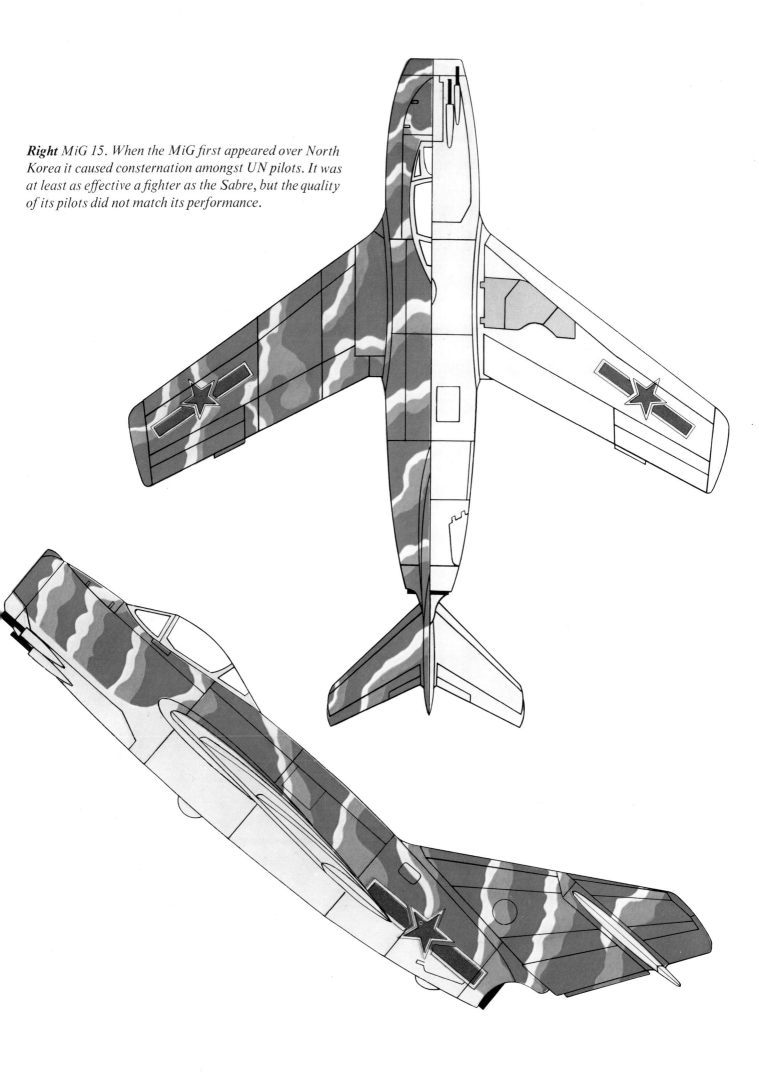

Right MiG 15. *When the MiG first appeared over North Korea it caused consternation amongst UN pilots. It was at least as effective a fighter as the Sabre, but the quality of its pilots did not match its performance.*

MiGs — the new menace

During the early part of the war, the UN airforce experienced little opposition from enemy aircraft, then, early in 1951, the Russian-built MiG swept-wing jet fighter arrived on the war-front, flown by Chinese pilots. Flying at near-sonic speed and armed with one 37mm and two 20mm cannons, they drastically altered the balance.

Gradually their numbers increased, and operations from behind the Yalu were stepped up. During February and March, several USAF B-29 strikes over the Sunchon area were met by these terrifying new jet fighters. On 12 April, forty-eight B-29s, escorted by seventy-two fighters, attacked the Antung-Sinuiju bridges, where they were met by a swarm of 80 MiGs. In a short, fierce battle, three B-29s were shot down for nine MiGs.

The Chinese Air Force became an increasingly important factor. By May they had over 1,000 aircraft and were building landing-strips in many parts of North Korea. Throughout the summer, increasing numbers of MiGs, vectored by GIC radar, intercepted UN formations. By September their number had risen to 1,400, and by October to over 3,000.

Now they flew across the Yalu in mass formations, seeking out targets in the Wonsan and Chinnampo areas, and attacking UN bombers and their fighter escorts, even reaching as far south as Seoul. And gradually the Mustangs and Meteors had to be withdrawn south of Chongchon, to be used for patrol and support duties. Only the Sabres were good enough to meet the MiGs in the daily battle for the control of the air over North Korea.

One of the most crucial encounters of the air war came on 23 October when eight B-29s attacked Namsi airfield, to be met by 150 MiGs. All eight bombers were hit and three were shot down.

For a week after the battle, large formations of MiGs came daily across the Yalu, forcing the USAF decision to stop daylight bombing.

Overnight, China had become one of the major air powers of the world.

***Right** The Dumbo, or SA-16, was an amphibious rescue plane brought into service to cut down the loss of valuable jet pilots who were shot down in North Korea.*

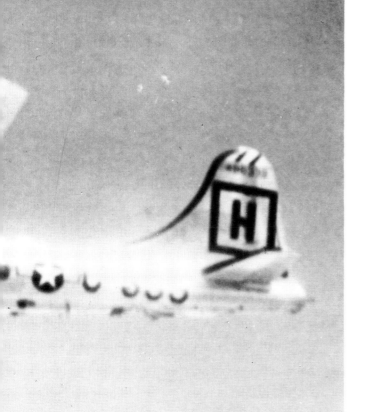

Combat — eight miles high

The Yalu was the political boundary over which the UN forces were not permitted to set foot. Consequently, the North Korean and Chinese MiGs could sit unmolested behind it. The UN pilots were not allowed to photograph them on their airfields, or attack them on the ground or while they were taking off. The Communist pilots, therefore, had the tremendous advantage of being able to climb unmolested behind the Chinese border to 40,000 feet, choose their position for attack, and wait for the UN patrols to run short of fuel before engaging them.

But then they would come – like avenging hawks out of the sun – and the fight would begin.

The UN pilots, greatly disadvantaged by having to fly 150 miles from the 38th Parallel to maintain air superiority over the ground forces and to allow the bombers and attack planes to prosecute 'Operation Strangle', lived in fear of being shot down in enemy territory. A downed pilot, probably injured, had little hope of ever getting out of one of the most rugged countries in the world, possibly in temperatures of 30 degrees below zero.

His only chance of getting out alive was to be picked up from the air, either out of the sea by an air-sea rescue unit, or from the ground by helicopter.

And this was one of the most vital aspects of the air war in Korea.

The morale of the whole fighter force depended on the efficiency and courage of the rescue system. To this end, General Everest, Commander of the US Fifth Air Force, had let it be known that he was prepared to lose two helicopters and crews in an effort to bring out one downed UN pilot from behind the lines.

He, at least, knew the dangers facing pilots in the battle for Korea – a battle fought for the bridges and reservoirs, for road and rail junctions,

Left A B-29 Superfortress drops its bombs on a target in North Korea. Heavy bombing was not as effective as had been anticipated.

Inset Rail junctions were important targets in the UN's bombing offensive. Code-named 'Operation Strangle', it was designed to isolate front-line Communist troops from their supply and communications centres.

and for anti-aircraft and searchlight installations – and in the sky, eight miles up.

In their zooming fire-spitting machines, men from the two halves of the world met daily, up there in the cold blue skies, in furious combat at sonic speeds. And it was in such combat, on a clear-skied day in May 1952, that Flight Lieutenant Swifte, an Australian serving with the UN forces, was jumped by MiGs over Chongchon and his plane shot down in flames.

A hazardous rescue

Swifte floated down. As he neared the ground he heard a rattle of fire and the whine of bullets. He hit the rocky ground on the side of a hill and rolled into the undergrowth. After releasing the harness, he got to his feet and moved in a crouching run to the other side of the valley from where the shots had come.

The flight leader reported to Ops Control that Swifte was down safely and supplied the map reference. Then he warned the controller that he and the other members of his flight were running out of fuel and would have to turn for home within the next four minutes.

Control told him:

'Baker Flight now approaching your position.'

At this point, six piston-engined fighters from Dumbo's escort flight arrived on the scene, flashing low over the hills, and a further formation of Sabres was coming in from 'MiG Alley'.

'Green Six to Able Leader.'

Swifte crouching behind an outcrop near the base of the hill, was using his small armpit radio.

Able Leader answered him.

Swifte described his position and warned him about the presence of enemy troops.

'Some fired on me as I landed.'

The flight came low over the area and climbed away so as not to draw attention to Swifte's hide-out. Some of the pilots saw troops moving across the hillside towards the spot where he had landed.

Meanwhile, a US helicopter had taken off from a forward base and was moving north under cover of six fighters. The distance to be covered was at extreme helicopter range, and a second helicopter was standing by, ready to follow at a moment's notice. If events made it necessary, it would take off and rendezvous at a point over the sea in Korea Bay, where the first helicopter carrying the

rescued pilot would ditch. The second helicopter would then hoist up the crew and the pilot and bring them back to base.

The second flight of Sabres appeared in the distance now, and Able Flight banked steeply in their turn for home. Swifte watched them go, their noses gently dipping, their silver canopies shining in the sun. He knew that they had over-stayed their limit and that most of them would 'flame out' before they reached base, meaning they would have to cover the last fifty miles and make their approach and landing without power.

It was eight minutes since Swifte's plane had been shot down, and presently the helicopter came on the air. Baker Leader, who had located Swifte, gave the American pilot the map position and warned him to expect enemy ground fire. Then he led his Sabres in on a strafing run to keep the Communists pinned down.

The chopper came in from across the sea, preceded by six escort fighters. They flashed in low with their guns churning up the ground on both sides of the hill.

The helicopter came quickly over the hills and set down gently on a flat spot at the bottom of the slope. Swifte stepped from behind the boulders and ran full tilt towards it, as the enemy troops opened fire.

Dumbo's six piston-engined fighters made their run one at a time, their guns blasting, at the same time as the Sabres attacked the troop positions.

Swifte reached the helicopter and was pulled

A rescue helicopter passes over a front line armoured unit on its way to pick up a pilot stranded behind enemy lines. Because jet pilots were so valuable every effort was made to recover them.

aboard, and a second later the chopper was off again, its great blades whirling, lifting off, lurching forward as it cleared the hills and swept away seawards.

Baker Leader reported back to Ops Control, and the show was over. The rattle of guns in the air and on the ground ceased. The chatter on the radio subsided to routine exchanges. The helicopter carrying Swifte, with its umbrella of fighters, moved south-west over the sea, then swung south towards the UN air-base and safety.

Jet war – a decisive factor?

Swifte was one of the fortunate pilots who survived being shot down in North Korea. Others were not so lucky – over 1,000 pilots, most of them Americans, were to die in that remote country. Whether they played a decisive role in ending the war is difficult to determine. Certainly the jet gave both sides immense striking power, but, just as in World War II, the ground forces and civilian population demonstrated that they could withstand this new and terrible weapon. Partly, of course, it was the rugged terrain which blunted the edge of the air-strikes. In such inhospitable country, it was impossible to come to grips with the enemy – a situation which was to be repeated in that other strife-torn Asian country – Vietnam.

'Operation Strangle' also failed because the source of raw materials and the main factories were beyond the Yalu River, where they were safe from air attack; and because of the ingenuity of the highly organised labour force in repairing roads, railways and bridges. But in the air the UN won a resounding victory. Whereas in January 1952 the Chinese Air Force flew 3,700 jet sorties, it was only able to fly 308 during June.

The cause was the poor standard of training; the Chinese pilots were not experienced enough to take on the Americans or the Australians, who shot them out of the sky in a ratio of ten to one; and all they could do by the end of the war was to try to preserve their precious aircraft.

Right An H-5 helicopter of the 3rd Air Rescue Squadron answers an emergency call for an aerial evacuation. To protect the helicopter as it lands, it will be escorted by a flight of fighters, whose job is to strafe enemy positions while the pick-up is made. Such missions saved the lives of many pilots shot down in North Korea.

PRE-EMPTIVE STRIKE

Arab-Israeli relations had deteriorated so badly by June 1967 that both sides knew a war was inevitable. The Israelis, confident that an Arab attack was imminent, decided to launch a pre-emptive air-offensive which would guarantee the success of their ground troops.

That morning the air was hot and breathless. The hills rose brown and empty on each side of the airfield. Beyond, withering in the harsh June sun, a wide panorama of vineyards fell away to the coast. To the south were broad acres of ploughed land, where a distant tractor crawled along the perimeter, a dust cloud shimmering in its wake.

At 0825, the first of five waves of Mirages began taking off amid billows of orange-red dust. They formed up into their separate groups over Jerusalem, then they wheeled toward the coast, flattening out as they reached the sea south of Bat Yam, and turned gently westward. All the pilots observed strict radio silence, and on the frequencies being monitored by Arab and Israeli intelligence there was no traffic; everything was normal.

The Israeli jets flew in five flat Vs, wing-tip to wing-tip, none more than 20 feet from the other. The Mediterranean this morning was cobalt-blue, brilliant and glistening in the slanting sun that glanced off the white-caps. Over the land, swelling white cumulus clouds had begun to form well under 10,000 feet. There was a slight haze which reduced visibility to about ten miles.

Presently, flight after flight, they turned gently eastward, now splitting up onto their pre-designated courses toward Sinai and Egypt. The leading flight headed for Cairo. Another turned toward the Suez Canal. Their targets were air-bases of the Egyptian Air Force – at Cairo West, Cairo International, El Mansura, Inchas, Abu Sueir, Fayid, Kabrit, Helwan, Beni Suef and El Minya.

It was 0835 Cairo Time on 5 June 1967.

In the Negev, where the Israeli Army was poised for a three-pronged attack on the 80,000-strong Egyptian troop concentration in Sinai, 15 twin-engine Vautour bombers were taking off from Hatzerim. Each plane carried two 500lb bombs and its maximum load of fuel.

They climbed steeply to 24,000 feet, forming up in two flights – one of seven aircraft, the other of eight – and headed due south on a course that would take them across the Gulf of Akaba, skimming over the edges of Saudi Arabian territory, and along the Red Sea to Luxor and Ras Banas.

Meanwhile, from other bases, squadrons of Mystères and Ouragans had taken off and were flying straight and low toward the string of Egyptian airfields in Sinai.

At 0845 the radio silence was shattered. A confused babble of voices burst over the R/T. All over Egypt the radio frequencies were suddenly jammed by incoherent chatter. Panic spread as the calls came from various bases.

'We are being attacked ... We are being attacked...'

Build-up to war

Ever since the Suez crisis ten years before, a United Nations peace-keeping force had occu-

Right Three Egyptian MiG 21 'Fishbed C' fighters destroyed on the apron at Abu Sueir in the '67 War. The accuracy of the Israeli attacks astounded both Arab and interested neutral observers.

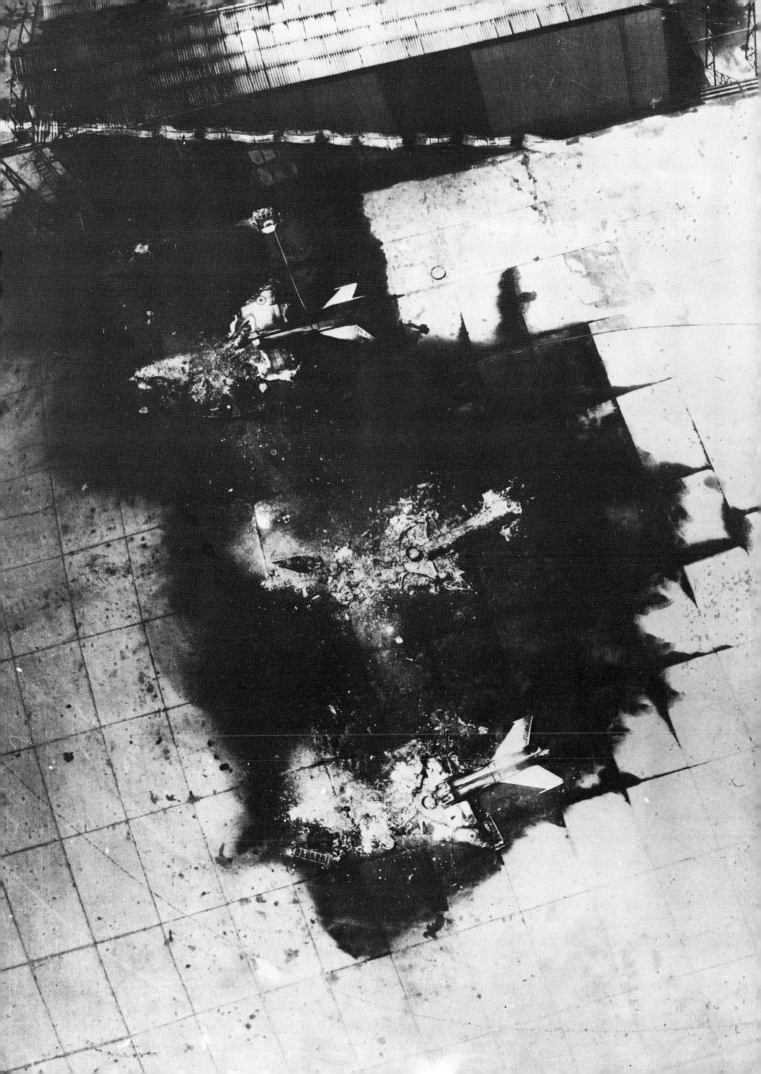

pied the Egyptian-Israeli border on the Gaza Strip and the heights of Sharm ash Shaykh, commanding the Strait of Tiran.

On 16 May, President Gamal Abd-al-Nasser came under pressure from the Arab world to close the Strait and to force a return to the pre-1956 borders.

On that same evening, Nasser dispatched a signal to the United Nations Secretary-General demanding that UN forces be withdrawn from the Sinai border so that his UAR troops could be moved up to face Israel.

U-Thant replied immediately, rejecting the Arab leader's request.

Nasser responded by moving his forces through Cairo and eastward into the Sinai desert; and on 22 May he closed the Strait of Tiran to Israeli shipping.

This move made him the champion of the Arab world. In one stroke he had defied the super-powers, established himself as the saviour of the Syrian regime, and reversed the decision of the 1956 war.

On 26 May, encouraged by his Arab neighbours, Nasser proclaimed:

'We feel strong enough to engage Israel in battle. With God's help we will triumph. On this basis we have decided to go ahead. Our objective will be to destroy Israel.'

Israel, under a new threat of extinction, immediately sent an emissary to the three Western great powers, but received little assurance. De Gaulle proclaimed French disinterest. Wilson voiced Britain's encouragement, but promised nothing concrete. Johnson promised the emissary that the United States would join with Britain in canvassing support in the United Nations for a declaration on the Strait of Tiran issue, and, if necessary, pledged intervention with international naval action.

But as the days passed, Israel felt herself increasingly threatened. On 30 May, King Hussein of Jordan gave way to pressure to join the Arab cause and concluded a pact with Nasser placing his forces under Arab command. There was intrigue in Moscow, Cairo, Damascus and Baghdad, and all through the Arab world there was the call for action.

Israeli intelligence plotted reports of troop concentrations near the UN-policed borders, and waited. The projected US-British action concerning Tiran was a hindrance which was tying Israel's hands. She had to survive *now*. She was in a precarious position. Her cities were only five minutes flying time from the nearest Arab airfields, and she had no natural strategic frontiers. She knew that she was too small to contemplate a defensive war. She could not wait for the first blow.

On Sunday, 4 June, the Israeli cabinet decided on war – and a pre-emptive air attack.

Pre-emptive strike

Flight One's Mirages swarmed down across the delta, flattening out in loose line-astern formation, to sweep in on West Cairo airbase. The leading jets neutralized the runways and strafed the control tower and maintenance buildings. Then they banked round and picked out their individual targets – 30 Tupolev Tu-16 bombers which

Below On the east bank of the Suez, a Russian-built SAM-2 surface-to-air missile lies damaged and abandoned after an Israeli air attack. Missile defences were caught napping by the speed of the Israeli attack and were not employed effectively. Poor training by Russian advisors was given as the reason for the failure.

were squatting snugly in their blast-proof revetments.

One by one, 16 of the sleek, Russian-built machines were destroyed, their fuel tanks exploding in ragged stabs of flame. As the first wave of Mirages turned for home, the second wave came in and dealt with the remaining 14, then poured a flood of thousands of bullets into everything in sight, hitting fuel waggons, hangars and installations, leaving the scene in a pall of smoke from 30 burning, twisted wrecks.

At nearby Cairo International Airport, another wave of Mirages swept in to find a whole squadron of MiG-21s conveniently lined up on the far side of the airfield. The first short burst of cannon-fire hit the first MiG, which exploded and set fire to three others. During three minutes every one of the remaining fighters on the airbase was smashed and set on fire. The runway was put out of action and the airport buildings strafed.

Meanwhile, in Sinai, Mystères had attacked all the Egyptian airfields, hitting the runways with jet-fired concrete dibber bombs. Then they came round again and strafed everything in sight. As they left the targets, flights of Ouragans swept in and finished the job. At Abn Sueir, Israeli fighters caught four MiG-21s taxiing toward the end of the runway and blasted them out of existence.

Over the Red Sea, the two flights of Vautours throttled right back and began a fast gliding descent towards the airfields of Ras Banas and Luxor. The Ras Banas flight found 16 Ilyushin Il-28s parked in neat ranks on the edge of the airfield. The two leading Vautours came in low and slow and raked the bombers with cannonfire. The whole squadron was destroyed in seconds.

At Luxor, the attack was met by heavy anti-aircraft fire. One of the Vautours was hit during the run-in and sheets of gasoline poured out of the left wing fuel tank. It turned over on its side and crashed onto a line of four parked MiG-17s with an enormous shattering explosion. Every Egyptian plane was destroyed on the ground in a matter of minutes; then the Vautours climbed out over the Red Sea, heading for the Israeli border.

By now the whole Canal Zone was mushrooming with palls of smoke. All EAF airfields had been knocked out, their machines on fire, their runways pock-marked with bomb-craters. Some of the Israeli planes had landed back at base and were being hurriedly refueled. Others were on their way, having dealt the first and most decisive blow of the war. Now the Israeli Air Force owned the skies.

Destruction on the ground

Egyptian Air Force commanders were desperately and belatedly trying to salvage something from the chaos – trying to muster some kind of combat force from the scattered remnants of their battered squadrons.

At Jebel Libni, three MiG-17s standing-by on operational readiness were manned and fueled up. As soon as the alarms sounded, ground-crew hurriedly wheeled up the battery trolleys and plugged them in for the pilots to start their engines. At that instant, four Israeli Mystères came swarming across the hills to attack the airfield. Two of them launched their rocket-powered concrete dibbers onto the runway intersection. The Egyptian pilots tore frantically at their harness and tried to get out of their aircraft – but too late. The other Mystères blasted a stream of cannon-shells into the hapless MiGs and blew them up as the ground-crews scattered in panic.

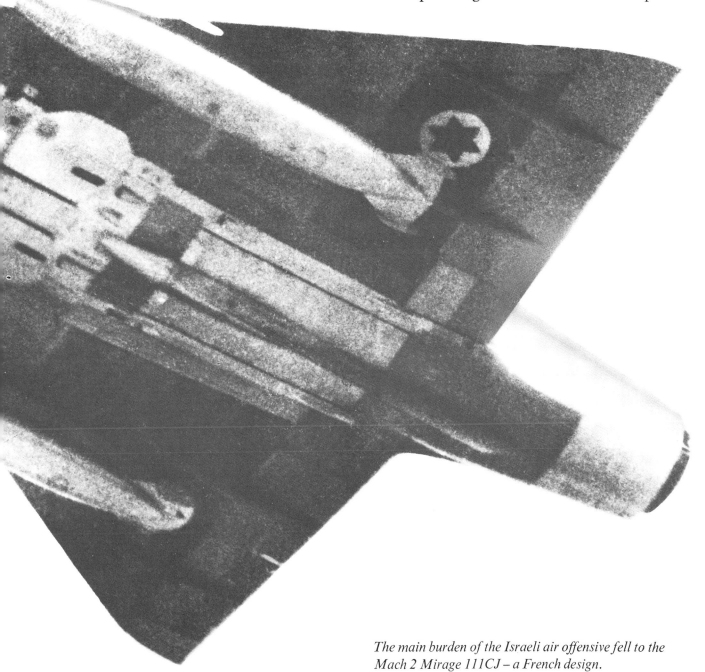

The main burden of the Israeli air offensive fell to the Mach 2 Mirage 111CJ – a French design.

The destruction caused by the IAF's surprise attacks is evident in this photograph of Kabrit Airbase. In the foreground are burnt out Il-14s – destroyed as they tried to take off. The smaller planes in the background are Yak-18 trainers, among which can be seen the shadow of an overflying Israeli Mirage. The photo inset shows a Russian-built TU-16 'Badger' burning outside its reinforced pen at Cairo West Airbase.

The other two Mystères came in again and strafed a row of 13 parked MiG-17s and MiG-19s and set them on fire. Then all four Israeli aircraft attacked 'targets of opportunity' around the airfield.

At Bir Gifgafa, a huge Mil Mi-6 helicopter had just got airborne and was hovering above the tarmac, poised before its forward thrust, trying to escape to the south, when two flights of Mystères came in low across the desert.

A burst of 30mm shells from the leading plane ripped off the main rotor and the huge chopper fell to the tarmac and crashed in flames. The other Mystères attacked four twin-engined Ilyushin Il-14 transports and two other helicopters on the ground.

On Bir Thamada, a big Antonov An-12 transport and two other transport planes were destroyed by Mystères. At El Arish, six MiG-17s, also caught on the ground, were knocked out by rockets from Super-Mystères.

The El Arish airstrip was saved for later use by Israeli transports; so was half the 7,000 feet long Jebel Libni runway.

Death of an Air Force

The first phase was over. The pre-emptive strike. The sudden sneak attack that had caught the Egyptians with their pants down. From now on, Egyptian anti-aircraft defences were ready, and the continuing Israeli attacks were met by heavy defensive ground fire.

Just after 0930, a squadron of MiG-21s from Hurghada, which had been covering the Canal Zone, flew north to engage the Israeli Mirages. They ran into 16 over Abu Sueir. In the first minutes, four MiGs were shot down. The Egypt-

ian pilots fought on valiantly in a whirling dog-fight. But they were hopelessly out-classed. The Egyptian force broke up and headed west, now short of fuel, the pilots looking for somewhere to land. Some got down safely, but others crashed onto cratered runways. A few ejected after their planes had run out of fuel.

In another engagement, eight MiG-21s which had just got airborne were jumped by a squadron of Mirages. The Egyptian pilots shot down two Mirages before their entire force was destroyed.

At 1050, four Jordanian Hunters from Mafraq strafed the Israeli airstrip at Kefar Sirkin and knocked out two Super Cubs and several vehicles. The RJAF planes returned to find their own base under attack by Israeli Mirages. Two were shot down and the other two exploded when trying to land on the bombed-out runway.

Throughout the morning the one-sided battle went on, the Arabs offering decreasing resistance. Strikes were made on Amman airport, which knocked out the whole Jordanian Air Force. A later strike by Mirages and Mystères on Habbaniya and Hotel Three destroyed nine MiG-21s, five Hunters and two Ilyushin Il-14s of the Iraqi Air Force.

The carnage went on throughout the day. At dusk, three flights of Mystères and Ouragans hit the Jebel Libni airfield to forestall any Egyptian attempt to repair the runways. They showered the field with delayed-action bombs, set to detonate throughout the night.

It had been a disastrous day for the Egyptians, whose worst fears had materialised. In Israel's surprise attack, made during the first minutes of the undeclared war, the great Russian-sponsored Egyptian Air Force had been reduced to scrap-metal by rockets, bombs and cannon-shells. And by nightfall, the Jordanian, Syrian and Iraqi air forces had been also knocked out of the war.

Nasser's dream of Arab conquest had been shattered, and Israel had assured herself of mastery of the air over the Sinai desert for the rest of the war.

This mastery was to prove the decisive factor, for, lacking both natural cover in the desert and the protection of their own air force, the UAR ground troops were at the mercy of the Israelis, who inflicted a humiliating defeat on the combined Arab forces within six days.

Below The aftermath. With total air superiority, the Israeli land forces dominated the battle in the desert – forcing the Arabs to abandon most of their equipment.

Overleaf Grim reminder of the Israeli air attack. Mi-6 helicopters blaze at Bir Gifgafa – an Egyptian base which was subsequently overrun by the Israelis.